FULL COVERAGE OF

**1997
IDEA AMENDMENTS**

What Do I Do When ...

The Answer Book on Individualized Education Programs

Susan Gorn

LRP
Publications

LRP Publications
Horsham, Pennsylvania 19044
(215) 784-0860

This publication was designed to provide accurate and authoritative information in regard to the subject matter covered. It is published with the understanding that neither the author nor the publisher is engaged in rendering legal, accounting, or other professional service. If legal advice or other expert assistance is required, the service of a competent professional should be sought.

Library of Congress Cataloging-in-Publication Data

Gorn, Susan, 1954-
    What do I do when — : the answer book on individualized education programs / Susan Gorn.
        p.   cm.
    Includes bibliographical references and index.
    ISBN 1-57834-003-9
    1. Handicapped children—Education—United States. 2. Individualized instruction—United States. 3. Curriculum planning—United States. 4. Education and state—United States.
I. Title.
LC4031.G65   1997
371.9'043—dc21
                                                        97-20412
                                                          CIP

Printed on acid-free paper.
Manufactured in the United States of America.

01 00 99 98 97   6 5 4 3 2 1

About the Author

Susan Gorn is a legal writer with a strong interest in the law concerning persons with disabilities. She is the author of *What Do I Do When . . . The Answer Book on Special Education Law* (1996), a question-and-answer treatment of the major areas of interest, and confusion, in special education. Gorn is a co-author, with Melinda Maloney and Vicki Pitasky, of *Special Education Regulation: The A-Z Guide to Part B* (1995), which provides a comprehensive section-by-section of 34 C.F.R. Part 300. She is also the editor of LRP's *Special Education Dictionary* (1997).

Before joining LRP, Gorn practiced in a mid-size law firm in the areas of health law, employee benefits, and business planning and taxation. She earned her Juris Doctor degree with honors from the Temple University School of Law in Philadelphia, Pennsylvania.

Table of Contents

Table of Contents

Table of Questions

Chapter 1. The Basics

Chapter 2. Contents of the IEP Document

Chapter 3. Formulating the IEP: Development, Review and Implementation

Chapter 4. Conducting IEP Meetings

Chapter 5. IEP Meeting Participants

Chapter 6. More on Parental Participation

Chapter 7. Behavior Management Plans and Other Special Needs

Chapter 8. Incarceration, Expulsion and Transfers

Chapter 9. Private School Students

Chapter 10. Transition Planning and Graduation

Chapter 11. Section 504, Part H (New Part C) and Public Agencies

Chapter 12. IEP Disputes and Remedies

How To Use The Answer Book

Overview of the Book

The individualized education program (IEP) has been called the "heart" of the Individuals with Disabilities Education Act (IDEA). That characterization vividly expresses that the related concepts of individualized consideration of needs and resulting educational programming are central to the law. This book analyzes these two key aspects of the IEP—the IEP process and the IEP document—in a series of questions and answers.

Who must attend an IEP meeting? When should such a meeting be held? What type of information ought to be included in the IEP document? These are the basic concerns addressed in this book. But they are addressed in fine detail, in anticipation of the wide range of circumstances that necessarily arise in the course of complying with a law that compels the recognition of individual needs.

IDEA Amendments of 1997

In late May 1997, both houses of Congress voted to reauthorize the discretionary programs of the IDEA and to amend Part B of the statute. As this book goes to print, the Individuals with Disabilities Education Act Amendments of 1997 await presidential signature, with President Clinton's approval anticipated. Most of the provisions, including those related to disciplinary removals of students with disabilities, will be effective immediately upon enactment. The provisions relating to IEPs, however, will not be effective until July 1, 1998.

According to the legislative history, the new law starts with the premise that the more than 20-year-old IDEA continues to serve vital national interests and is basically sound. Nevertheless, experience has shown that modifications are needed to better serve the interests of children with disabilities and students and educators generally.

Consistent with the premise that the IDEA needed only fine-tuning, rather than an overhaul, the language of the legislation concerning the development, review and revision of IEPs remain relatively unchanged. Further, according to the legislative history, the amendments affirm statutory interpretations contained in the Part B regulations and other regulatory guidance and policies from the Department of Education.

To keep you as current as possible, the author alerts you to any changes in the IEP process or document that will result from the new legislation (referred to within as "the 1997 Amendments") whenever pertinent. When the 1997 Amendments are not mentioned in the response, the author sees no impact at this point. In this regard, recognize that many IEP compliance issues—and thus many of the questions in this publication—have been addressed on the level of regulations, judicial decisions and Department of Education guidance (such as OSEP Policy Letters), rather than in the statute itself.

Citation to Authorities

The answers are based on a variety of sources, such as statutes and regulations, court decisions, state educational agency due process hearing decisions, administrative review decisions, Office for Civil Rights Letters of Findings, and policy letters promulgated by the Office of Special Education Programs. Naturally, the amount of authority and degree of deference that should be accorded to these sources varies. In many instances court and administrative decisions are cited for their illustrative, rather than precedential, value. While authoritative and influential court decisions are cited, the nature of the subject matter lends itself to extended discussions of many well-reasoned administrative rulings.

All of these sources are cited to LRP Publications' *Individuals with Disabilities Law Report*® (IDELR) or *Early Childhood Law and Policy Reporter* (ECLPR). Citations to the IDEA are made to the pertinent section of the Part B regulations (34 C.F.R. Parts 300 and 301), rather than the statutory provisions under which the regulation was promulgated, even when the regulation essentially repeats the statutory language. In addition, a shorthand citation used throughout the chapters, Appendix C to 34 C.F.R. Part 300, refers to the Department of Education's Notice of Interpretation on IEP Requirements.

Acronyms

Special education incorporates a number of terms specific to the field. Because these terms are so frequently used, they are known only in their abbreviated form. The reader should be aware of the following acronyms commonly used in this, and any discussion of the IDEA and its implementing regulations.

ADD	attention deficit disorder
ADHD	attention deficit hyperactivity disorder
ALJ	administrative law judge
BMP	behavior management plan
DSM-IV	Diagnostic and Statistical Manual of Mental Disorders—Fourth Edition
ED or DOE	United States Department of Education
EDGAR	Education Department General Administrative Regulations
ESY	extended school year

FAPE	free appropriate public education
FERPA	Family Education Rights and Privacy Act
IDEA	Individuals with Disabilities Education Act
IEE	independent educational evaluation
IEP	individualized education program
IFSP	individualized family service plan
ITP	interim transition plan
IU	intermediate unit
LEA	local educational agency
LRE	least restrictive environment
MDT	multidisciplinary team
M-team	multidisciplinary team
OCR	Department of Education's Office for Civil Rights
OSEP	Department of Education's Office of Special Education Programs
OSERS	Department of Education's Office of Special Education and Rehabilitative Services
SEA	state educational agency

The term "district" or "school district" is used throughout as an abbreviation for "local school district" or, to the extent appropriate, any other public agency within a state involved in the education of children with disabilities.

Chapter 1

The Basics

The Individuals with Disabilities Education Act (IDEA), codified at 20 U.S.C. §§ 1400-1485, was enacted in 1975[1] to address the failure of state educational systems to meet the educational needs of children with disabilities in this country. Congress' enactment was in part a response to two well-publicized cases, *Mills v. Board of Education of the District of Columbia,* 348 F. Supp. 866 (D.D.C. 1972), and *Pennsylvania Association of Retarded Children v. Commonwealth of Pennsylvania,* 343 F. Supp. 279 (E.D. Pa. 1972), both contesting the exclusion of children with mental disabilities from the public school system. It was also a response to the persistent efforts of persons with disabilities and organizations interested in the rights of persons with disabilities. In both cases, the courts held that children with disabilities had a constitutional right to education. In excluding such children states and local school districts were violating the equal protection clause of the Fourteenth Amendment.

The concerns that led Congress to enact the IDEA are manifested in the general provisions of the law. Among these concerns were two facts: In the mid-1970s more than half of the approximately 8 million children with disabilities in the country were not receiving appropriate educational services, and one million were excluded entirely.

Stepping in to remediate the deficiencies in the state systems revealed in Congressional hearings, Congress stated that the purpose of the IDEA was:

> to assure that all children with disabilities have available to them . . . a free appropriate education which emphasizes special education and related services designed to meet their unique needs, to assure that the rights of children with disabilities and their parents or guardians are protected, to assist States and localities to provide for the

---

[1] Formerly called the Education of the Handicapped Act (EHA) and the Education for All Handicapped Children Act (EAHCA).

education of all children with disabilities, and to assess and assure the effectiveness of efforts to educate children with disabilities.

20 U.S.C. § 1400(c).

Twenty-two years later Congress enacted the Individuals with Disabilities Education Act Amendments of 1997 (1997 Amendments), declaring that the lofty goals of the IDEA, for the most part, have been achieved. Nevertheless, believing that the law should be changed to help improve post-school prospects for many children with disabilities and to remove the law's distracting emphasis on paperwork, Congress rewrote the law to address those issues and other emerging concerns.

One of the themes that runs consistently through the 1997 Amendments is the need to improve educational results for children with disabilities. "The critical issue is now to place greater emphasis on improving student performance and ensuring that children with disabilities receive a quality public education." (S. REP. No. 105-17, at 3 (1997)) Taking a cue, perhaps, from current trends in health care, the act establishes new federal requirements for data collection and outcome analysis.

Members of the general public may not be aware of this aspect of the 1997 Amendments, though. The headline-grabbing aspects of the law address changes in discipline procedures for students with disabilities intended to make schools safer. Less publicized aspects of the act include the focus on enhancing the role of parents while decreasing the potential for contention as the parties work together; ensuring access of children with disabilities into the general curriculum; and resolving current uncertainty about items such as continuing services for properly expelled students or students unilaterally placed in private schools. Overall, the 1997 Amendments address a wide variety of concerns that have puzzled or troubled educators and school attorneys for some time.

Prior to enactment of the 1997 Amendments, the IDEA contained eight parts, Part A through Part H, with Part B being its "heart"—a series of procedural safeguards designed to protect the interests of "school age" (generally from ages three to 21) children with disabilities. Congress was loath to establish substantive educational standards, education being within the traditional scope of state authority. The 1997 Amendments restate and consolidate the statute into four parts, Part A through Part D. Part B remains the section providing federal assistance for education of children with disabilities.

Within Part B, the "individualized education program," or IEP, is the the cornerstone. The IEP is the translation of Congress' idealistic vision of children with disabilities receiving meaningful education into a specific mandate to be followed for millions of children, no matter what their circumstances and their needs.

As discussed in this chapter, the IEP concept of the IDEA is, in fact, two distinct, but related, imperatives. First, the IEP is a document, ideally developed in a collaborative and cooperative effort between parents and school personnel, that describes the disabled child's abilities and needs and prescribes the placement and services designed to meet that child's unique needs.

But the IEP is not only a document. It is also the culmination of a mandated process that substantially alters the means by which educators plan programming for children with disabilities. Under the IDEA, educators must now work with parents, who are made mandatory participants in the IEP process and who are provided procedural safeguards if they disagree with the educators responsible for educating their children.

The IDEA, now being over two decades old, has become an established part of the educational landscape. So we may forget just how revolutionary the two IEP concepts—individualized curriculum and parental participation in curriculum development—were at the time of enactment, and remain today.

In fact, the core principles of the IDEA—those establishing the parameters of the entitlement of a child with a disability to educational services—are unique in the history of public education. This chapter sets out the basic contours of the IEP provisions of the IDEA, beginning with the following brief explanations of key IDEA terminology and concepts central to an understanding of the IEP process.

Children with disabilities. Not all children with disabilities are covered by the IDEA. Only those children who are *educationally* disabled fall within the scope of the Act. The IDEA lists those disabilities that are recognized as educational disabilities. That listing, intended to be exhaustive, is set out in the statute at 20 U.S.C. § 1401(a)(1) as including those children "with mental retardation, hearing impairments, including deafness, speech or language impairments, visual impairments, including blindness, serious emotional disturbance, orthopedic impairments, autism, traumatic brain injury, other health impairments, or specific learning disabilities . . . who, by reason thereof, need special education and related services." IDEA regulations at 34 C.F.R. § 300.7 further define these disabilities.

Special education. The term "special education" is defined as "specially designed instruction . . . to meet the unique needs of a child with a disability." 20 U.S.C. § 1401(a)(16). It is the combination of being specially designed and meeting the unique needs of a given child that makes special education, in a word, "special." Because of its child-specific character, special education cannot be more precisely defined. For example, neither the statute itself nor its regulations include a definition of "specially designed instruction."

In some instances, the use of regular education curriculum materials to meet the needs of a student with a disability may satisfy a school district's obligation to provide special education. In other instances, certain modifications provided to students in the regular classroom, such as an interpreter for a hearing-impaired student or modified materials for students with visual or physical impairments, could constitute "specially designed instruction." The implications of the limited statutory definition, however, are significant. One clear ramification is that special education is not restricted to traditional academic instruction in the classroom; it also can be provided in a physical education classroom, at home, or in a hospital or other institution. Special education can be related to, or in support of, regular academic instruction. It also can include vocational instruction, or it can focus on daily living skills, community living skills, pre-vocational skills or whatever is appropriate for the particular child in question. Thus, the nature of special education will vary as required to address the individual child's needs.

Related services. Under the IDEA, related services are defined as including transportation and developmental, corrective and other supportive services designed to help the disabled child benefit from special education. 20 U.S.C. § 1401(a)(17). Related services also include speech pathology, audiology, physical therapy, occupational therapy, recreation, counseling, psychological services and medical services provided solely for diagnostic and evaluative purposes. The statutory listing is not exhaustive; neither is the regulatory one (34 C.F.R. § 300.16). However, in specifically identifying school health services as a related service, the regulatory listing raised the stakes substantially for the school districts and engendered a body of litigation that includes *Irving School District v. Tatro,* 1983-84 EHLR 555:511 (1984), one of the handful of IDEA cases heard by the United States Supreme Court.

Free appropriate public education. A free appropriate public education (FAPE) is the entitlement the IDEA confers upon each eligible child. The term is defined under the IDEA at 20 U.S.C. § 1401(a)(18) as comprising special education and/or related services provided at public expense that meet the standards of the state educational agency (SEA) and that are provided in accordance with the IEP devised for each child with a disability. Twenty-plus years have shown that the statutory definition is only the beginning of the story, for interpretation of the statute has shown that the words "properly formulated and providing an adequate educational benefit" are implied in connection with the requirement for provision in accordance with an IEP.

The substantive part of that implied requirement—the quantum of benefit—is generally understood to be at issue when one considers the appropriateness of the educational program set out in an IEP. This publication does not address substantive appropriateness of the IEP. The procedural aspect—the consideration of whether an IEP has been properly formulated—is what we address here.

1. *What is an "individualized education program"?*

The individualized education program (IEP) is the cornerstone of the IDEA. It is the written document that sets forth the free appropriate public education (FAPE) that is to be or has been offered to a child with a disability eligible to receive individualized programming and related services under Part B of the IDEA. As stated by the U.S. Supreme Court in *Burlington School Committee v. Massachusetts Department of Education,* 1984-85 EHLR 556:389 (1985), "[t]he IEP is, in brief, a comprehensive statement of the educational needs of a handicapped child and the specially designed instruction and related services to be employed to meet those needs."

Under the IDEA, the IEP document must be in writing and must always include the following five components:

(A) a statement of the present levels of educational performance of such child,

(B) a statement of annual goals, including short-term instructional objectives,

(C) a statement of the specific educational services to be provided to such child and the extent to which such child will be able to participate in regular educational programs,

. . .

(E) the projected date for initiation and anticipated duration of such services, and

(F) appropriate objective criteria and evaluation procedures and schedules for determining, on at least an annual basis, whether instructional objectives are being achieved.

20 U.S.C. § 1401(a)(20).

In addition, when a student with a disability reaches age 16 (or before, when provision of transition services is appropriate for a younger child), the IEP must also include:

(D) a statement of the needed transition services for students beginning no later than age 16 and annually thereafter (and, when determined appropriate for the individual, beginning at age 14 or younger), including, when appropriate, a statement of the interagency responsibilities or linkages (or both) before the student leaves the school setting.

20 U.S.C. § 1401(a)(20).

IDEA regulations at 34 C.F.R. § 300.341(a) succinctly define an IEP as "a written statement for a child with a disability that is developed and implemented in accordance with §§ 300.341-300.350." While the regulations at 34 C.F.R. § 300.346 address the required content of an IEP—the description of the programs and services that comprise the provision of FAPE—the balance of the regulations set out the procedural requirements governing the formulation of the IEP.

The 1997 Amendments at Section 614(d)(1)(A) essentially continue the IDEA statutory definition, providing modified or more detailed versions of the five already required components (with one required statement divided into two modified statements) and adding one entirely new requirement:

(v)(I) a statement of any individual modifications in the administration of State or districtwide assessments of student achievement (or part of such an assessment); and

(II) if the IEP Team determines that the child will not participate in a particular State or districtwide assessment of student achievement (or part of such an assessment), a statement of—

(aa) why that assessment is not appropriate for the child; and

(bb) how the child will be assessed.

The 1997 Amendments' version of each of the other components will be set out in full where appropriate in chapter 2. A modified statement of transition services is also part of the 1997 Amendments and is discussed in chapter 10.

2. Who is responsible for developing the IEPs of children with disabilities?

While the ultimate responsibility for providing FAPE lies with the state educational agency (SEA), 34 C.F.R. § 600, the public agency within the state that is responsible for providing FAPE to a child with a disability is also responsible for developing and implementing his or her IEP. 34 C.F.R. § 341(a). "Public agency," as defined in IDEA regulations at 34 C.F.R. § 300.14, includes local school districts (local educational agencies), intermediate educational units, or other political divisions or subdivisions within a state charged under state law with providing education to children with disabilities.

Generally, the school district in which the parents reside is the responsible public agency for a child with a disability, although state law may establish another responsible agency, such as the state department of mental health and mental retardation, for some students.[2]

In the typical case of a school district, that public agency is responsible for developing an IEP for each of the following children with disabilities, in addition to those within its jurisdiction attending schools it operates (34 C.F.R. § 300.341(b)):

- Children the district refers to or places in a private school or agency. 34 C.F.R. § 300.348.

- Children placed by their parents in a parochial or other private school to whom the district is providing special education or related services. 34 C.F.R. 300.403(a).

3. What is an "IEP meeting"?

The IDEA requires the school district, or other public agency responsible for providing FAPE to a child with a disability, to initiate and conduct IEP meetings for

---

[2] *See* Questions 12 and 13 in chapter 11, *infra,* for further discussion identifying the public agency responsible for providing FAPE to a particular student.

the purpose of working jointly with parents to develop, review and revise the IEP of a child with a disability. According to the Department of Education's Notice of Interpretation on IEP Requirements, "[t]he IEP meeting serves as a communication vehicle between parents and school personnel, and enables them, as equal participants, to jointly decide what the child's needs are, what services will be provided to meet those needs, and what the anticipated outcomes may be." Appendix C to 34 C.F.R. Part 300, Question 32.

Not every meeting held among school district representatives to discuss educational programming for a student with a disability is an IEP meeting. In fact, one would expect staff to meet beforehand to review and prepare for the IEP meeting. Appendix C to 34 C.F.R. Part 300, Question 55.

Similarly, parents may meet with representatives of the school district to discuss educational planning without triggering the IEP procedural requirements. For example, according to *Letter to Blades*, EHLR 213:169 (OSERS 1988), a parent's visit to his or her child's classroom for observation is ordinarily not considered an IEP meeting.

While IEP meetings may sometimes become contentious, it is important to distinguish them from other types of more adversarial meetings or procedures that are convened to determine a student's IEP, for different procedural safeguards apply to those proceedings. For example, sometimes the line between an IEP meeting and a mediation may blur. However, the Department of Education made it clear in its *Letter to Decker*, 19 IDELR 279 (OSERS 1992), that a mediation should not be confused with an IEP meeting. Rather, a mediation is a post-IEP meeting, a voluntary precursor to a due process hearing at which none of the procedural safeguards for the conduct of IEP meetings apply.

4. Is a "staffing" the same as an IEP meeting?

Yes. Like the Department of Education, the author uses the term "IEP meeting" in this publication. The exact name used to identify and describe these meetings can vary, however, as state and local practice typically controls the name. In various regions of the country, the IEP meeting is given names such as staffing, multidisciplinary team (M-team) meeting, multidisciplinary staff conference and IEP conference. Within a given locality, the variations on the terms may have separate, defined meanings.

5. Is there a required format for an IEP meeting?

No, not as a matter of federal law. Instead, state or local practice typically controls the format of IEP meetings. Federal regulators left the format open, apparently relying on the professionalism of the participants the school district assembles for the meeting.

Federal regulations do impose some ground rules, however, including, most significantly, the requirement that parents be treated as "equal participants" in the meetings, contributing to the discussion about the child's needs and joining with the other participants in deciding what services the child will receive. Appendix C to 34 C.F.R. Part 300, Question 26. We identify and discuss these and other ground rules throughout this publication.

6. Is there a required format for an IEP document?

No. Unlike, for example, IRS Form 1040, there is no federal IEP form. Assuming the IEP adequately describes the student's educational program—that is, all the content requirements of IDEA regulations at 34 C.F.R. § 346 are met—the specific format is left to the discretion of state or local authorities. Appendix C to 34 C.F.R. Part 300, Question 56; *Letter to Anonymous,* 24 IDELR 854 (OSEP 1996).

One caveat to keep in mind: To comply with federal law, any format chosen by a public agency must be understandable to parents. In *Rockford (IL) School District #205,* EHLR 352:465 (OCR 1987), OCR found that the school district's use of computer-generated IEPs violated the requirements of Section 504 (34 C.F.R. § 104.33(b)(1)) because the documents were not readily comprehensible to parents.

Desktop publishing has undoubtedly become more sophisticated in the 10 years since OCR's investigation in *Rockford.* Nevertheless, the importance of keeping the parents-readers in mind when designing IEP document format is emphasized in OCR's description of the school district's IEPs:

> OCR's review indicated that the IEP document consists of a computer print-out. An individual IEP is developed by choosing among hundreds of possible goals and objectives, which are then printed out with corresponding code numbers. The face sheet of the IEP similarly contains identifying information concerning the child along with computer symbols, markings, codes, etc. While nearly all significant information is printed out in English, the simultaneous use of codes and computer markings makes the IEP difficult to read for persons not familiar with computer print-outs. OCR also reviewed the explanatory material which is supposed to accompany the IEP. While this material provides a basic description of the IEP format, it does not explain the use of codes and other markings found on the document.
>
> OCR interviewed five parent witnesses with respect to whether they understood the IEP process used by the district. All of the interviewees indicated that they felt intimidated by the process given the brevity of the format. . . . They indicated that they did not think the format provided sufficient information to enable them to ask questions.

EHLR 352:465 at 467.

7. How long should an IEP document be?

Like format, length of the IEP document is a matter left to state and local discretion. According to the Notice of Interpretation on IEP Requirements, "[t]he IEP should be as long as necessary to adequately describe a child's program." Appendix C to 34 C.F.R. Part 300, Question 56. The Notice of Interpretation opines that an IEP document "usually" can contain all the required information (34 C.F.R. § 300.346) in a one-to three-page form.

Illustrating how one cannot generalize about individual requirements, most school districts find one to three pages inadequate for a substantial range of students. On the other hand, a very lengthy document can be counter-productive, confusing and full of extraneous materials.

The IEP for a 14-year-old student with physical disabilities, low-average intelligence and profound deafness shows how long an IEP *can* be. As described in *French v. Omaha Public Schools,* 17 EHLR 811 (D. Neb. 1991), the IEP was 35 pages, largely single-spaced. Four pages described the student's present educational performance; another 23 pages were devoted to a description of the goals and objectives. Seems detailed enough, but the parents still challenged its adequacy —unsuccessfully— claiming that some of the statements of present educational performance were unclear and subjective and that some of the objectives were inconsistent with the assessment of the student.

The 1997 Amendments expanded IEP content requirements as a result of the emphasis on improving results for students with disabilities in the general curriculum and the likely desire to document discussion of the new mandatory IEP meeting special consideration items. *See* Question 14 in chapter 4 infra. Thus, it is likely that IEP documents will have to be longer. Nevertheless, in the Committee Report that accompanies the Senate's Reauthorization bill, Congress stated that it did not intend the new content requirements to result in "major expansion in the size of the IEP." S. REP. No. 105-17, at 20 (1997).

8. What is the "IEP process"?

Essentially, the IEP process is the set of procedures set out in the IDEA that governs how school districts should determine the educational services that a student with a disability requires to receive the free appropriate public education to which he or she is entitled—and more. As explained quite articulately by the review officer in *Independent School District No. 625,* 22 IDELR 920 (SEA Minn. 1995):

> The IEP process should be more than an exercise in paying lip service to what the law requires. The IEP should be the key for the handicapped student to receiving the necessary *individual,* instructional services that a district recognizes and provides to that student so that he/she can receive some educational benefit. Educational benefit should be a direct benefit of the delivery of the IEP, not educational benefit that a student achieves by osmosis from sitting in classrooms for a school year.

22 IDELR at 928.

As an exercise in meeting the requirements of the law, the U.S. Supreme Court made clear in *Board of Education of Hendrick Hudson Central School District v. Rowley,* 1981-82 EHLR 553:656 (1982), that review for compliance with the procedural requirements of the IDEA is essential in assessing if a school district has met its obligation under the IDEA to offer a FAPE to a child with a disability. In connection with the IEP process, compliance means developing and implementing the detailed, legally mandated procedures concerning the conduct of IEP meetings prescribed in Part B regulations at 34 C.F.R. §§ 300.341-300.350.

These sections, in turn, establish requirements concerning, among other things:

- when an IEP meeting must be initiated (34 C.F.R. § 300.342),

- how an IEP meeting must be conducted (34 C.F.R. § 300.343),

- who may or must attend IEP meetings (34 C.F.R. § 300.344), and

- rights of parents to participate in the IEP process (34 C.F.R. § 300.345).

Taken as a whole the process established in those regulations substantially altered the means by which educators plan programming for children with disabilities. Even more so than with children with disabilities eligible for services under Section 504, the IEP process requirements of the IDEA require educators to include parents as mandatory participants in the planning process. In addition, parents also are provided with procedural safeguards in the event they disagree with the educators about the program proposed as the child's IEP.

One of the stated purposes of the 1997 Amendments was to involve parents even more in the IEP process and also make them required participants in decision-making concerning eligibility and placement decisions.

9. What purposes are served by compliance with the requirements for the IEP meeting process and the IEP document?

Clearly, compliance evidences due regard for the mandates of providing FAPE and involving parents in educational programming. In its Notice of Interpretation on IEP Requirements, the Department of Education identifies six distinct functions and purposes for the IEP requirement. When the school district has not carried out the IEP process to meet these standards, set out below, litigation often results.

a.   The IEP meeting serves as a communication vehicle between parents and school personnel, and enables them, as equal participants, to jointly decide what the child's needs are, what services will be provided to meet those needs, and what the anticipated outcomes may be.

b.   The IEP process provides an opportunity for resolving any differences between the parents and the agency concerning the special education needs of a child with a disability: first, through the IEP meeting, and second, if necessary, through the procedural protections that are available to the parents.

c. The IEP sets forth in writing a commitment of resources necessary to enable a child with a disability to receive needed special education and related services.

d. The IEP is a management tool that is used to ensure that each child with a disability is provided special education and related services appropriate to the child's special learning needs.

e. The IEP is a compliance/monitoring document that may be used by authorized monitoring personnel from each governmental level to determine whether a child with a disability is actually receiving the FAPE agreed to by the parents and the school.

f. The IEP serves as an evaluation device for use in determining the extent of the child's progress toward meeting the projected outcomes.

Appendix C to 34 C.F.R. Part 300.

With respect to the IEP document itself, OCR has stated that "[t]he IEP sets forth the commitment of resources necessary to enable the student to benefit from an education, is a management tool used to ensure the provision of an appropriate education, serves as a means of evaluating student progress, and provides the chief mechanism for parental participation." *Rockford (IL) Sch. Dist. #205*, EHLR 352:465 (OCR 1987).

10. Is the IEP a contract?

Yes and no. The IEP obligates the school district or other public agency responsible for providing FAPE to provide the special instruction and related services identified in the IEP. On the other hand, while the IEP includes the objectives hoped to be achieved by the child through the provision of such services, it does not guarantee that the child will achieve them.

IDEA regulations at 34 C.F.R. § 300.350 require school districts to provide the special education and related services to a child with a disability set out in his or her IEP. The Notice of Interpretation on IEP Requirements makes the obligatory nature of the IEP clear in its answer to this question: "Is the IEP a commitment to provide services, i.e., must a public agency provide all the services listed in the IEP?" The answer is yes. "The IEP of each child with a disability must include all services necessary to meet the child's identified special education and related services needs; *and* all services in the IEP must be provided in order for the agency to be in compliance with the Act." Appendix C to 34 C.F.R. Part 300, Question 45 (emphasis added).

Thus, the school district in *In re Child with Disabilities*, 21 IDELR 624 (SEA Conn. 1994), denied FAPE to 17-year-old twins, both learning disabled, by failing to provide the work-study program component identified in each student's IEP. One student was to work in the field of auto body repair; the other in auto mechanics. That programming was never provided during the school year, the school district contending that it was unable to find a work site for either. Under the district's regular education cooperative work program, the district was not obliged to provide such services for a student if no work site could be found; the district claimed that policy applied to work opportunities identified in IEPs as well.

The hearing officer disagreed. "Regardless of the Board policy, when a service is identified as necessary to provide a FAPE, the Board is required to procure that service. If it is unable to do so, the [IEP team] should reconvene to discuss alternative methods of implementing the IEP." 21 IDELR at 629.

The reader should note carefully the implication of the Notice of Interpretation. Including an item of special instruction or related service on an IEP arguably creates a commitment to provide it even if it is not required for FAPE. *See, e.g., Dougherty County (GA) Sch. Dist.,* 23 IDELR 843 (OCR 1995) (the district's failure to supply tutoring was not a denial of FAPE as it was not a service included in the student's IEP). Thus, a school district will have to comply with the IDEA procedural safeguards if it later wishes to cease provision of that item or service.[3]

Another implication of the Notice is that a school district cannot provide programming or services that meet the definition of special education and related services on an informal basis, without documenting its intention to provide them in the IEP document. The school district in *Hillsborough County School Board,* 21 IDELR 191 (SEA Fla. 1994), violated the procedural requirements of the IDEA relating to the formulation and implementation of the IEP for a six-year-old student with multiple disabilities including Down syndrome and speech and language impairments in many ways. One of the more significant violations related to the district's unwritten policy of not specifying on an IEP document a requirement to provide individual speech/language services, irrespective of any showing of individual need for those services. Instead, the provision of such services was left to the discretion of the speech therapist. The hearing officer rightly recognized that this policy permitted the school district to avoid making a binding commitment to provide the resources needed for the provision of FAPE to the student.

34 C.F.R. § 300.350 also makes it clear, however, that an IEP is not an educational contract guaranteeing that a student will achieve a certain level of achievement in meeting that IEP's goals and objectives. Rather, the district's responsibility is limited to ensuring that all involved personnel make a good faith effort to assist the child in achieving those goals and objectives. (34 C.F.R. § 300.350 note.) For example, in *Hannibal (MO) #60 School District,* 20 IDELR 1346 (OCR 1993), OCR found the parent's allegation that the school district allowed the learning disabled student to sleep

---

[3] *See also* Question 13 in chapter 3, *infra,* concerning school districts ceasing to provide services included on an IEP.

in class was without merit. OCR found credible the district's statement that the student was not allowed to sleep in class; he was uncooperative and often pretended to be sleeping. School district personnel had therefore met their obligations by carrying out the goals and objectives in the student's IEP to the maximum extent possible.

11. Are all decisions made at IEP meetings considered contractual obligations of the school district?

No. While decisions made at an IEP meeting concerning the special education and related services set out in the student's IEP (in accordance with 34 C.F.R. § 300.346[4]) are binding obligations that cannot be changed unilaterally, other decisions are not binding. *Letter to Anonymous,* 20 IDELR 1222 (OSEP 1993). In response to that inquiry, OSEP stated that, in particular, decisions made at IEP meetings concerning parental participation at MDT meetings are not binding since they do not relate to a required component of a child's IEP. The 1997 Amendments make parents required participants in school groups making eligibility and placement decisions.

12. Does a verbal IEP comply with the IDEA?

Until October 1996 the answer would have been no. (In fact, this question would not have been included at all.) The IDEA statute itself makes it clear that an IEP is, by definition, a written document. 20 U.S.C. § 1401(a)(20).[5]

But in *Lincoln Consolidated Schools,* 25 IDELR 92 (SEA Mich. 1996), the hearing officer held that parents could assert the doctrine of promissory estoppel to compel the school district to provide services it had agreed to provide in an IEP meeting with parents, even though an IEP consistent with that agreement was not produced. In *Lincoln,* school officials and the parents of a five-year-old student with autism agreed in a meeting in March 1996 that the student would receive a range of services that included 30 hours per week of at-home discrete trial training. That agreement was not reduced to a written IEP. Instead, the school district met several times after that without the parents. As a result of those meetings, two months later the district produced a written IEP that did not include discrete trial training and otherwise excluded services agreed to in March. The parents refused to approve the written IEP and requested due process.

The hearing officer held that the school district had entered into a verbal contract to provide the services agreed to at the March meeting and that contract was enforceable

---

[4] *See* Question 28 of chapter 2, *infra.*

[5] *See also* Letter to Donnelly, EHLR 211:349 (OSEP 1994) (delays in formulating a written IEP may in some instances be excusable, though) and Question 21 of chapter 3, *infra.*

by reason of promissory estoppel, the parents having established the four elements of such a claim under generally applicable state law.[6]

This is a unique holding in the published annals of special education law, and, in the author's view, not particularly well-reasoned. The hearing officer seems to have gone out on a limb for no particular reason. According to the hearing officer, the fact that the school district held IEP meetings without the parents in attendance invalidated the May IEP in any event.[7] Further, as a substantive matter, the program proposed in that written IEP was held to be inappropriate.

---

[6] For a discussion of the doctrine of promissory estoppel and the elements needed to support a claim, see *Lincoln,* 25 IDELR at 100.

[7] *See* Question 1 in chapter 5.

Chapter 2

Contents of the IEP Document

The IEP document has been termed both the "heart" and the "centerpiece" of the IDEA. The IEP process has as one of its main purposes design of IEP documents in conformity with the objectives of the law. Yet after two decades, both educators and legislators have identified various ways in which the IEP content requirements—both what is required and what is not—have turned out to be counterproductive.

As the Department of Education stated in its explanation of its proposed Individuals with Disabilities in Education Act Amendments of 1995, the structure of the IEP document results in planning efforts being focused on what has come to be seen as minutiae, concerns that may have only a tangential relationship to the student's overall needs and ability to succeed in the "real world."

> Experience offers insight into why this is the case: IEP meetings too frequently focus only on the time each day or each week the child is "in" special education and on the detailed short-term objectives that bear little relation to how children learn or their parents' aspirations for them. . . . In effect, IEP meetings focus on access to special education rather than on access to an overall high-quality education. Moreover, because of the requirement that the IEP contain short-term objectives for every goal, teachers may spend significant time and energy developing a multitude of detailed and lengthy objectives that have little instructional utility. As a result, the IEP process often results in a paper exercise characterized by fragmented objectives, lower expectations, and instructional irrelevance.[1]

One thought that may strike anyone concerned about the interplay between state and federal government is the extent to which the Department of Education's critique about the effectiveness of IEPs is premised on reservations about how states are discharging their general authority to educate all students, disabled and nondisabled alike.

---

[1] Accessed by the author at <hhtp://www.ed.gov/IDEA/amend95/prin2.html> at p.3.

aside, though, the actual changes to the IEP document contained in the 1997 ?nts are relatively modest. Most focus on articulating the importance of the articipating in regular education to the extent possible and as effectively as possible and shifting the IEP planning emphasis from special education to integration into the regular curriculum. Changes to the IEP document include:

- The contents of the statement of the student's present levels of educational performance has to include a statement of how the child's impairment affects his or her participation and progress in the general curriculum. (For preschoolers, the statement would address how the impairment affects his or her access to developmentally appropriate activities.)

- There is a statement of measurable annual objectives relating to meeting the student's needs that result from his or her disability, enabling him or her to participate in the general curriculum, and to meeting any other educational needs that relate to the disability.

- As a new item, there is a statement of any modifications in the administration of general State or district assessments required to permit the student to participate, or, in the event participation is not appropriate, a statement of alternative assessment measures to be used to measure the student's educational achievement.

- The statement of program modifications needed to allow participation in the regular classroom environment is supplemented to also include participation in extracurricular and other nonacademic activities.

- The IEP of any student who is not being educated or will not participate in extracurricular activities with nondisabled students must include a justification of why separation to the extent specified was approved.

- The IEP team must consider the language needs of the student as they relate to the student's IEP.

- When a disabled student's behavior impedes his or her or other student's learning, the IEP team is required to consider strategies, including a behavior management plan, to address the problem behavior.

In the author's view, any educational approach, whether for disabled or nondisabled students, will start to show some wear-and-tear after two decades. Legislation as well may need fine-tuning, as experience shows improvements that could be made. But the author suspects that any new IEP document—no matter how retooled—will have its own weaknesses.

To show that, where IEPs are concerned, every silver lining has a cloud, the National Association of State Directors of Special Education lists items that once were thought to be the strengths of the IEP document—with their accompanying limitations:[2]

- The IEP memorializes the school district's compliance with the IDEA. *But* the IEP is too often designed to be and is viewed as being legal evidence of compliance with legal requirements, rather than a blueprint for educational programming.

- The IEP serves as the disclosure to the parents of the services and programming being provided for their child. *But* the IEP contains so much educational jargon and legal terminology that it is incomprehensible to many parents.

- The IEP details the disabilities the child faces that impact his or her education and the services that must be provided for the receipt of FAPE. *But* the IEP fails to consider the total child, his or her other non-disability-related needs and objectives.

- The IEP addresses the needs and programming for the child one year at a time in order to allow phased planning to achieve goals. *But* the one-year horizon lacks continuity and perspective on longer-term goals.

- The IEP is individualized because each child with a disability has unique needs. *But* the emphasis on individuality makes assessment of the student's achievement and accountability of the school system for achieving results much more difficult to measure.

Generally

1. What information must be included in an IEP?

34 C.F.R. § 300.346(a)(1)-(a)(5) lists the five types of information that must be included in each IEP. 34 C.F.R. § 300.346(b) adds a sixth requirement concerning transition services that must be addressed in the IEP of every student with a disability beginning no later than age 16.[3]

The five required IEP elements are:

- a statement of the student's present levels of educational performance (34 C.F.R. § 300.346(a)(1));

---

[2] "Enhancing Individual Student Accountability Through the IEP: Report of the Wingspread Conference on Accountability in Special Education: Enhancing Student Accountability," National Association of State Directors of Special Education, Inc., held October 7-9, 1996.

[3] *See* chapter 10, *infra,* concerning transition services.

- a statement of annual goals, including short-term instructional objectives (34 C.F.R. § 300.346(a)(2));

- a statement of both the special education and related services the student will receive and the extent to which he or she will participate in regular education (34 C.F.R. § 300.346(a)(3));

- the dates services will begin and are expected to terminate (34 C.F.R. § 300.346(a)(4)); and

- appropriate objective criteria and evaluation procedures and scheduling for determining, on at least an annual basis, whether the short-term instructional objectives are being achieved (34 C.F.R. § 300.346(a)(5)).

The regulations make it clear that mere recitation of the services to be provided to the student does not comply with the IDEA. In one state supreme court decision, the court rejected a proposed program and placement for an elementary school student with Down syndrome on the ground that the IEP, though it provided a statement of the needed services, lacked such items as annual goals and objectives, objective criteria and a statement of the amount of time the student would participate in regular education. *Thorndock v. Boise Indep. Sch. Dist.*, 1987-88 EHLR 559:486 (Sup. Ct. Idaho 1988).

The 1997 Amendments turned the five required statements into six, and in the process added new subparts and more specific information disclosures throughout. Here is where you can find the text of each element set out in full, along with a very brief discussion (all in chapter 2 herein):

Present educational level—Question 6

Annual goals—Question 11

Services to be provided—Question 28

Extent of inclusion—Question 25

When services are to be provided—Question 22

Determination of progress—Question 32

In addition, the 1997 Amendments add a range of items that must be considered at some or all IEP meetings. Sections 614(d)(3)(A) and (B). While statements documenting the discussion of these items—identified in Question 14 of chapter 4—are not included in the definition of an IEP at Section 614(d)(1)(A)(i)—(viii), it is possible that future regulations will so require or best practice will make it advisable to so include.

2.   May a school district include information in an IEP that is over and above the information required by the IEP content requirements of the IDEA (at 34 C.F.R. § 300.346)?

The IDEA does not prohibit states or school districts from including additional information in the IEP document. While the Notice of Interpretation does remind educators and administrators that the "IEP is not intended to be a detailed instructional plan" (Appendix C to 34 C.F.R. Part 300, Question 56), the inclusion of additional statements concerning specific aspects of programming is left to the discretion of state and local agencies.

The following is a sampling of additional information a school district may choose to include in IEPs.[4]

- Present levels of educational performance

- Annual goals and short-term objectives

- Appropriate objective criteria, evaluation procedures, and schedules for determining, on at least an annual basis, whether the short-term objectives have been met

- A statement of the specific special education services and the amount of time for each service

- A statement indicating the extent to which the student will participate in general education programs, and nonacademic and extracurricular services and activities

- A statement justifying removal from the regular education environment

- A statement indicating any medical information

- Appropriate indicators of related services that are required to assist the student

- Appropriate indicators of special transportation, if necessary

- A statement as to whether the student will be receiving regular or specially designed physical education

- A statement as to whether the student will be receiving regular or modified special education vocational education

- A statement as to whether the student will participate in standardized testing

- A statement as to whether a student with a visual disability needs to be taught braille

- Appropriate indicators of transition services

- A statement reflecting if the student needs extended school year services

---

[4] From the web site of the Kenosha Unified School District No. 1 (<hhtp://ksud.ksud.edu/ssps/web-doc3.htm>).

3. How standardized may an IEP document be while still complying with the IDEA's requirement for individualization?

Over time and across an entire student population, there likely will be substantial similarities between the disabilities and resulting educational needs of some eligible students with disabilities. Plus, accepted principles of organizational efficiency demand the use of standardized forms to the extent possible. Thus, given that individualized education is not individual education, it is reasonable to expect that no IEP will be altogether unique.

The First Circuit Court of Appeals recognized the real-world of education in *Roland M. v. Concord School Committee,* 16 EHLR 1129 (1st Cir. 1990). Rejecting the parents' claims of procedural inadequacies in the development of the IEP for their multi-disabled son, the court held that school districts may use computerized forms and need not "exhaustively and explicitly" document every personal detail about the child that was considered in formulating the IEP program.

Nevertheless, because an IEP is the foundation of a student's individualized special education program, a school district's compliance with the IDEA may be suspect if many of the district's IEPs are identical or if they contain generalized information. IEPs that reflect little personal information about the students do not have the requisite indicia of individual consideration of the student's situation. Thus, when a school district developed identical IEPs for students with similar disabling conditions, it denied those students FAPE. *Letter to New,* EHLR 211:464 (OSEP 1987); *see also Tipp City (OH) Exempted Village Sch. Dist.,* 25 IDELR 240 (OCR 1996) (school district's IEP for a student with multiple disabilities was based on the student's individual needs and was not substantially equivalent to the IEPs of other students in the multiple handicapped class).

Parents challenging an IEP on the basis of lack of individualization need not allege and prove that their child's IEP is identical to any other student's. Rather, a parent who can convince an administrative or judicial decision-maker that the IEP at issue is "generic" has more likely than not prevailed. In reviewing these allegations, courts and hearing officers look beyond facial compliance to closely analyze the actual language used in the IEP, in terms of its applicability to the student and his or her needs. The following cases illustrate how courts and review officers analyze the IEP document.

The court in *Chris D. v. Montgomery County Board of Education,* 17 EHLR 267 (M.D. Ala. 1990), ordered that the district implement the IEP developed by a private consultant for a 13-year-old boy with emotional and learning disabilities. In finding that the program proposed by the school district did not provide FAPE, the court held, among other things, that the IEP contained generic academic goals. In a footnote, the court specified why the goals were deficient.

> As a written document, this IEP, like other ones later adopted for [the student], consisted of two parts. The first was a preprinted form, with a heading for "specific

goals and objectives", and space for other related information beside it. However, despite the specificity suggested by this heading, the information included for [the student] was far from individualized. One typical objective read simply: "Student will participate in reading activities in the regular classroom," and indicated which reading textbooks [the student] would use. The second part of the IEP also consisted of several pre-printed pages, which listed various more specific-sounding "objectives" or "competencies," such as "the student will be able to: Read and write numbers 0-999", each followed by the phrase, "with _____% accuracy". On [the student's forms], the teacher simply filled in each blank with a number. There is no indication on these forms how the teacher arrived at these numbers.

17 EHLR at 273 n.9.

In *Evans v. Board of Education of the Rhinebeck Central School District,* 24 IDELR 338 (S.D.N.Y. 1996), the court ordered the school district to reimburse private school tuition paid by the parents of an adolescent with severe dyslexia. Among other procedural and substantive deficits in the IEP process, the court found that the objectives stated in the IEP were both broad and generic.

Interesting administrative decisions finding the school district violated the IDEA by including generic items in a student's IEP include: *Board of Education of the Lawrence Union Free School District,* 20 IDELR 1423 (SEA N.Y. 1994) (IEP's description of the management needs of a 10-year-old student with learning disabilities was generic and conclusory because it did not reflect the fact that the student had exhibited off-task and perseverative behaviors), *In re Child with Disabilities,* 19 IDELR 448 (SEA Ver. 1992) (IEP for an 18-year-old student with learning disabilities and ADD failed to offer FAPE because many of its provisions were generic in nature, with little mention made of strategies to address his particular disorders).

A final example of how use of a non-individualized IEP results in a denial of FAPE is the outrageous IEP described in *Hingham Public School,* 1986-87 EHLR 508:289 (SEA Mass. 1987):

> The proposed IEP was developed using a computer bank of curriculum goals and objectives. . . . It does not address Peter's [the student's] individual learning needs, styles or goals. From one look at the document this is obvious. . . . The proposed IEP in this matter is virtually unreadable. It contains no description of Peter's current functioning level. . . . The goals and objectives listed in the document are the same for all four quarters of the year, reflecting either extremely low expectations for Peter's progress or poor instructional planning. Moreover, the goals and objectives listed in Peter's IEP are remarkably similar to those for the other students in the Learning Center, despite admittedly varying learning needs, bolstering the conclusion that they were not individually tailored goals. Furthermore, undisputed testimony at the hearing supports the finding that three of the four major goals listed on the IEP were not appropriate for Peter and that 51 of the 77 specific objectives had already been mastered by Peter at the time the IEP was developed.

1986-87 EHLR at 508:294.

4. *What is the standard for review of the contents of the IEP?*

Facial compliance with the regulatory requirements is not enough. As made clear in the questions that follow concerning specific aspects of the content requirements of 34 C.F.R. § 300.346, administrative decision-makers review the IEP document for both procedural and substantive compliance with the IDEA. In fact, they frequently give the document an extremely rigorous line-by-line analysis that takes no prisoners. Illogic, inconsistency, vagueness are all noted.

Here's a good example: the review officer's analysis of the school district's IEPs for a gifted student with a learning disability and behavior problems in *Independent School District No. 625*, 22 IDELR 920 (SEA Minn. 1995).

> IEP #1 is devoid of present level of functioning information. While the District is permitted to attach the Assessment Team Summary Report with this first IEP, there is no evidence to suggest that the summary was in fact attached. Special Education needs are so vague that this need could conceivably apply to *any* student in *any* grade. Short-term objectives focus on what the student will do rather than on what "instruction" he needs to allow him to achieve each objective. IEP periodic review is incomplete. The "Adaptation of regular and special education" section is overly vague.

> Similarly, IEP #2 contains the identical, vague special education needs. Percent level of performance is described but is not consistent with his annual goal. His reading level is reported to be at the 3rd grade level, yet his goal is stated as "[Student] will improve his reading skills a minimum of 1 year. He needs to improve from 2.8 to 3.8 grade level." His short-term objectives remain unchanged except for levels of accuracy—even though the periodic review of his last IEP indicated he hadn't come close to meeting those objectives. Pages five and six remain identical to those of IEP #1. The IEP periodic review gives no indication as to how he is doing!

> IEP #3 comes closer to meeting *procedural* requirements, but still misses the mark. Interestingly, his annual goal for reading accounts for only minimal gains to be made and places him only four months ahead of his goal of two years earlier! Special education needs are vague. Again, only a few instructional goals are evident. Social work goals and objectives are vague, reflecting lack of personalization. Adaptations for regular classroom references a menu type checklist that is attached and reportedly incorporated by reference. However, the only adaptation listed is "A daily monitor sheet will be used daily [sic] to keep up with home behavior and missing assignments."

22 IDELR at 927-28.

Another good example of a "bad" IEP is found in *Elizabethtown Area School District*, 25 IDELR 353 (SEA Pa. 1996). In that decision the review panel affirmed the award of both tuition reimbursement and compensatory education for an elementary school student with reading, writing, spelling and math disorders. The IEP was found to be "woefully inadequate" because it failed to include all necessary elements and those it did include were vague and lacked specificity. At this point the school district was willing to concede that the IEP *was* vague. But tuition reimbursement was too harsh a remedy, it claimed. An order to reconvene the IEP team to make the IEP more specific would be enough. The panel responded that it was "not persuaded by the District's claim that vagueness is 'a subjective determination for which the sanction of reimbursement is much to (sic) strong.'" 25 IDELR at 356.

Statement of Present Levels of Educational Performance

5. Why must the IEP include a statement of the child's present levels of educational performance?

This section of the IEP helps to describe the problems that interfere with the child's education so that annual goals can be developed. The needs must be set forth in the IEP so that everyone working with the child knows the level at which the child is functioning and can develop an IEP that will provide the child with an appropriate education.

As stated by OSEP in its Notice of Interpretation on IEP Requirements:

> There should be a direct relationship between the present levels of educational performance and the other components of the IEP. Thus, if the statement describes a problem with the child's reading skill level and points to a deficiency in a specific reading skill, this problem should be addressed under both (1) goals and objectives, and (2) specific special education and related services to be provided to the child.

Appendix C to 34 C.F.R. Part 300, Question 36.

Thus, the statement of present levels creates a baseline for designing educational programming and measuring future progress.[5]

6. What information must a school district include in the statement of the child's present levels of educational performance?

This first required section of the IEP should provide relevant background information about the child's areas of need, strengths, interests and learning style. The description

---

[5] *See* also Questions 7 and 13 in this chapter, *infra,* about determining goals and objectives on the basis of the child's present level of performance and educational needs and Question 11 in this chapter, *infra,* about how to measure progress from that baseline toward the agreed goals.

should consider reports from each person who evaluated the child in preparation for the IEP meeting.

Specifically, the IEP statement should include:

- the child's academic achievement;

- the child's testing scores (with an evaluation of the scores);

- a report of the child's physical condition;

- a description of the child's emotional maturity, self-help skills, social adaptation, and development (social history); and

- a statement of the child's prevocational and vocational skills.

The child's strengths and weaknesses in each area should be specified, as should an explanation of how the child is best able to learn (including, for example, a description of the methodologies or modalities that are most effective for the child). The child's social and emotional behavior (including his or her interactions with adults and peers) should be described since these behaviors may affect learning.

The student's current status also should include a physical assessment and description of any medical or health problems that may impact instructional programming. This might include, for example, information concerning seizures, medications, equipment needs, allergies, heart defects, physical limitations, movement problems, hearing or visual problems, prosthetic needs, positioning difficulties, and any gross or fine motor skill problems.

If the child is currently in school, a report from the student's present teacher, including a discussion of the child's progress toward the annual goals in any previous (current) IEP, belongs in this section.

Because educational performance is such a broad term under the IDEA, this section of the IEP must be all-encompassing so as to provide a baseline that reflects the entire range of the child's needs, including both academic (e.g., reading, math, communication) and nonacademic (e.g., daily life activities, mobility) areas. Appendix C to 34 C.F.R. Part 300, Question 36.

As just one example of the emphasis placed on increasing the access of students with disabilities to the general curriculum, the 1997 Amendments at Section 614(d)(1)(A)(i) require that the statement of present levels of educational performance includes the following:

(I) how the child's disability affects the child's involvement and progress in the general curriculum; or

(II) for preschool children, as appropriate, how the disability affects the child's participation in appropriate activities.

7. Can a deficient statement of present levels of educational performance result in denial of FAPE?

Yes. If the statement does not consider the unique needs of the child, establish a baseline for establishing goals and monitoring progress or allow informed parental participation in the IEP process, then the IEP may be found to be fatally deficient.

The author knows of no better illustration of how problems with the description of needs at the outset infects the entire IEP than *Friedman v. Vance*, 24 IDELR 654 (D. Md. 1996). In that case, the IEP team did not take into account the elementary school student's needs related to her learning disability, as well as her speech impairment. The court described what happened next:

> The problems inherent in the failure to appreciate the importance of making the full diagnosis of the extent of the child's disabilities flow into deficiencies in the remainder of the IEP. By missing the learning disability problems, over and above the speech and language problems, the IEP lacks a full set of goals and objectives, and those that are present consist of mere sketches of the full range of services needed. It is not enough to say that certain services are inherent in a certain placement. . . .

24 IDELR at 657.

Similarly, the hearing officer in *Portland Public Schools*, 24 IDELR 1196 (SEA Me. 1996), faulted the school district for failing to appreciate the student's present level of educational performance in determining what services should be provided to deliver FAPE. The IEP proposed by the school district for a 15-year-old student with a learning disability was inappropriate because it reduced the amount of services the district would be providing in the face of decreasing standardized test scores.

8. Can the description of the present levels of educational performance simply identify the student's disability?

No. Consistent with the premise of the IDEA, each child's needs are unique; the resulting present levels of educational performance that must be included—and how they should be described—are also unique to that child.

As stated by OSEP in its Notice of Interpretation on IEP Requirements: "The statement of present levels of educational performance will be different for each child with a disability. Thus, determinations about the content of the statement for an individual child are matters that are left to the discretion of participants in the IEP meetings. . . ." Appendix C to 34 C.F.R. Part 300, Question 36.

A Note to that Notice section emphasizes that the statement must be both specific and unique. "Labels such as mental retardation or deafness may not be used as a substitute for the description of present levels of educational performance."

In *Letter to New*, EHLR 211:464 (OSEP 1987), OSEP explained why a school district could not lawfully prepare IEPs with the same statement of current levels of educational performance for all the students in a self-contained program for students with mental retardation.

> [W]hile some children within a category of disability may share some relevant behavior characteristics and educational needs, the possibility of finding sufficient clusters of children with identical behavior characteristics, identical levels of educational performance and identical educational needs is . . . remote. . . . Consequently, it is impermissible for public agencies to have the IEP for each student in a class contain identical statements of present levels of educational performance.

EHLR at 211:465-66.

Even in 1996, some school districts still fail to appreciate that generic descriptions of a student's current levels may lead to trouble. For example, in *Conemaugh Township School District*, 23 IDELR 1233, 1235 (SEA Pa. 1996), the review panel invalidated the IEP of a student which, among its other procedural deficits, contained a statement of current educational levels that "actually tells us nothing about where [the student] actually (sic) stands."

Even individual test scores may not adequately state a student's particular needs. The Notice of Interpretation states that, to the extent possible, the statement should be written in objective measurable terms and, in an effort to present objective information, "[t]est scores that are pertinent to the child's diagnosis might be included, if appropriate." Appendix C to 34 C.F.R. Part 300, Question 36.

One would think that standardized test scores from a student's evaluation are objective measurable terms that should be incorporated into the IEP of a student with a learning disability. But, as the decision in *Evans v. Board of Education of the Rhinebeck Central School District*, 24 IDELR 338 (S.D.N.Y. 1996) illustrates, inclusion of test scores does not always result in a compliant statement of current educational performance. Some uses of test scores can be problematic. In *Evans* the court held that the statement of present levels of educational performance in the IEP for a student with dyslexia failed to establish with precision his individual needs. By basing the student's programming on his broad scores in reading and writing, rather than testing designed to pinpoint his particular areas of weakness in spelling and word attack, the IEP masked the student's deficits and understated his need for more intensive programming. *Accord Board of Educ. of City Sch. Dist. of City of White Plains*, 20 IDELR 1475 (SEA N.Y. 1994) (recitation of the results of group-administered standardized reading and mathematics tests did not comprise an adequate statement of present levels of academic performance for a student with learning and emotional disabilities). *Contra Independent Sch. Dist. No. 625*, 22 IDELR 920 (SEA Minn. 1995) (school district was permitted to attach the preplacement evaluation, as it purported to do, although it would have helped if they had actually attached it).

Even when appropriate test scores are included, use of such scores in the statement of present levels of educational performance can result in the denial of FAPE. In the Notice of Interpretation on IEP Requirements, DOE stated that test scores, if used, should be "self-explanatory (i.e., they can be interpreted by all participants without the use of test manuals or other aids), or . . . an explanation should be included." Appendix C to 34 C.F.R. Part 300, Question 36. Failure to follow that guidance contributed to the decision in *Pocatello School District No. 25,* 18 IDELR 83 (SEA Idaho 1991), that procedural deficiencies in the description of the present levels of educational performance of an elementary school student with autism had a detrimental impact on her ability to receive FAPE. The hearing officer held that the parents could not fully understand the proposed educational program and participate in the IEP process because, among other things, numeric test scores were neither explained nor self-explanatory.

9. Can a school district reference an evaluation to comply with the IEP requirement for inclusion of a statement of present levels of educational performance?

There is nothing in the IDEA specifically prohibiting such an approach, although it is likely that by simply incorporating an evaluation the district will simultaneously provide both more information and less information than is required for purposes of the IEP. Put another way, the information in the evaluation may be thought of as raw data needing editing and focus to become the baseline for monitoring the student's educational progress.

For example, the hearing officer in *Fayetteville-Perry Local School District,* 20 IDELR 1289 (SEA Ohio 1994), held that the school district which incorporated by reference the student's end-of-the-year evaluation for the prior year as the present level of educational performance complied with 34 C.F.R. § 300.346(a)(1) because the report reasonably related to progress made on the previous year's long-term goals and short-term instructional objectives. On the other hand, the evaluation report from the private school at which the student was unilaterally placed could not be incorporated by reference as the statement of present levels of educational performance in *Board of Education of the City School District of the City of White Plains,* 20 IDELR 1475 (SEA N.Y. 1994), because it was too "cursory."

Statement of Goals and Objectives

10. Why are goals and objectives required in an IEP?

The statement of goals and objectives enables both prospective and retrospective review of a child's educational program. "In effect, these requirements provide a way for the child's teacher(s) and parents to be able to track the child's progress in special education." Appendix C to 34 C.F.R. Part 300, Question 37.

With regard to prospective review of the adequacy of a student's educational program, proposed placement and services should be analyzed to ensure that all such elements of the student's program are logically and educationally related to achievement of the goals and objectives identified in the IEP. The statement of goals and objectives also highlight gaps in programming. Each IEP goal should have corresponding items of instruction or services identified. Having goals without related programming indicates that the school district is not providing FAPE.

That was the case in *Burlington School District,* 20 IDELR 1303 (SEA Ver. 1994). The school district's IEP for a seriously emotionally disturbed teenager contained detailed goals and objectives in the areas of study skills and social and emotional development in school. However, because it included no specific related services to address the student's identified needs for social and emotional development in his home or community, it did not offer FAPE.

That same analysis can be done retrospectively as well, when using the current year's program to plan for the next year. The statement of goals and objectives may be used in retrospective analysis as a mechanism for determining "whether the anticipated outcomes for the child are being met (i.e., whether the child is progressing in the special education program)." Appendix C to 34 C.F.R. Part 300, Question 37.

Without meaningful goals, the provision of an appropriate program of services and instruction that actually meets the identified needs of the child is almost accidental. Generally speaking, an IEP that lacks meaningful educational goals is likely to be fatally defective. As just one example, consider the IEP proposed by the school district for a high school student with a learning disability in *Susquentia School District v. Raelee S.,* 25 IDELR 120 (E.D. Pa. 1996). In that case the parents were entitled to two years' reimbursement at a private school because the student's IEP lacked meaningful educational goals and, as a result, also lacked adequate short-term objectives, criteria for measuring progress and adequate programming or services to address the student's identified problem areas.

As the review panel in *Conemaugh Township School District,* 23 IDELR 1233, 1236 (SEA Pa. 1996) observed: "[N]o program can appropriately address a student's needs without first defining the goals it is expected to achieve." Thus, the panel in that case held that the IEP for a post-high school student with unspecified disabilities was fatally defective because it did not contain a goal for each of his identified needs, while, on the other hand, it promulgated a goal for an area that arguably was one of his strengths. The review panel also found more global deficits with the IEP related to its establishment of goals.

> Finally, we believe the deficiencies in the program/IEP content find their genesis in a basic failure to decide upon, in conjunction with [the student], what the overall goal of his education is. Whether that be to attend college, some other postsecondary

institution, or pursue a vocational career, no program can appropriately address a student's needs without first defining the goals it is expected to achieve.

23 IDELR at 1236.

The 1997 Amendments likely will change the response to this question, as explained in Question 11 in this chapter.

11. Must the school district develop goals and objectives relating to all aspects of the education of a child with a disability?

No, according to the Notice of Interpretation on IEP Requirements, goals and objectives need only be formulated for those areas in which the IEP identifies an educational need resulting from the child's disability. 34 C.F.R. Part 300, Question 36. As stated in the response to Question 40:

> IEP goals and objectives are concerned primarily with meeting the needs of a child with a disability for special education and related services, and are not required to cover other areas of the child's education. Stated another way, the goals and objectives in the IEP should focus on off-setting or reducing the problems resulting from the child's disability that interfere with learning and educational performance in school.

Relying on that section of the Notice of Interpretation did not save the school district in *Los Angeles Unified School District,* 24 IDELR 503 (SEA Cal. 1996). The district was found to have crafted a defective IEP for a six-year-old child with orthopedic and hearing impairments, because it failed to include academic goals and objectives in the student's IEP. The district argued, unsuccessfully, that no academic goals or objectives were required because the student was placed in regular education classes and was not receiving special education instruction.

The hearing officer found that argument "without merit," although the author finds erroneous the reasoning articulated in support of that conclusion—that goals and objectives must always be included for regular education classroom instruction. The better position is that goals and objectives are required when the student is receiving special education or supplementary aids and services, in either a regular or special education classroom. The author is not alone in that view. The administrative law judge in *Clarion-Goldfield Community School District,* 22 IDELR 267 (SEA Iowa 1994), found that academic goals must be included in the IEP for an eight-year-old with Down syndrome and other cognitive disabilities, despite the fact that he was receiving his academic instruction—indeed spending 75% of his day—in the regular education classroom.

The 1997 Amendments have broadened the focus from providing special education services to improving overall educational results for children with disabilities. As a result, DOE's Notice of Interpretation, discussed immediately above, likely narrows impermissibly how goals and objectives should now be approached.

The IEP definition in Section 614(1)(A)(ii) provides that the IEP must include the following:

> (ii) a statement of measurable annual goals, including benchmarks or short-term objectives, related to—
>
> > (I) meeting the child's needs that result from the child's disability to enable the child to be involved in and progress in the general curriculum; and
> >
> > (II) meeting each of the child's other educational needs that result from the child's disability.

12. *How are annual goals developed?*

Annual educational goals should be developed to correlate directly with the child's present educational levels, as delineated in the first portion of the child's IEP (34 C.F.R. § 300.346(a)(1)).

Goals should not be too broad or too vague, nor should they be as specific as the short-term objectives.[6] According to the administrative law judge in *Edmonds School District*, 16 EHLR 1049 (SEA Wash. 1990), the statement need not include the exact number of minutes per class and number of minutes in each class spent toward achieving each objective. Further, both the goals and objectives should be written to allow objective measurement of the extent to which the student is making progress in achieving them.[7]

Overall, as the district court in *Friedman v. Vance*, 24 IDELR 654, 656 (D. Md. 1996), stated: "The [IEP] form is not a mere formality. Rather, the goals and objectives must match the plans. The goals and objectives, moreover, must be complete and thorough, and not merely superficial." As just one example, consider how the school district in *French v. Omaha Public Schools*, 17 EHLR 811 (D. Neb. 1991), presented its 80 objectives for a 14-year-old student with multiple disabilities, along with related measurement criteria and schedule:

> For each objective there is a description of the person who is to implement the objective, a narrative description of the objective, a statement of what evaluation procedures will be used, and a schedule for when those evaluation procedures will be implemented. [An example] will serve to illustrate how the IEP approaches this area.

> One of the objectives for language was the following:

> OBJECTIVE FOR: LANGUAGE

---

[6] *See* Question 14 in this chapter, *infra.*

[7] *See* Question 10 in this chapter, *supra.*

IMPLEMENTED BY: CLASSROOM TEACHER

Given reading paragraph with three to ten specified events at second to third grade reading level, student will retell the content of the story, using key vocabulary cue list without teacher assistance (independently) at 80% accuracy.

EVALUATION PROCEDURE:

Independently read paragraph and asked to retell story content of the ten events, given list of key vocabulary.

EVALUATION SCHEDULE:

Weekly

17 EHLR at 820.

When developing annual goals it is also important to capitalize on the child's strengths. Both the child's past and present educational performance, his or her preferences, the priority of various needs and the amount of time anticipated for the child to attain each of the goals should be considered. While seeking to foster a child's strengths, the IEP team also should develop goals that will help the child overcome or minimize his or her areas of need so that the disability will be of as little a hindrance as possible to the child's ability to function in daily life.

If a school district formulates unrealistic annual goals it serves neither the student nor its own staff well. For example, a hearing officer found that a school district should not have permitted either parental pressure or a misguided desire to accommodate the parents to result in the formulation of an IEP for an eighth-grade student with a learning disability which contained unreasonably demanding goals and objectives. *Vallejo Unified Sch. Dist.,* 16 EHLR 571 (SEA Cal. 1989).

13. How many annual goals must be included in an IEP?

The IDEA does not establish a specific number. That would be inconsistent with the overall emphasis on individualization. As a general rule, there should be at least one annual goal to address each area of need. But the relevance and practicality of the goals in light of the child's total needs and the remaining amount of time the child will continue to be in the educational system needs to be taken into account in setting priorities. As explained by the hearing officer in *Clarion-Goldfield Community School District,* 22 IDELR 267 (SEA Iowa 1994):

> It is truly a judgment call by the multidisciplinary team as to what goals to include in an IEP. The IEP should not include so many goals that the child cannot reasonably be expected to complete them but yet the team must guard against overlooking an important area for the child.

22 IDELR at 274.

Each of a student's recognized needs must be addressed by the IEP committee. Thus, school officials at the IEP meeting for an eight-year-old student with Down syndrome, developmental delays and communication deficits violated the IDEA when they refused to consider the student's recreation and leisure needs. In that case, *Clarion-Goldfield Community School District*, 22 IDELR 267 (SEA Iowa 1994), the hearing officer found that the IEP team should have addressed whether the student's recreation and leisure needs were items that should be addressed in the IEP, even though the student's priority needs clearly were in the areas of speech and communication.[8]

Similarly, the hearing officer in *Richardson Independent School District*, 21 IDELR 333 (SEA Tex. 1994), found that a 15-year-old student with a pervasive developmental disorder (PDD) was denied FAPE because his IEP failed to include goals and objectives addressing his identified need of anxiety management. As a remedy the student's parent was awarded reimbursement of private school tuition and the costs of psychotherapy services necessary for him to cope with his anxiety.

14. What is the relationship between annual goals and short-term objectives?

Annual goals set out, for each area in which a child with a disability has an identified need, what he or she has a reasonable chance of attaining in a year. Those goals are then broken down into short-term objectives.

The Notice of Interpretation on IEP Requirements describes annual goals as "statements that describe what a child with a disability can reasonably be expected to accomplish within a twelve month period, in the child's special education program." Appendix C to 34 C.F.R. Part 300, Question 38.

The Notice also describes how short-term objectives relate to annual goals:

> Short term instructional objectives (also called IEP objectives) are measurable, intermediate steps between the present levels of educational performance of a child with a disability and the annual goals that are established for the child. The objectives are developed based on a logical breakdown of the major components of the annual goals, and can serve as milestones for measuring progress toward meeting the goals.

Appendix C to 34 C.F.R. Part 300, Question 39.

Short-term objectives should describe a subskill of an annual goal, not merely restate the goal. The objectives should be written in a sequential order that reflects a progression through the various skills needed to meet the annual goals and permit monitoring of progress throughout the year. The IEP for the student with autism in *Pocatello School District #25*, 18 IDELR 83 (SEA Idaho 1991), was suspect because

---

[8] In a classic example of what not to do at an IEP meeting, some members of the IEP team laughed when the student's mother suggested provision of recreation services.

the short-term objectives concerning fine motor skill development all had the same start date (the first day of the year) and the same target date (the end of the year), rather than being broken down into smaller, more achievable components that build upon each other over the course of the school year.

The IEP at issue in *Hingham Public School,* 1986-87 EHLR 508:289 (SEA Mass. 1987), similarly had short-term objectives that remained constant throughout the school year. It is not clear if that was the tip-off to the hearing officer that the IEP had a myriad of both substantive and procedural deficits, but it is true that in many cases failure to show a progression in the objectives reflects a significant programming problem that implicates FAPE. That was certainly the case in *Hingham,* in which the violations were egregious.

While annual goals are distinct from short-term objectives, the administrative decision in *Board of Education of Waterford-Halfmoon Union Free School District,* 20 IDELR 1092 (SEA N.Y. 1994), illustrates how appropriately drafted short-term objectives may compensate for inadequate annual goals. In that case the annual goals for a student with a learning disability, such as "will increase reading comprehension, improve study skills and increase writing skills," were impermissibly vague. Nevertheless, the lack of specificity was not fatal to the IEP because the short-term objectives both set the general direction to be taken by those charged with implementing the IEP and provided a basis for developing detailed instructional plans. *See also Board of Educ. of Rondout Valley Cent. Sch. Dist.,* 24 IDELR 203 (SEA N.Y. 1996).

15. Should the IEP include goals and objectives for related services?

Generally no, although if the student receives instruction during the course of being provided with the related service, then goals and objectives are necessary.

There is no IDEA requirement to include separate annual goals and objectives for related services, assuming the related service is being provided to meet an identified need for which an annual goal and objective is otherwise included in the IEP. *Letter to Hayden,* 22 IDELR 501 (OSEP 1994). Thus, OSEP states, goals and objectives for related services such as air conditioning or catheterization are not required to be included in an IEP if the service is necessary only to enable the student to attend school and is not intended to provide an educational benefit in itself.

A related service such as transportation also may fall into that category, depending on the purpose for which it is being provided. Assuming it is being provided solely to enable the student to attend school, then no goals and objectives are required. But if the mode of transportation is intended to provide some other benefit related to the student's education—such as enabling the student to increase independence or have increased opportunities for socialization—then goals and objectives relating to independence or socialization must be included for the transportation service, so progress can be monitored and measured. *Letter to Hayden, supra; accord Letter to Smith,* 23 IDELR 344 (OSEP 1995).

Applying the same reasoning, the administrative decision-maker in *Urban v. Jefferson County School District R-1,* 21 IDELR 985 (SEA Col. 1991), concluded that the IEP for a multi-disabled student did not have to include annual goals and objectives for the student's aide. The student's own goals and short-term objectives should take into account the progress expected to be achieved through the services provided by the aide.

16. What is the relationship between the short-term objectives of an IEP and those contained in classroom instructional plans?

Short-term objectives should not be as specific as those in daily lesson plans, although they should be specific enough to serve as the basis for those plans. Appendix C to 34 C.F.R. Part 300, Question 41.

The Notice of Interpretation on IEP Requirements distinguishes the objectives of the two planning documents as follows:

> In some respects, IEP objectives are similar to objectives used in daily classroom instructional plans. For example, both kinds of objectives are used (1) to describe what a given child is expected to accomplish in a particular area within some specified time period, and (2) to determine the extent that child is progressing toward those accomplishments.

> In other respects, objectives in IEPs are different from those used in instructional plans, primarily in the amount of detail they provide. IEP objectives provide general benchmarks for determining progress to be accomplished over an extended period of time (e.g., an entire quarter or semester). On the other hand, the objectives in classroom instructional plans deal with more specific outcomes that are to be accomplished on a daily, weekly, or monthly basis. . . .

Appendix C to 34 C.F.R. Part 300, Question 39.

17. Must the objectives contained in instructional plans also be included in the student's IEP?

No, although the preparation of lesson plans with detailed objectives is good practice, that level of detail is not appropriately made a part of an IEP. Appendix C to 34 C.F.R. Part 300, Question 42.

18. Can an IEP include goals that will require more than one school year to accomplish?

No. According to OSERS, while the planning process for a child with a disability is not limited to a one-year span, the goals and objectives contained in the IEP are.

Letter to Butler, EHLR 213:118 (OSERS 1988). Even when the school district anticipates needs that must be met over several future years, only the components of those long-range goals that must be addressed—and can be reasonably expected to be accomplished—in the year under consideration should be included in that year's IEP.

Notwithstanding the parameters for setting out goals in the IEP, IEP teams should keep in mind that the ultimate goal of the IDEA is to provide children with disabilities with a future. The purpose of education is to produce productive citizens who can live in and contribute to their communities to the maximum extent possible. This should be the long-term goal for nondisabled students and students with disabilities alike.

19. Must a school district convene an IEP meeting before changing short-term objectives?

Generally yes, although a 1995 decision of the Fifth Circuit Court of Appeals suggested an exception—in a footnote, no less.

Long-standing interpretation of the IDEA mandates the convening of an IEP whenever a school district proposes to change a short-term objective contained in a student's IEP. As stated in the Notice of Interpretation on IEP Requirements: "Since a change in short term instructional objectives constitutes a revision of the child's IEP, the agency must (1) notify the parents of the proposed change (see § 300.504(a)(1)), and (2) initiate an IEP meeting." Appendix C to 34 C.F.R. Part 300, Question 43.

In *Buser v. Corpus Christi Independent School*, 22 IDELR 626 (5th Cir. 1995), the court held that a school district did not change the short-term objectives set out in the IEP for an adult student with autism when it discontinued those objectives that had been mastered by the student.

> Mastering a short-term objective is not a 'change' under 20 U.S.C. § 1415(b)(1)(C) [concerning the requirement for prior notice to parents], but merely constitutes the completion of a listed objective in the IEP. The successful completion of a short-term objective is a necessary step in the implementation of the IEP if the annual goal is to be achieved.

22 IDELR at 628 n.5.

20. Must a school district periodically report to parents about their children's progress in accomplishing their short-term objectives?

Yes and no under the IDEA, and an unqualified yes under the 1997 Amendments.

While the IDEA does not require a school district to issue periodic reports on students' progress with their IEP programs, *Letter to Anonymous*, 21 IDELR 998 (OSEP 1994), general reporting procedures typically provide periodic updates for all students.

Further, while the IDEA does not require school districts to include in IEPs specific "checkpoint intervals" (i.e., meeting dates) for reviewing a child's progress, school districts should grant any reasonable requests for IEP meetings. Appendix C to 34 C.F.R. Part 300, Question 11. In addition, an IEP team could decide to include specific meeting dates in the IEP document, if all members of the team believe that would be appropriate for that student. Appendix C to 34 C.F.R. Part 300, Question 34.

The new IEP definition in the 1997 Amendments makes it clear that districts must periodically report progress toward IEP goals. Section 614(d)(1)(A)(viii)(II) states that the IEP must include a statement of

> how the child's parents will be regularly informed (by such measure as periodic report cards), at least as often as parents are informed of their nondisabled children's progress, of—(aa) their child's progress toward the annual goals described [in the law]; and (bb) the extent to which that progress is sufficient to enable the child to achieve the goals by the end of the year.

21. What is the relationship between annual goals and the provision of FAPE?

According to the Ninth Circuit Court of Appeals, whether a student makes adequate progress toward achieving appropriate goals set out in his or her IEP is the standard by which one can evaluate retrospectively if that student has received FAPE. As the court opined in *County of San Diego v. California Special Education Hearing Office*, 24 IDELR 756 (9th Cir. 1996):

> [I]n any particular case, the student's IEP defines what goals are relevant in providing the measure of whether a student is getting an educational benefit in the place-ment. . . . [T]he correct standard for measuring educational benefit under the IDEA is not merely whether the placement is "reasonably calculated to provide the child with educational benefits," but rather, whether the child makes progress toward the goals set forth in her IEP.

24 IDELR at 760-61.

Progress toward IEP goals is the standard typically used in deciding if a student with a disability should be graduated,[9] but the standard for determining if a student has received FAPE *is,* in fact, whether the IEP was reasonably calculated to provide educa-tional benefit, *Board of Education of the Hendrick Hudson Central School District v. Rowley,* 1981-82 EHLR 553:656 (1982), the Ninth Circuit's view notwithstanding.

IDEA regulations at 34 C.F.R. § 300.350 also cast doubt on the Ninth Circuit's blanket pronouncement. That section states that: ". . . Part B of the Act does not require

---

[9] *See* Question 17 in chapter 10, *infra.*

that any agency, teacher, or other person be held accountable if a child does not achieve the growth projected in the annual goals and objectives."

Well-reasoned opinions in the Third Circuit further support the view that whether an IEP is reasonably calculated to provide educational benefit is determined prospectively. *Fuhrmann v. East Hanover Bd. of Educ.*, 19 IDELR 1065 (3d Cir. 1993); *Susan N. and David N. v. Wilson Sch. Dist.*, 23 IDELR 526 (3d Cir. 1995); *accord Roland M. v. Concord Sch. Comm.*, 16 EHLR 1129 (1st Cir. 1990) (appropriateness of the school district's IEP could not be judged exclusively in hindsight); *Manchester Sch. Dist. v. Christopher B.*, 19 IDELR 143 (D.N.H. 1992), *rev'd. on reconsideration on other grounds*, 19 IDELR 389 (D. N.H. 1992); *Portland Pub. Schs.*, 20 IDELR 596 (SEA Me. 1993) (failure to meet the majority of goals in the IEP is not cause for finding the IEP inappropriate).

As explained by the *Fuhrmann* court:

> *Rowley* requires, at the time the initial evaluation is undertaken, an IEP need only be "reasonably calculated to enable the child to receive educational benefits." . . . Our understanding of *Rowley* comports with that of the district court: that the measure and adequacy of an IEP can only be determined as of the time it is offered to the student, and not at some later date.
>
> Judge Mansmann's concurring opinion [in the court below] underscores and emphasizes the importance of this threshold determination. Neither the statute nor reason countenance "Monday morning quarterbacking" in evaluating the appropriateness of a child's placement. Thus, Judge Mansmann and I are in complete agreement as to the time when we must look at the "reasonable calculation" made pursuant to *Rowley*.

19 IDELR at 1069.

Statement of Special Education, Related Services and Extent of Participation in Regular Education

22. Must the IEP specify the amount of the specific special education and related services to be provided in terms of hours or minutes?

No, although expression in such terms should be adopted when most appropriate, considering the nature of the service.

It is clear that the IEP must specify the amount of services to be provided in some way. It is not enough simply to list the services. "The amount of services to be provided must be stated in the IEP, so that the level of agency's commitment of resources will be clear to parents and other IEP members." Appendix C to 34 C.F.R. Part 300, Question 51. OSEP also made it clear in its 1994 *Letter to Copenhaver,* 21 IDELR 1183 (OSEP

1994), that school districts are not required to specify in the IEP the amount of services the student will receive in terms of hours and minutes. Nonetheless, when the nature of the service (for example, direct physical therapy) lends itself to such description, statements of precise daily allotments of service are preferable. When, on the other hand, the service is one that cannot be expressed meaningfully by use of a daily allocation (for example, the services of an aide for a behaviorally disordered student placed in a regular education classroom), then an estimated weekly allocation should be included in the IEP.

Echoing the requirement in the Part H regulations (at 34 C.F.R. § 300.344(d)(1)(i)) that an IFSP specify the "frequency, intensity, location, and method" of delivering early intervention services, the 1997 Amendments at 614(d)(1)(A)(vi) require that the IEP contain a statement of "the anticipated frequency, location, and duration" of the special education, related services and supplementary aids and services called for in the IEP. Here again, though, there is no explicit requirement that hours and minutes be stated.

As a related matter, the Committee Report to accompany the Senate's Reauthorization bill posits the following rationale for adding the new requirement for identification of the location where services will be provided:

> The location where special education and related services will be provided to a child influences decisions about the nature and amount of these services and when they should be provided to a child. For example, the appropriate place for the related service may be the regular classroom, so that the child does not have to choose between a needed service and the regular educational program.

S. Rep. No. 105-17, at 22 (1997).

23. Is placement in a regular education classroom with auxiliary aids and services considered participation in a regular education or special education program?

Placement in a regular education classroom with auxiliary aids and services is considered participation in a regular education classroom, for purposes of drafting an IEP that complies with 34 C.F.R. § 300.346(a)(3). The term "regular education program" is undefined in the IDEA or its regulations. In responding to an inquiry about whether a class wholly consisting of children with disabilities, but taught by a regular education teacher, is a regular education placement, OSEP acknowledged the LRE mandate[10] of

---

[10] The directive to segregate children with disabilities as seldom as possible, set out in the IDEA at 20 U.S.C. § 1412(5)(B): "To the maximum extent appropriate, children with disabilities, including children in public or private institutions or other care facilities, are educated with children who are not disabled and that special classes, separate schooling, or other removal of children with disabilities from the regular educational environment occurs only when the nature or severity of the disability is such that education in regular classes with the use of supplementary aids and services cannot be achieved satisfactorily."

the IDEA has resulted in a blurring of the lines between regular and special education. *Letter to Mancuso,* EHLR 211:433 (OSEP 1987).

Nevertheless, compelled to make a distinction by the requirements of 34 C.F.R. § 300.346(a)(3), which mandates a statement of the extent to which a child with a disability will be educated in the regular education program, OSEP opined that for that purpose, a regular education program is education in a class in which most students are not receiving special education.

24. Must the IEP indicate the amount of time a student will be educated in the regular education program in terms of hours or minutes?

No, while the IEP for each child with a disability must include "a statement of . . . the extent that the child will be able to participate in regular educational programs (34 C.F.R. § 300.346(a)(3))," neither the statute nor the regulations specify a particular format. According to the Notice of Interpretation on IEP Requirements, "one way of meeting this requirement is to indicate the percent of time the child will be spending in the regular education program with non-disabled students. Another way is to list the specific regular education classes the child will be attending." Appendix C to 34 C.F.R. Part 300, Question 52.

25. Must the IEP include a statement justifying why any removal from the regular education environment is appropriate?

No under the IDEA, but yes under the 1997 Amendments.

Neither 34 C.F.R. § 300.346(a)(3) (requiring a statement of the extent that the child will be able to participate in regular educational programs) or any provision of the IDEA regulations impose such an informational requirement. A concise written articulation of the basis for the placement decision does not appear to be a required element of any IDEA documentation, although certainly the multidisciplinary team's preplacement evaluation should justify such a determination. Nevertheless, the IDEA does not prohibit including such a statement in the IEP and it is possible that a state or local law or policy mandates its inclusion.

The 1997 Amendments presume that children with disabilities should be educated in the regular classroom. S. Rep. No. 105-17, at 21 (1997). Proceeding on that basis, Section 614(d)(1)(A)(iv) states that an IEP must include "an explanation of the extent, if any, to which the child will not participate with nondisabled children in the regular class and [extracurricular and other nonacademic activities]."

26.   Should any modifications needed to place a child with a disability in a regular education program or classroom be included in the IEP?

Yes. While regular education programming is not considered an item of specialized instruction or service in an IEP, a description of any supplementary aids and services[11] needed to allow such placement is required. That was the view of DOE in its Notice of Interpretation on IEP Requirements, Appendix C to 34 C.F.R. Part 300, Question 48 and in the more recent *Letter to Anonymous,* 20 IDELR 541 (OSEP 1993). In that response OSEP stated that when modifications to the regular education program are necessary to ensure the participation of a child with a disability in that program, then such modifications must be provided to the child and included in the IEP. *Accord Letter to Shelby,* 21 IDELR 61 (OSERS 1994) (determinations about whether a student with disabilities requires modifications such as large print text books and one-on-one assistance must be made by the participants on the student's IEP team and incorporated in his or her IEP); *Bridge Creek (OK) Sch. Sys.,* 25 IDELR 325 (OCR 1996).

The Notice of Interpretation does not recite the only possible interpretation of the IDEA's requirement in connection with documentation of regular education classroom modifications. The hearing officer in *School District of Beloit,* 25 IDELR 109 (SEA Wis. 1996), for example, opined that a school district was not required to enumerate accommodations that might assist the student in regular education activities. Such modifications, not needed to assist a student in benefiting from special education, were not related services; only related services needed to be included in the IEP under 34 C.F.R. § 300.346.

The extent of the required description is not addressed in the Notice of Interpretation, however, leaving the matter to the discretion of the school district or state department of education. While there is little published case law addressing this issue, the court in *Lascari v. Board of Education,* 1988-89 EHLR 441:565 (N.J. 1989) affirmed a hearing officer's finding that the school district's failure to identify in the IEP the supplementary aids, such as special reading materials, a calculator, and modified homework and testing arrangements, did not justify an award of tuition reimbursement.

On the other hand, the hearing officer in *Saddleback Unified Sch. Dist.,* 23 IDELR 477 (SEA Cal. 1995), found that the IEP's three "general guidelines" for including a student with severe migraine headaches in regular education kindergarten was not a

---

[11] Supplementary aids and services have been understood to be modifications to the regular education program made to ensure the satisfactory participation of a student with a disability. Common examples include a one-to-one aide, curriculum adaptations, special seating arrangements and assistive technology. The 1997 Amendments added a statutory definition at Section 602(29) which provides that supplementary aids and services means "aids, services, and other supports that are provided in regular education classes or other education-related settings to enable children with disabilities to be educated with nondisabled children to the maximum extent appropriate in accordance with [the least restrictive environment provision of the law]."

statement of specific modifications, as required by the IEP content requirements of the IDEA. Those guidelines were: "1. regular team meetings with parents; 2. developing school/classroom contingencies for dealing with headaches and their physical ramifications; and 3. adapting instruction to ensure maintenance of positive attitude toward school." 23 IDELR at 479.

While the school district maintained that the general guidelines in the IEP, developed in the spring preceding the start of the student's kindergarten year, were intended to be supplemented in the fall before the student started his schooling, the hearing officer properly held that the IEP must stand on its own and, as written, was deficient.

Confirming the DOE Notice of Interpretation, Section 614(d)(1)(A)(iii) mandates the identification of the supplementary aids and services to be provided to the student. *See also* Question 28 in this chapter, in which Section 614(d)(1)(A)(iii) is set out in full.

27.   Is the failure of an IEP to indicate the amount of time a student will be educated in the regular educational program necessarily a denial of FAPE?

Not always. Although "a statement of . . . the extent that the child will be able to participate in regular educational programs" is a required element of an IEP under IDEA regulations at 34 C.F.R. § 300.346(a)(3), its omission will not always be fatal. Normally, such a statement is an essential item because of the IDEA's goal of placing students in their least restrictive environments. As explained by OSEP in *OSEP Memorandum 95-9*, 21 IDELR 1152 (OSEP 1994):

> The relationship of IDEA's LRE requirements to the IEP process is key, since under IDEA, the student's IEP forms the basis for the student's placement decision.[12] . . . At the student's IEP meeting, the extent that the student will be able to participate in regular educational programs is one of the matters to be addressed by all the participants on the student's IEP team before the student's IEP is finalized.

21 IDELR at 1154.

Despite this general rule, the review officer in *Board of Education of Greenwood Lake Union Free School District*, 23 IDELR 1032 (SEA N.Y. 1996), held that a school district's failure to indicate in a student's IEP the extent to which she would be participating in regular education was harmless. The student was a young child with autism whose program was based on the TEACCH method. The mother had visited the school and was well-informed about the programming set out in the IEP. Thus she was clearly aware that the program was self-contained and opportunities for inclusion with nondisabled students at recess, lunch and the like was very limited.

---

[12] *See* Question 27 in chapter 3, *infra,* with regard to school districts reversing that process, referred to frequently as predetermining placement.

28. Should the IEP include all the special education and related services needed for that student to receive FAPE?

Yes, the IEP must include all the specific special education and related services needed by the student. Thus, for example, health-care related services, such as tube feeding or clean intermittent catheterization, the provision of which the IEP team determines are necessary for the student to receive FAPE in his or her LRE must be included in the IEP, despite the seemingly "non-educational" nature of the services. *See, e.g., Letter to Williams*, 25 IDELR 634 (OSEP 1996).

As explained in the Notice of Interpretation on IEP Requirements,

> Each public agency must provide FAPE to all children with disabilities under its jurisdiction. Therefore, the IEP for a child with a disability must include all of the specific special education and related services needed by the child—as determined by the child's current evaluation. This means that the services must be listed in the IEP even if they are not directly available from the local agency, and must be provided by the agency through contract or other arrangements.

Appendix C to 34 C.F.R. Part 300, Question 44.

As the Notice of Interpretation states, a responsible public agency does not have to directly provide (i.e., with its own employees) an item of service listed in the student's IEP.[13] In addition, a responsible public agency may not even be financially responsible for all items identified on an IEP.[14]

Recognize also that a student with a disability may need supportive services that are not considered special education and related services and thus are not the responsibility of the school district (or other public agency responsible for providing FAPE). Appendix C to 34 C.F.R. Part 300, Question 47; see Question 34 in this chapter, *infra*.

An IEP which fails to state all the special education and related services needed by a student fails to meet both the procedural and substantive requirements of the IDEA.[15] Further, an IEP which fails to clearly specify the nature and type of services to be provided is inadequate. *E.g., Board of Educ. of Carmel Cent. Sch. Dist.*, 21 IDELR 633 (SEA N.Y. 1994) (although the board recommended that a 12-year-old student with Down syndrome receive the services of a special education teacher to provide technical support in the classroom and a teaching assistant, the IEP made no specific mention of these services).

This is the case even with preschool services, such as discrete trial training, that are not as easily described as the services more typically provided in the school

---

[13] *See* Question 14 in chapter 11, *infra,* concerning contracting with other providers.

[14] *See* Questions 13 in chapter 11, *infra.*

[15] *See, e.g.,* the discussion of Hillsborough County School Board, 21 IDELR 191 (SEA Fla. 1994), in Question 11 in chapter 1, *supra.*

environment to school age students with disabilities. For example, the hearing officer in *Board of Education of the Ann Arbor Public School*, 24 IDELR 621 (SEA Mich. 1996), held that the parents of a preschool child with autism were entitled to reimbursement of their costs for a home-based program of Lovaas therapy because the IEP failed to address issues such as: how many hours of Lovaas training it proposed providing, the format for the training (one or two persons), the length of the school day, and how the home and school components of the program would be coordinated. The district had included these items in a separate document; but, because it was not prepared at the same time as the IEP or distributed to the parents, it did not cure the IEP defects.

Conversely, an IEP should not identify services that are not provided or are no longer to be provided. Failure to revise an IEP to delete services that are no longer being provided constitutes discrimination on the basis of a disability. *Rockdale County (GA) School District*, 22 IDELR 1047 (OCR 1995) (the district discriminated against a student with muscular dystrophy in violation of Section 504 and the ADA when it failed to remove provisions calling for physical therapy and adaptive physical education from the student's IEP after it discontinued providing those services at the request of the parents).

The 1997 Amendments retain the requirement that the IEP include a statement of all the special education and related services required to provide FAPE. In addition, the new law expands the range of items and services the provision of which must be identified in the IEP. Section 614(d)(1)(A)(iii), set out in full below (with newly required documentation italicized), requires that the IEP include:

> (iii) a statement of the special education and related services and *supplementary aids and services* to be provided to the child, *or on behalf of the child, and any program modifications or support for school personnel* necessary for the child—
>
> > (I) to advance appropriately toward attaining the annual goals;
> >
> > (II) to be involved and progress in the general curriculum in accordance with [the student's annual goals] *and to participate in extracurricular and other nonacademic activities;* and
> >
> > (III) to be educated and participate with other children with disabilities and nondisabled children in the activities described in this paragraph.

In explaining the new requirement for a statement of supplementary aids and services in the IEP, the Committee Report to accompany the Senate's Reauthorization bill made it clear that not every adjustment made to help a student with a disability rises to the level of a "program modification" for purposes of inclusion on the IEP. "Specific day-to-day adjustments in instructional methods and approaches that are made by either a regular or special education teacher to assist a disabled child to achieve his or her annual goals would not require action by the child's IEP Team." S. Rep. No. 105-17, at 20 (1997).

29. What type of information about a student's educational program does not have to be included in an IEP?

While 34 C.F.R. § 300.346(a)(1)-(a)(5) delineates mandatory IEP elements, it is not always clear what additional types of information a school district might be expected to provide in the document. According to OSEP, the following generally are *not* necessary elements of an IEP:

- identification of particular teachers or other educational personnel (*Letter to Hall,* 21 IDELR 58 (OSEP 1994));

- identification of educational materials (*Letter to Hall,* 21 IDELR 58 (OSEP 1994));

- Title I or other non-special education services that the student may need (*Letter to Montano,* 18 IDELR 1232 (OSEP 1992));

- recommendations submitted to or discussed at IEP meetings, but not adopted (*Letter to Anonymous,* 20 IDELR 1460 (OSEP 1994));

- evaluation procedures and schedules (Appendix C to 34 C.F.R. Part 300, Question 54.);

- extracurricular activities that are not considered part of a student's appropriate educational program (*Letter to Anonymous,* 17 EHLR 180 (OSEP 1994));

- educational methodology (*Letter to Hall,* 21 IDELR 58 (OSERS 1994); *Letter to Anonymous,* 21 IDELR 573 (OSEP 1994); the Committee Report to accompany the Senate's Reauthorization bill confirmed that under the 1997 Amendments methodology is not "expected to be written into the IEP." S. Rep. No. 105-17, at 21 (1997));

- selection of particular classroom or teacher (*Letter to Fisher,* 21 IDELR 992 (OSEP 1994));

- personal devices such as hearing aids and eyeglasses (*Letter to Seiler,* 20 IDELR 1216 (OSEP 1993));

- class size and teacher/pupil ratios (*Letter to Williams,* 25 IDELR 634 (OSEP 1996)); and

- behavior management plans (*Letter to Huefner,* 23 IDELR 1072 (OSEP 1995)).

Despite the requirement in the 1997 Amendments that the IEP include a statement of services or programming modifications necessary for involvement in extracurricular activities (Section 614(d)(1)(A)(iii)(II)), there appears to be no change to the definition of FAPE vis-à-vis participation in extracurricular activities. Further, there is no requirement that such activities be included in the IEP when participation is not necessary for FAPE. On the other hand, the 1997 Amendments may require districts to include behavior management plans in IEPs. *See* Question 14 in chapter 4, *infra.*

Courts and administrative decision-makers have recognized other items that are neither individualized instruction nor related services and thus do not have to be included in a student's IEP:

- teacher training (*Sioux Falls Sch. Dist. v. Koupal*, 22 IDELR 26 (S.D. 1994), *Prins v. Independent Sch. Dist. No. 761*, 23 IDELR 544 (D. Minn. 1995));

- provision of teacher's manuals to parents (*Maine Administrative District #35*, 22 IDELR 907 (OCR 1995));

- specific scheduling of programming included in the student's IEP (*Maine Sch. Admin. Dist. No. 74*, 21 IDELR 1218 (SEA Me. 1995));

- provision of home notes to parents (*Granite Sch. Dist.*, 19 IDELR 402 (SEA Utah 1992)); and

- identification of classroom characteristics, such as class size, class age range, classroom management and teaching style (*Morgan Hill Unified Sch. Dist.*, 19 IDELR 557 (SEA Cal. 1992)).

The *Koupal* decision might be different under the 1997 Amendments, since Section 614(d)(1)(A)(iii) requires inclusion of support for school personnel to the extent necessary for a particular child. In that case the support at issue was training in the TEACCH method for the teacher of an autistic child.

Concerning the inclusion of recommendations that were considered but rejected: Do not assume that just because such information is not a required part of the IEP it is not a sound idea to document in some way what proposals were reviewed at the IEP. This is particularly true when the school district declines to incorporate proposals for provisions of services advanced by the parents. An alternative to including this item in the IEP itself is to include a discussion of proposals reviewed and rejected in the minutes of the meeting.[16]

With regard to delineating the required contents of an IEP, the IDEA's emphasis on meeting the child's individual needs trumps, as always, the application of general rules. Thus, in *Letter to Seiler*, OSEP stated that if the IEP team determines that a child needs a hearing aid to receive FAPE, the IEP should reflect the need for the hearing aid and the public agency should provide it at no cost to the parents. Similarly, in *Board of Education v. Scotia-Glenville Central School District*, 23 IDELR 727 (SEA

---

[16] *See* Question 14 in chapter 4, *infra.*

N.Y. 1995), the state review officer held that an IEP team could be required to identify individual service providers by name if the student's needs were so unique that he or she would not be able to benefit from instruction from anyone else. This is a heavy burden to bear, though, placed squarely on the parents advocating such identification.

The instruction and related services needed to provide FAPE is a floor, not a ceiling. Thus, a school district may elect to provide additional instruction or services. When it does so, the IEP could reflect those supplemental items, as well. *Prins v. Independent Sch. Dist. No. 761,* 23 IDELR 544 (D. Minn. 1995) (teacher training can be included in a student's IEP).

30. Can interscholastic sports (or other extracurricular activities) be included in an IEP?

Yes, they are, although one federal district court decision suggests that, even if they are included, the school district may have a lesser obligation to provide them if the student is barred from participation by application of nondiscriminatory eligibility rules.

Usually, participation in interscholastic sports or other extracurricular activities is not considered a necessary component of an appropriate education. This conclusion follows from the standard of appropriateness propounded in *Board of Education of Hendrick Hudson Central School District v. Rowley,* 1981-82 EHLR 553:656 (1982). In the regular education environment, extracurricular activities are, by definition, "extra." They are for enrichment—a maximization of a student's educational opportunities.

For this reason, interscholastic sports or other extracurricular activities are not expressly included in the related service of "recreation" under 34 C.F.R. § 300.16(b)(9). *See Rettig v. Kent City Sch. Dist.,* 1985-86 EHLR 557:308 (6th Cir. 1986); *Letter to Miller,* EHLR 211:468 (OSERS 1987). As a result, it is not unusual to find that participation in athletic programs is not included in the IEP of a student with a disability. *See, e.g., Rhodes v. Ohio High Sch. Athletic Ass'n,* 24 IDELR 936 (N.D. Ohio 1996) (high school athlete with learning disabilities was not required to exhaust IDEA administrative remedies to contest exclusion based on athletic association's maximum semester rule because there was no indication that his participation was included in his IEP).

Nonetheless, participation in an interscholastic sport or other extracurricular activity can be included in an IEP if the IEP team determines that such participation is a necessary component of FAPE and includes participation as a specific related service in the student's IEP. *Letter to Anonymous,* 17 EHLR 180 (OSEP 1990).

Whether or not participation in athletics (or another extracurricular activity) is included in a student's IEP can be critical. When participation is not included, a student with a disability may be barred from participating because of failure to meet generally applicable maximum age or minimum grade level requirements.[17] On the other hand,

---

[17] Courts are split on whether such rules, when applied to students with disabilities, violate the antidiscrimination requirement of Section 504 and the ADA. A leading case upholding the maximum

if the activity is included in a student's IEP, then participation cannot be barred by any otherwise applicable age or time limiting rules. The school district is obligated to provide the services identified on the student's IEP. "[A]ll services in the IEP must be provided in order for the agency to be in compliance with the Act." Appendix C to 34 C.F.R. Part 300, Question 45; *see also* Question 11 in chapter 1, *supra*.

At least that's what OSEP opined in *Letter to Anonymous, supra.* The District Court for the District of Connecticut also held to that effect in *Dennin v. Connecticut Interscholastic Athletic Conference, Inc,* 23 IDELR 704 (D. Conn. 1996). The court ruled that, while there generally is no constitutional right to participate in interscholastic sports, a student with a disability whose IEP included competitive swimming on his high school team has a federally protected right to challenge his exclusion from the team on the basis of generally applicable age eligibility rules. The inclusion of team swimming in the student's IEP transformed it into a federally protected right. *Accord M.H. v. Montana High Sch. Ass'n,* 25 IDELR 42 (Mont. 1996) (for a student with a disability to have a federally protected right to participate in interscholastic sports, the student must have an IEP under the IDEA which includes participation in sports).

That interpretation of the IDEA was rejected by the federal district court for the Eastern District of Pennsylvania in its decision in *Beatty v. Pennsylvania Interscholastic Athletic Association,* 24 IDELR 1146 (W.D. Pa. 1996). In that decision, the 19-year-old student with a learning disability had continued participation on his high school volleyball and basketball teams listed on his IEP. Seeking to defeat application of the athletic association's maximum age rule, the student filed suit. In its decision denying the student's request for a preliminary injunction, delivered from the bench, the court discounted the importance of inclusion of the activity in the student's IEP. Looking beyond the four corners of the IEP document, it held that participation in sports was not an essential part of the student's educational program. Thus, the rights accruing to items related to the provision of FAPE did not attach.

31. Why is educational methodology not required to be included in the IEP?

Essentially, in enacting the IDEA Congress elected to defer to state and local governments on decisions about educational methodology. That discernment of congressional intent was expressed in the seminal case of *Board of Education of Hendrick Hudson Central School District v. Rowley,* 1981-82 EHLR 553:656 (1982), and it still holds sway as a prime consideration in resolving disputes about the provision of FAPE.

Educational methodology is a set of working methods or techniques, procedures and rules used in the education of children, as distinguished from a special educational

---

age limitation of an athletic association is Pottgen v. Missouri State High School Activities Association, 21 IDELR 929 (8th Cir. 1994). A well-reasoned decision requiring case-by-case analysis is Sandison v. Michigan High School Athletic Association, Inc., 21 IDELR 658 (E.D. Mich. 1994).

program or placement. Thus, it has been treated as outside the scope of concerns that trigger parental involvement under the IDEA.[18]

As the Supreme Court explained in *Rowley:*

In assuring that the requirements of the [IDEA] have been met, courts must be careful to avoid imposing their view of preferable educational methodology upon the States. The primary responsibility for formulating the education to be accorded a handicapped child, and for choosing the educational method most suitable to the child's needs, was left by the [IDEA] to state and local educational agencies in cooperation with the parents and guardians of the child. . . . [I]t seems highly unlikely that Congress intended courts to overturn a State's choice of appropriate educational theories in a proceeding brought pursuant to Section 1415(e)(2) [of the IDEA].

We previously have cautioned that courts lack the "specialized knowledge and experience" necessary to resolve "persistent and difficult questions of educational policy." We think that Congress shared that view when it passed the [IDEA]. . . . Therefore, once a court determines that the requirements of the Act have been met, questions of methodology are for resolution by the States.

1981-82 EHLR 553:663 (footnotes and citations omitted.)

The law is thus clear that parents cannot compel the choice of methodology, assuming the method offered by the school district is reasonably calculated to provide educational benefit. However, as the district court observed in *Brougham v. Town of Yarmouth,* 20 IDELR 12 (D. Me. 1993), one cannot easily separate questions of methodology from questions of appropriateness. In those instances, though, when the school district succeeds in characterizing a dispute with parents as one concerning a choice between competing methodologies, both of which provide FAPE, the school district prevails.

Nevertheless, parents litigate, quite passionately, whether the school district's chosen methodology provides FAPE. Such disputes have been more common when the child has a low-incidence disability, such as deafness or autism, but parents of learning disabled students also have litigated quite strongly for certain methods for teaching reading. Authoritative court decisions concerning disputes about methodology include:

- *Lachman v. Illinois State Board of Education,* 1988-89 EHLR 441:156 (7th Cir. 1988)—hearing impairment

- *Bonnie Ann F. v. Calallen Independent School District,* 22 IDELR 615 (6th Cir. 1994)—hearing impairment (cochlear implant)

- *Barnett v. Fairfax County School Board,* 17 EHLR 350 (4th Cir. 1991)— hearing impairment

---

[18] *See* Question 29 in this chapter, *supra.*

- *Dreher v. Amphitheater Unified School District,* 20 IDELR 1449 (9th Cir. 1994)—hearing impairment
- *Delaware County Intermediate Unit v. Martin and Melinda K.,* 20 IDELR 363 (E.D. Pa. 1993)—autism
- *Board of Education of Downers Grove Grade School District No. 58 v. Steven L. and Christine L.,* 23 IDELR 36 (N.D. Ill. 1995)—learning disability

This is not to say that methodology should not be discussed at IEP meetings; it should. *Broughan v. Town of Yarmouth, supra.* As discussed above, it is conceptually difficult to cleanly separate issues of methodology and appropriateness. And there is no good purpose served in prohibiting discussion of items that are often of the most concern to parents. OSEP thus supports discussion of issues of methodology in the interest of parental participation. In *Letter to Anonymous,* 21 IDELR 573 (OSEP 1994), the inquirer focused on the use of phonics with learning disabled students. While advising that the federal government does not require school districts to use any specific instructional method, it also stated that a parent can appropriately raise the use of a particular teaching method during an IEP meeting.

The Committee Report to accompany the Senate's Reauthorization bill endorsed discussion of methodology issues at IEP meetings, stating that "teaching and related services methodologies or approaches are an appropriate topic for discussion and consideration by the IEP team." S. Rep. No. 105-17, at 21 (1997).

Other Issues

32. Must the IEP include objective criteria for monitoring a student's progress for that student to receive FAPE?

Yes, the IDEA requires that such criteria be included in the IEP; failure to so include generally will not be treated as a mere technical defect. 34 C.F.R. § 300.345(a)(5) provides that "[a]appropriate objective criteria and evaluation procedures and schedules for determining, on at least an annual basis, whether the short-term instructional objectives are being achieved" must be included in the IEP.

Three judicial decisions illustrate the importance of including adequate objective monitoring criteria in the student's IEP: *Lascari v. Board of Education,* 1988-89 EHLR 441:565 (N.J. 1989); *Chris D. v. Montgomery County Board of Education,* 17 EHLR 267 (M.D. Ala. 1990); and *Evans v. Board of Education of Rhinebeck Central School District,* 24 IDELR 338 (S.D.N.Y. 1996). In all three cases, the courts characterized the criteria for monitoring as "vague." When something in an IEP is found to be vague, one can be fairly certain it does not comply with the IDEA.

In *Lascari* the district court explained the importance of including such criteria and evaluation procedures, stating that an IEP program incapable of being evaluated for appropriateness—with no objective way to measure the student's progress—is itself inappropriate because it impedes the informed participation of parents and does not allow identification of any needed changes. The court found that the school district erred in the first instance when it designed the goals and objectives for a junior high school student with dyslexia who had an IQ of 126 but read on a second-grade level. His IEP had five goals:

- to continue a phonetic-linguistic reading program to strengthen skills;

- to develop math skills to include all areas necessary for practical math;

- to develop a language arts program;

- to build self-esteem and self-worth; and

- to develop vocational skills.

The problem is clear: The goals are incapable of objective measurement. While self-esteem and self-worth may be amorphous concepts, the hearing officer correctly pointed out that objective tests scores well measure progress in word recognition, spelling or mathematics, yet they were not included.

In *Chris D.* the criteria for monitoring academic progress seemed concrete and objective on the surface, but the court found them "vague." Review of those criteria, provided by the court in a footnote, suggests that the difficulty may have been with the sole use of classroom tests and work to assess progress.

> [T]he first objective in [the student's] new IEP, provided in standard form: "The student will maintain a/an _____ % average in math on the 3rd grade level," with 80% written in the blank space, and stated that [the student] would be evaluated by reference to his "Daily work" and "Chapter tests." . . . [A] supplement to the IEP also consisted of several pre-printed pages which listed more specific-sounding "objectives" or "competencies" such as "The student will be able to: Identify periods to punctuate sentences with _____ % accuracy," with the figure "80" again written in. The supplement also indicated that the student would be evaluated by means of "unit tests."

17 EHLR at 273, n.14.

The court in *Evans* uses the same type of barely suppressed sarcasm as did the *Chris D.* court in holding that the school district's IEP was fatally defective as a result of its vague and subjective methods for monitoring progress. Again, believing that some of the best learning comes from seeing what to avoid, we quote the court's description of the offending IEP:

> [T]he first goal in Frank's [the student's] October 1994 IEP provided that he would be evaluated on the listed objectives by reference to "teacher observation" and "80% accuracy." With reference to the second goal, the October 1994 IEP provided that Frank would be evaluated by "teacher evaluation" and "80% success." Although the IEP repeatedly incants these phrases—"teacher observation," "80% success"— because there is little indication of what Frank's level of success was when the IEP was written, it fails to specify strategies for adequately evaluating Frank's academic progress. . . . Again, . . . with regard to the June 1994 IEP, which used the same mantra to a large extent, . . . it did not set forth measurable criteria to assess progress.

24 IDELR at 346.

On the administrative level, concerns about hindering parental participation caused the hearing officer in *Pocatello School District #25,* 18 IDELR 83 (SEA Iowa 1991), to invalidate the IEP for a student with autism. Because the student's behavior, socialization and awareness of others were critical educational issues, the failure of the IEP to establish objective ways to measure her progress in these areas was material.

Another administrative decision shows that a school district's failure to comply with 34 C.F.R. § 300.345(a)(5) need not always be fatal. In *Sioux City Community School District,* 20 IDELR 107 (SEA Iowa 1993), the IEP for a 13-year-old girl with a hearing impairment lacked statements of present level of educational performance, objective criteria and evaluation procedures. The school district was forced to concede at due process that no specific measure or test was used to assess either initial levels of performance or progress toward objectives. Nevertheless, the hearing officer found, based on testimony of two of the student's teachers, that the student did derive significant benefits from her program. That being the case, the ALJ concluded that "[i]nadequate measurement procedures specified *in the IEP* do not render the educational program inappropriate." 20 IDELR at 109.

The evidence the school district submitted to show progress was extensive and, to a certain extent, fortuitous. Here is what the school district had to present to dig itself out of the hole it created by failing to properly design the student's IEP:

- Daily work samples
- Classroom observations
- Unit test scores
- Passing grades, including "legitimate" Bs in language arts classes
- Two formal academic evaluations

See also *Board of Educ. of Casadaga Valley Cent. Sch. Dist.,* 20 IDELR 1023 (SEA N.Y. 1994) (IEP for a 12-year-old student with Tourette syndrome and attention deficit disorder was defective because it failed to set forth objective criteria and evaluation procedures).

Although the 1997 Amendments use different language than the IDEA, inclusion of a statement of objective criteria appears to remain a requirement. Section 614(d)(1)(A)(ii) mandates inclusion of "measurable" annual goals. Section 614(d)(1)(A)(viii)(I) requires a statement of "how the child's progress toward the annual goals described [in the law] will be measured." In the Report to accompany its Reauthorization bill, the Senate Committee terms the requirement for a statement of measurable annual goals "crucial." S. Rep. No. 105-17, at 20 (1997).

33. Do the same IEP content requirements apply to both school age and preschool children?

Yes. In *Letter to Anonymous,* 23 IDELR 342 (OSEP 1994), the inquirer questioned whether some of the mandates of the IDEA (Part B) make sense when applied to pre-kindergarten children with disabilities. Pertinent to our purposes, the inquirer questioned whether educational goals, the statement of which is a required part of a child's IEP under 34 C.F.R. § 300.346(a)(3), are appropriate for this population.

In response OSEP stated that, after determining that a preschool child is eligible for special education and related services, a school district must develop an IEP for that child that is based on his or her individual needs. The contents to be included in that IEP are all those specified in 34 C.F.R. § 300.346, the same as it is for children attending elementary or secondary school.[19]

One distinction the 1997 Amendments make between the content requirements for school age and preschool age children is found in Section 614(d)(1)(A)(i) with regard to the statement of present levels of educational performance. Subsection (I) mandates description of "how the child's disability affects the child's involvement and progress in the general curriculum," while subsection (II) requires "for preschool children, as appropriate [a description of] how the disability affects the child's participation in appropriate activities."

34. Should the IEP document describe the total education of the student with a disability?

No. The Department of Education makes it clear that the IEP needs to include only: (1) the provision of special education and related services and (2) the extent to which the student can participate in regular education programs, with or without supplementary aids and services. Appendix C to 34 C.F.R. Part 300, Question 47.

As DOE further explains in the Notice of Interpretation:

---

[19] *See also* Questions 5 through 11 in chapter 11, *infra,* concerning the IEP process when children transition from Part H to Part B.

For some children with disabilities, the IEP will only address a very limited part of their education (e.g., for a child with a speech impairment, the IEP would generally be limited to the child's speech impairment). For other children (e.g., those with profound mental retardation), the IEP might cover their total education. An IEP for a child with a physical disability with no mental or emotional disability might consist only of specially designed physical education.[20] However, if the child also has a mental or emotional disability, the IEP might cover most of the child's education.

The 1997 Amendments taken as a whole confirm the movement toward viewing the education of a child with a disability in a more holistic way. With the the emphasis on improving results in the general curriculum and increasing access to the regular school environment, the IEP seems likely to become less focused on special education and services. Nonetheless, there is no suggestion in the 1997 Amendments that the IEP process is intended to supplant the traditional rights of states and local school districts to design or implement the general curriculum. Likewise, there is no requirement that the general curriculum itself be described or contained in the IEP.

35. Can an IEP team make either the provision of special education or the placement contingent upon the administration of Ritalin to the student?

No, an IEP team may not condition the provision of special education and related services or the placement upon the administration of Ritalin or any other medications to a student. The Department of Education specifically addressed this type of situation in its Notice of Interpretation of IEP Requirements:

> There may be instances where the parents and agency are in agreement about the basic IEP services (e.g., the child's placement and/or special education services), but disagree about the provision of a particular related service (i.e., whether the service is needed and/or the amount to be provided). In such cases, it is recommended that (1) the IEP be implemented in all areas in which there is agreement, (2) that the document indicate the point of disagreement, and (3) that the procedures be initiated to resolve the disagreement.

Appendix C to 34 C.F.R. Part 300, Question 35.

Based upon that reasoning, a federal district court held in *Casey J. v. Derry Cooperative School District*, 17 IDELR 1095 (D.N.H. 1995), that a school district violated the IDEA when it insisted, over parental objections, on the administration of Ritalin to a child diagnosed with attention deficit disorder as a prerequisite to the provision of special education and related services.

---

[20] What if the student with a physical disability only does not need adaptive physical education either? Can he or she be IDEA-eligible? That was the question answered in the affirmative in Yankton School District v. Schramm, 24 IDELR 704 (8th Cir. 1996).

It seems unlikely that there will be factual circumstances under which a school district would wish to proceed to due process over the content of an IEP where it feels the child needs medication in spite of the objection of the parents. In such a case, the school district would be better advised to prepare an IEP based on the individual needs and circumstances of the child, when he or she is unmedicated.[21]

36. Are parents required to sign IEPs?

No, according to the Notice of Interpretation, neither the IDEA nor its regulations mandate the signature of parents. Appendix C to 34 C.F.R. Part 300, Question 29. Nonetheless, the Department of Education notes three reasons why having parents' signatures on the IEP, as well as the signatures of the other IEP team members, is useful.

- To serve as record of attendance at IEP meeting

- To document for parents the services the school district has agreed to provide

- To indicate the parents' approval of the programming contained—or not contained—in the document

With regard to the last item, parents do not waive their rights to contest the IEP if they sign it, but their credibility suffers. Many opinions thus reflect attempts by parents to say they were coerced into signing the IEP or misunderstood the significance of affixing their signatures. Signatures also defeat allegations of lack of notice of IEP changes. For example, the court in *Buser v. Corpus Christi Independent School District,* 20 IDELR 981 (S.D. Tex. 1994), rejected the parent's claim that the student's IEPs were changed without notice to them because IEPs submitted in evidence showed that the parents had signed and approved all IEPs from 1978 to 1984.

Under the 1997 Amendments, parents who do sign the IEP may, however, jeopardize their rights to tuition reimbursement or attorneys' fees in the event of a later dispute. *See* Question 2 in chapter 12, *infra,* for citation to and a brief discussion of the pertinent law changes.

---

[21] Such a placement, although likely to be more restrictive, could nevertheless satisfy the school district's legal obligations. District officials also may consider their obligations under state child neglect statutes, in the event the refusal to allow administration of medication results in alarming behavioral problems.

Chapter 3

Formulating the IEP: Development, Review and Implementation

In proposing amendments to the IDEA in 1995, the Department of Education had occasion to review the impact of the IDEA on the education of children with disabilities over the 20 years since enactment. Overall, it found substantial achievement; the exclusion of children with disabilities is largely a thing of the past. Beyond the basic protection of constitutional rights, the IDEA has substantially improved educational outcomes for students with disabilities, the Department of Education found.

Because the initial objectives of the IDEA have been largely accomplished, the time was right, according to the Department, to refocus the IDEA more on improving post-school outcomes for students with disabilities. While the law had been intentionally process-oriented, it was now time to modify aspects of the law to focus on improving results. School districts, among others, claimed that more resources could be devoted to outcomes if various changes could be made in the law. Among those changes, reduce the focus on paperwork and process.

The Department of Education's Reauthorization proposal did, in fact, propose a wide array of changes to virtually all aspects of the IDEA, almost all of which were reflected in some way in the 1997 Amendments. These proposals were themselves results-oriented, with specific amendments proposed to accomplish six specific goals:

- Align the IDEA with state and local educational reform efforts so that students with disabilities can benefit from them.

- Improve results for students with disabilities through higher expectations and access to the general curriculum.

- Address individual needs in the least restrictive environment.

- Provide families and teachers—those closest to the students—with the knowledge and training to effectively support students' learning.

- Focus resources on teaching and learning.

- Strengthen early intervention to help ensure that every child starts school ready to learn.

Interestingly, the 1997 Amendments make virtually no changes in the IEP process itself: IEP development, review and implementation would continue essentially unchanged. The only significant change, though, addresses an issue that has generated a fair amount of litigation: the relationship between IEP determinations and placement decisions.

Prior to the 1997 Amendments, parents did not have a federal right to participate in placement decisions. While by no means the sole factor, this exclusion of parents from a critical decision while it is being made can lead to an adversarial relationship, as often the only way a parent can have input is through the more adversarial due process. As discussed in this chapter, the 1997 Amendments remedy that situation by creating a federal right to parental participation in both eligibility and placement decisions.

It is not surprising that the 1997 Amendments contain virtually no changes to the sections of the IDEA dealing with the timelines and process for developing, reviewing and implementing IEPs. The guiding principles are eminently sensible: a student with a disability should be provided appropriate programming as soon as possible after his or her eligibility has been determined and that programming should be periodically reviewed for continuing suitability, being modified as required. The statute and regulations themselves are clear and, especially in comparison to the arcane nature of some other federal laws, simple.

Yet, this chapter cites not just the law, but many judicial and administrative decisions in which a school district was found to have not complied with these relatively straightforward requirements. Worse, from the school district's perspective, many instances involve serious disputes about what programming should be provided and relationships between parents and school officials that are anything but collaborative. Those instances in which the school district should be on guard to comply precisely with all the procedural requirements are, in effect, the ones in which the press of the officials' administrative burdens seems to overwhelm them.

Developing the Initial IEP

1. How soon after a student is identified as IDEA-eligible must the IEP meeting be convened?

IDEA regulations require that a meeting to develop a student's initial IEP be held within 30 calendar days of the date on which the student was found to be IDEA-eligible. 34 C.F.R. § 300.343. The stated purpose of the 30-day requirement is to ensure that there be no significant delays between the time the student is evaluated and the time he or she begins to receive needed services. Appendix C to 34 C.F.R. Part 300, Question 7.

The 30-day timeframe sometimes can be a problem, particularly when the evaluation is made shortly before the summer vacation. Recognizing that difficulty, OSEP opined in its *Letter to Lillie,* 23 IDELR 714 (OSEP 1994), that, while the Part B regulations clearly contemplate that IEP meetings be held after eligibility determinations are made, they do not preclude a school district from developing an IEP in anticipation of the student being determined to be eligible.

Difficult as it may be to schedule IEP meetings within the 30-day timeframe, some school districts are faced with even tighter timelines established under state special education law. In *Hall v. Detroit Public Schools,* 20 IDELR 18 (E.D. Mich. 1993), for example, the court held that 34 C.F.R. § 300.343(c) establishes a floor; states may establish a shorter timeline.

Interestingly enough, there is no specific timeline established for the time between the identification of a possible disabling condition and the preplacement evaluation or for the time between finalization of the IEP document and implementation. 34 C.F.R. § 300.342. Nevertheless, the establishment of the 30-day timeline for convening the initial IEP meeting shows the direct connection the IDEA makes between timely decision-making and the provision of FAPE. *Reusch v. Fountain,* 21 IDELR 1107 (D. Md. 1994).

The court's decision in *Gerstmyer v. Howard County Public Schools,* 20 IDELR 1327 (D. Md. 1994), illustrates the importance of timely scheduling of IEP meetings for initial programming. In that case the court awarded private school tuition reimbursement to the parents of a first grader because, among other things, the school district scheduled an IEP meeting on September 25, almost 60 days after being advised of the student's exceptionality.

In *Gerstmyer* the district also delayed evaluating the student and ultimately proffered a one-size-fits-all IEP, so the precise impact of that particular violation—delay in scheduling—is difficult to assess. It was significant, though, that the delay resulted in the dyslexic child starting his school career with no special preplanning in place to assist him in his adjustment and to give him a good start in his school career.

A hearing officer similarly awarded reimbursement for an in-home Lovaas program to the parents of a five-year-old with autism because the district waited almost five months after an initial eligibility determination to develop a complete IEP. The district in *Cobb County School System,* 24 IDELR 875 (SEA Ga. 1996), claimed it had received "too many applications" for the needed services to process them in accordance with the IDEA timeline. "This does not constitute a legal excuse," the hearing officer held, "but rather an admission that the school system could not live up to its first responsibility." 24 IDELR at 875.

Two court decisions—*Salley v. St. Tammany Parish School Board,* 22 IDELR 878 (5th Cir. 1995) and *Myles S. v. Montgomery County Board of Education,* 20 IDELR 237 (M.D. Ala. 1993)—show that, on the other hand, failure to meet the 30-day timeline is not always fatal. In *Salley,* the district's failure to hold an IEP meeting for a fourth-grade transfer student with learning disabilities within 30 days of her May enrollment did not violate the IDEA. At that time, only 14 days remained of the school year and the student's records were not forwarded until after the end of the school year. In *Myles,* the court held that the school district's delay in convening an initial IEP meeting for a preschool age child with multiple disabilities was a "technical violation" that should be excused because the school made a good faith effort to comply with the regulations, gave the parents an opportunity for meaningful participation and provided a meaningful educational benefit in the interim period before finalization of the IEP.

Part of the difficulty in *Myles,* like in *Salley,* was an intervening summer vacation. The court made it clear, though, that ordinarily summer breaks do not excuse compliance with 34 C.F.R. § 300.343(c). "[W]hen students enter the program for the first time, the school system must hold meetings to develop an actual IEP and establish the actual IEP before the school year begins, even if that requires meeting with the child and the parents during the summer." 20 IDELR at 239.

2.   How soon after a student with a disability is referred for evaluation must an IEP be approved by the parents?

There is no specific period of time under the IDEA, although the amount of time required should be reasonable and without undue delay.

The timeline for conducting a preplacement evaluation starts running from the time the district suspects or has reason to suspect that a child has a disability. Preplacement evaluations procedures at 34 C.F.R. § 300.531 do not, however, provide a specific timeline in which the evaluation must be conducted. According to OSEP, each state must establish and implement standards to ensure that the right of each student with a disability to receive FAPE is neither denied nor delayed because the school district fails to conduct an initial evaluation within a reasonable period of time. *Letter to Barnett,* 18 IDELR 1235 (OSEP 1992).

The timeline for convening a meeting to develop a student's initial IEP is within 30 days of the date the student is determined to be IDEA-eligible. 34 C.F.R. § 300.343(c). There is no timeline for completion of the IEP meeting or the creation of the IEP document which should result from the meeting. Again reasonableness is the rule, as far as federal requirements are concerned.

Thus, the amount of time that elapses from referral for evaluation to approval of the IEP may vary. As an example of what was found appropriate in a particular instance (under Section 504), OCR held in *Huntsville City (AL) School District,* 24 IDELR 1195 (OCR 1996), that a student with a learning disability who was referred for evaluation, evaluated and had an IEP designed and approved by his parents within a six-week time period was not denied FAPE; the district's actions were timely.

State laws, however, may establish specific timelines assuming they are at least as protective of the student's right as those under the IDEA. North Carolina, for instance, requires that the provision of special education and related services be implemented within 90 calendar days of the date of the initial referral. *See Beaufort County Schools v. Roach,* 21 IDELR 113 (N.C. Ct. App. 1994).

3. Can an IEP meeting be combined and held concurrently with a meeting to determine eligibility?

The IDEA regulations generally contemplate a three-step process for determining a child's FAPE: multidisciplinary team determination of eligibility (34 C.F.R. § 300.532); IEP meeting to design a program of appropriate programming and services (34 C.F.R. § 300.343); and another multidisciplinary team determination of the appropriate, i.e., least restrictive environment, placement in which to implement the IEP (34 C.F.R. § 300.533).

Nevertheless, according to the Department of Education, states are free to determine whether or not to hold separate eligibility meetings before the IEP meetings or to combine the two steps in one. Appendix C to 34 C.F.R. Part 300, Question 8. Consistent with that stance, OSEP opined in *Letter to Neveldine,* 20 IDELR 181 (OSEP 1993), that if a multidisciplinary team is composed of all the participants required for an IEP team meeting, the determination of special education and related services may be made by the MDT.

Substantially stricter regulatory requirements govern IEP meetings, as opposed to multidisciplinary team decisions. Rather than the specific identification of individuals who must participate in IEP meetings (34 C.F.R. § 300.344), the regulations for evaluation procedures (34 C.F.R. § 300.352(e)) generally require only that at least one team member be knowledgeable in the area of suspected disability. In the case of placement decisions, the regulations are a bit more specific (34 C.F.R. § 300.533(a)(4)), but still allow wide discretion.

Most notably, in neither case need parents be included as multidisciplinary team members. As a result, the formality requirements regarding notice for and conduct of meetings—indeed, the requirement to hold meetings in the first instance—associated with the IEP process are not carried over into the evaluation and placement arenas in federal IDEA regulations.

The 1997 Amendments follow through on the finding that the parents of children with disabilities should be more involved in educational decision-making by creating a federal right to participate in both eligibility (Sections 614(a)(4)(A) and 615(b)(1)) and placement (Sections 614(f) and 615(b)(1)) decisions. Concerning placement decisions, the Committee Report to accompany the Senate's Reauthorization bill states "the committee expects that the majority of placement decisions will be made by the IEP team, but in those unique cases where it is not, the committee expects parents to be involved in the group making the decision." S. Rep. No. 105-17, at 24 (1997). In this regard the 1997 Amendments realign the IDEA to be consistent with the special education laws already on the books in many states.

4. Do special rules govern who should attend the IEP meeting for a child with a disability who has been evaluated for the first time?

IDEA regulations have such rules but the 1997 Amendments do not. In addition to the generally applicable requirements set out in IDEA regulations at 34 C.F.R. § 300.344(a),[1] special requirements applying to the first IEP meeting held after a determination of eligibility appear in § 300.344(b). That section mandates the participation of either a member of the multidisciplinary team that conducted the evaluation *or* another representative of the school district (or other public agency) who "is knowledgeable about the evaluation procedures used with the child and is familiar with the results of the evaluation." In the latter instance, the individual attending the meeting as the required "representative of the public agency" (34 C.F.R. § 300.344(a)(1)) or as the "child's teacher" (34 C.F.R. § 300.344(a)(2)) also may meet this attendance requirement.

While the issue of whether the school district fulfilled the attendance requirement of this section has not generated many disputes on either the judicial or administrative level, it was discussed by the Court of Appeals for the District of Columbia Circuit in *Holland v. District of Columbia,* 23 IDELR 552 (D.C. Cir. 1995). In that case, the school district claimed it had the right not to accept the independent educational evaluation (IEE) funded by the parent because it could not compel the evaluator's attendance at the student's IEP meeting and, without such attendance, could not assemble a properly constituted IEP meeting under 34 C.F.R. § 300.344(b).

The court disagreed with that reasoning (although it supported on other grounds the district's right to use its own personnel to perform evaluations), holding that section 300.344(a) does not prohibit a school district from finding a student eligible for special education and related services on the basis of an evaluation performed by non-school district personnel. The individual who conducts an evaluation need not be present at the initial IEP meeting, as long as some other individual who is knowledgeable about the evaluation of the student participates.

On the other hand, a small number of administrative decisions make it clear that failure to have any individual meeting the criteria set out in 34 C.F.R. § 300.344(b) is a significant procedural violation of the IDEA. *See, e.g., Evanston-Skokie Community Consol. Sch. Dist.,* 17 EHLR 1072 (SEA Ill. 1991).

---

[1] *See* Chapter 5, *infra,* concerning IEP meeting participants.

The 1997 Amendments no longer contain such a requirement, although they do promulgate a new requirement concerning attendance of individuals knowledgeable about evaluations. *See* Question 9 in chapter 4 for a citation to this provision.

5. Do special rules govern who should attend the initial IEP meeting for a child with a disability as that child's teacher?

No. The requirement of 34 C.F.R. § 300.344(a), that an IEP meeting be attended by "the child's teacher," applies without further refinement in the case of an initial IEP. OSEP provides further guidance in the Notice of Interpretation on IEP Requirements, stating that the teacher may be either a teacher qualified to provide special education in the child's area of suspected disability or the child's regular teacher. The Notice of Interpretation goes on to state that "[a]t the option of the agency, both teachers could attend. In any event, there should be at least one member of the school staff at the meeting (e.g., the agency representative or the teacher) who is qualified in the child's area of suspected disability." Appendix C to 34 C.F.R. Part 300, Question 15; *see also* Question 5 in chapter 5, *infra.*

The 1997 Amendments do not contain any special requirements regarding attendance at initial IEP meetings. There are, however, significant changes to the generally applicable requirements addressing attendance of teachers at IEP meetings. In this regard, *see generally* Chapter 5.

Reviewing and Revising IEPs

6. How often must a school district review an IEP?

IDEA regulations at 34 C.F.R. § 300.343(d) provide that "each public agency shall initiate and conduct meetings to review each child's IEP periodically and, if appropriate, revise its provisions. A meeting must be held for this purpose at least once a year."

This requirement does not mean that a school district always discharges its duty by simply reviewing each student's IEP on an annual basis. The changing needs of some students with disabilities may demand more frequent reviews and revisions. According to the Notice of Interpretation, "the legislative history of the Act makes it clear that there should be as many meetings a year as any one child may need." Appendix C to 34 C.F.R. Part 300, Question 10. For example, in *Letter to Borucki,* 16 EHLR 884 (OSEP 1990), OSEP advised that a student's failure to cooperate with school staff may indicate the need for, among other things, revision of his or her IEP, making it necessary to convene IEP meetings.

Generally, whenever a school district proposes to substantially or materially alter a student's then-current educational program, it should convene an IEP meeting beforehand. *Letter to Green,* 22 IDELR 639 (OSEP 1995). Occasionally, parents claim that the school district changed an element of the student's IEP without first convening an IEP meeting, but the school district claims that the particular item at issue was neither an aspect of programming, or a related service required to be addressed in the IEP in the first instance.[2] The proposed termination of IEP programming or services is, of course, a substantial alteration of a student's program and thus should trigger an IEP meeting.[3]

State laws may specify other, more specific, requirements for review. For example, Pennsylvania state education law requires that an IEP meeting be convened within six months of a reevaluation. *See Rose v. Chester County Intermediate Unit,* 24 IDELR 61 (E.D. Pa. 1996).

Of course, not every meeting to discuss the programming for a student with a disability or the progress he or she is making needs to be an IEP meeting, subject to parental notice and participation. School district personnel may meet informally to the extent appropriate for the particular student. *See, e.g., Buser v. Corpus Christi Indep. Sch.,* 22 IDELR 626 (5th Cir. 1995).

The IDEA requirements for review and revision continue substantially unchanged in the 1997 Amendments, although there is now more statutory guidance about conducting reviews. Section 614(d)(4)(A) provides in relevant part:

(A) In general.—The local educational agency shall ensure that . . . the IEP Team—

(i) reviews the child's IEP periodically, but not less than annually to determine whether the annual goals for the child are being achieved; and

(ii) revises the IEP as appropriate to address—

(I) any lack of expected progress toward the annual goals and in the general curriculum, where appropriate;

(II) the results of any reevaluation conducted under this section;

(III) information about the child provided to, or by, the parents. . . . ;

(IV) the child's anticipated needs; or

(V) other matters.

7. Why must a school district review a student's IEP at least annually?

Children's needs change over time. An educational program that met the student's individual needs at the time it was implemented, cannot be modified as the child ages

---

[2] *See* Question 29 in chapter 2, *supra.*

[3] *See* Question 22 in chapter 10, *infra.*

based on general assumptions about the learning and maturation process of children who have been diagnosed as having the same disabilities.

At each annual review meeting the team needs to consider if the IEP still reflects the individual needs of the student. To answer that question, the IEP team reviews the extent to which the student has accomplished his or her annual goals. Based on the student's level of success, the team members can then decide which adjustments, if any, are necessary. It also may decide that modifications to the criteria for measuring progress should be made.

Thus, neither an IEP nor items of service contained in an IEP can be considered effective for more than one year. A state court who disregarded that limitation was overruled in *Tanya v. Cincinnati Board of Education,* 21 IDELR 1120 (Ohio Ct. App. 1995). In that instance the court held that a lower state court exceeded its authority under the IDEA when it ordered a school district to provide an inclusive placement, with an aide to provide tracheotomy care, to an eight-year-old student with spina bifida for the remainder of her school career.

Similarly, in *Board of Education of City School District of City of New York,* 21 IDELR 265 (SEA N.Y. 1994), a state review officer overturned the order of the hearing officer directing a school board to provide a lap-top computer for a 15-year-old student with a learning disability on a 12-month basis until the student either reached the age of 21 or graduated. Using the same reasoning, the hearing officer in *Birmingham Board of Education,* 20 IDELR 1281 (SEA Ala. 1994), struck down a state policy requiring accommodations to be a part of a student's educational program for a period covering two IEPs, holding that it contravened the annual review requirement of the IDEA.

8. Are there circumstances that relieve a school district of its obligation to review IEPs at least annually?

Generally no, although an IEP is not required for a student with a disability who has been unilaterally placed by his or her parents, assuming that student is neither requesting nor receiving services. *See Letter to Champagne,* 22 IDELR 1136 (OSEP 1995). When a privately placed student is either requesting or receiving services, IEP review requirements apply.[4]

Is it a different story when parents file for due process claiming that the proffered IEP fails to provide FAPE? From the school district's perspective, it is futile to conduct a meeting to review the rejected IEP and plan next year's program when the parties are in the midst of administrative or even judicial proceedings to decide the appropriateness of that very IEP. Regardless of the surface logic of that reasoning, federal courts have come down squarely in favor of conducting annual reviews even under such contentious circumstances.

---

[4] *See* Questions 13 and 14 in chapter 9, *infra.*

In *Town of Burlington v. Department of Education for Massachusetts,* 1983-84 EHLR 555:526 (1st Cir. 1984), the First Circuit Court of Appeals held that, in the absence of a stipulation between the parties stating how the outcome of the due process review will affect educational programming (a stipulation the parties are unlikely to make), the school district should continue the IEP process. The court explained why it reached this conclusion:

> The [IDEA] omits any reference to whether IEPs are to be revised during the pendency of review. We, therefore, must fashion a rule to facilitate implementation of the Act. We think that pending review of an earlier IEP, local educational agencies should continue to review and revise IEPs in accordance with applicable law, at least in the absence of a stipulation between the parties providing for how the outcome will affect later years. Without an IEP as a starting point, the court is faced with a mere hypothesis of what the [school district] would have proposed and effectuated during subsequent years, an hypothesis which at the time of trial would have the unfair benefit of hindsight. Such a rear view proposal could not comply with the statutory requirements for drafting IEPs, could not have been submitted in a timely fashion to the parents, and could not constitute evidence at trial. IEPs for subsequent years could be appealed to the state agency; and appeals from the state agency's "findings and decisions" on the subsequent IEPs could be consolidated with the original appeal to the district court. The continuation of the IEP process during the pendency of litigation may assist in promoting settlements. Also, subsequent IEPs that have not been appealed to the state agency may still provide useful evidence for the district court in fashioning "appropriate relief."

1983-84 EHLR at 555:537.

Ten years after the First Circuit's decision in *Town of Burlington,* the Ninth Circuit Court of Appeals held to the same effect and further noted that there had been no published opinions in which futility of review was found to be a basis for relieving a school district of its obligation to review and revise IEPs according to applicable timetables. In *Union School District v. Smith,* 20 IDELR 987 (9th Cir. 1994), the court recognized that the doctrine of futility had been acknowledged in the context of relieving parents of their obligations to exhaust administrative remedies, but the court declined to extend application of that doctrine to provide relief for school districts. To the contrary, a school district cannot escape its obligations to complete the IEP, formally offer a placement and indicate what educational assistance is being offered to supplement the placement by arguing that a disabled child's parents expressed an unwillingness to accept that placement.

The district court for the Eastern District of Pennsylvania weighed in to the same effect in *Delaware County Intermediate Unit #25 v. Martin & Melinda K.,* 20 IDELR 363 (E.D. Pa. 1993). In finding for parents alleging substantial procedural violations of the IDEA, the court concluded that nothing in the law expressly exempts public agencies from the requirement to review IEPs at least annually in those instances when the parties are engaged in ongoing disputes about the appropriateness of the past year's IEP and the agency knows to a certainty that the parents will reject the proposed IEP.

Most recently the District Court for the District of New Hampshire found that the school district in *Briere v. Fair Haven Grade School District*, 25 IDELR 55 (D. Vt. 1996), violated the IDEA when it failed to convene a meeting for the school year following the year in which the parent had challenged the IEP in due process. The school district tried to excuse its failure to review the IEP by saying that the mother's unilateral placement of her daughter disrupted the process. No dice, said the court.

> Educational agencies are bound to adhere to provisions of the IDEA whether or not the child has been placed in a private or public facility. The IDEA requires special educators and administrators to encourage parental participation. . . . This court refuses to adopt a principle which would in any way shift responsibility for compliance with the IDEA to parents.

25 IDELR at 61.

There is one quirky case, however, in which the court did excuse the school district from scheduling an IEP meeting. Although it was not an annual meeting, the opinion may be helpful in the case of such meetings. In *Kutin v. Anne Arundel County Board of Education*, 24 IDELR 666 (D. Md. 1996), the parents failed to prevail on their request for private placement, although the hearing officer ordered substantial modifications of the school district's proposed IEP. The hearing officer directed the school district to modify the IEP as directed. The parents appealed the decision and, on the advice of counsel, chose not to participate in the IEP meeting promptly scheduled by the school district, until the outcome of the appeal. When the hearing officer's decision was affirmed on appeal, the school district did not schedule another meeting, surmising the parents would not attend that one either pending the result of their civil action.

In that action, the parents added to their complaint by claiming that the school district violated the IDEA by failing to schedule an IEP meeting after the administrative review decision. The court could see the parent's point on an abstract level, but found that "this argument loses steam when the relevant background of the case is taken into consideration." 24 IDELR at 670. The school district acted justifiably in not scheduling a meeting they knew the parents—well-informed and well-represented—would not attend. The evidence established that if the parents had requested such a meeting the school district would have scheduled it.

9. Must the school district convene an IEP meeting prior to making a change in placement?

It depends on whether the change in placement is considered a change in educational placement, in which case the answer is yes, or a change in location, in which case the answer generally is no.

While neither the IDEA nor its regulations define "change in placement" or "change in educational placement," both terms generally are used interchangeably to mean modifications of the program or services set out in a student's IEP, including a cessation of services for 10 or more days. According to the Fifth Circuit Court of Appeals, "a change in placement occurs where there is a fundamental change in a basic element of the educational program." *Sherry A.D. v. Kirby,* 19 IDELR 339 (5th Cir. 1992).

Whenever a school district proposes to change an item of programming contained in an IEP, it must convene an IEP meeting. *See* Question 6 in this chapter, *supra.* Any proposal to move a student along the continuum of alternative placements—either to a more restrictive or a less restrictive placement—implicates a change in programming. Thus, an IEP meeting would be necessary in these instances, as well.

On the other hand, some proposals to change the location at which a student receives his or her educational program are not proposals to change that student's educational placement, and thus do not require the school district to convene an IEP meeting prior to making the change.[5]

Assuming the student's then-current IEP will be implemented without change in the new placement the district generally does not have to convene an IEP meeting, nor must it seek the consent of the parents. This principal, sometimes surprising to parents, flows from the distinctions drawn between programming and placement decisions in the IDEA, as discussed in Question 27.

Two circuit courts have issued authoritative decisions affirming this interpretation of the IDEA: the Fifth Circuit in *Daniel R.R. v. State Board of Education,* 1988-89 EHLR 441:433 (5th Cir. 1989) and *Clyde K. v. Puyallup School District,* 21 IDELR 664 (9th Cir. 1994). In the latter case, a student with Tourette syndrome was moved from the regular classroom to a self-contained placement because of his overly disruptive effect on his classmates. One of the bases for the parents' challenge was that the school district failed to convene an IEP meeting before placing the student in the more restrictive setting. The court ruled, however, that the parents had not been denied the procedural protections of the IDEA. The district did not err in failing to draft a new IEP, since the student's then-current IEP could be implemented in the proposed placement.

OCR takes the same position with respect to Section 504. For example, the school district in *Conejo Valley (CA) Unified School District,* 22 IDELR 1140 (OCR 1995), was not required to conduct IEP meetings prior to transferring three preschoolers with disabilities from their neighborhood school to another site in the district. The neighborhood school was overcrowded and nondisabled students were transferred, as

---

[5] Although they may be considered to trigger the prior notice and due process requirements of 34 C.F.R. §§ 300.500-300.513. According to OSEP a change in location may be considered a change in educational placement for purposes of prior notice on the basis of a multifactorial analysis that considers, in addition to whether or not the IEP should be revised, whether the student will be educated with nondisabled peers to the same extent or will have the same opportunities to participate in extracurricular and nonacademic activities. Letter to Fisher, 21 IDELR 992 (OSEP 1994).

well. After examining the IEPs, OCR found that all the educational services and related aids and services were being provided in the new location.

10. Is a school district required to schedule an IEP meeting upon parental request?

No, but it certainly makes sense to accommodate such a parent to the extent possible. That is the gist of the guidance and suggestions provided by the Department of Education in its Notice of Interpretation, in which it states that

> if the parents of a child with a disability believe that the child is not progressing satisfactorily or that there is a problem with the child's current IEP, it would be appropriate for the parents to request an IEP meeting. The public agency should grant any reasonable request for such a meeting.

Appendix C to 34 C.F.R. Part 300, Question 11.

The one instance in which a school district would be required to schedule IEP meetings upon parental request, or in accordance with a schedule previously agreed to by the parties, would be if such a requirement were incorporated into the child's IEP.[6]

While the IDEA thus does not establish a specific requirement for convening an IEP at parental request, state law may. California, for example, requires that a school district convene an IEP meeting within 30 days, not counting days in July and August, of a parent's written request. *Butte Valley Unified Sch. Dist. & Siskiyou County Office of Educ.*, 22 IDELR 465 (SEA 1994) (school district complied with state law when it convened an IEP meeting on August 15 in response to the parent's request of June 27).

While a school district is not required to always convene an IEP meeting upon parental request, it must provide written notice when it declines to change a child's IEP and include in the notice an explanation of why it refuses to make the proposed change. 34 C.F.R. § 300.504(a); *see, e.g., Myles S. v. Montgomery County Bd. of Educ.*, 20 IDELR 237 (M.D. Ala. 1993).

11. Must a school district review the student's IEP at the beginning of each school year?

No. While IEPs must be in place at the beginning of each school year (34 C.F.R. § 300.342(a)) and must be reviewed at least annually (34 C.F.R. § 300.343(d)), they need not be reviewed at the beginning of each school year. According to the Note following 34 C.F.R. § 300.343(d), the IDEA does not specify when the required review

---

[6] *See* Question 20 in chapter 2, *supra*, concerning specific checkpoint intervals for parents to review their children's IEP.

must be held. It can be held at any time throughout the year as long as the IEPs themselves are in effect at the beginning of the school year.

The Notice of Interpretation on IEP Requirements provides a bit more guidance, suggesting that three alternative compliant approaches are: (1) convening the meeting at the end of the prior school year; (2) convening the meeting during the summer, before the new school year starts; or (3) convening the meeting on the anniversary date of the immediately preceding IEP meeting. Appendix C to 34 C.F.R. Part 300, Question 9.

Thus, in the administrative decision *In re Child with Disabilities,* 19 IDELR 203 (SEA Conn. 1992), the school district complied with the IDEA when it developed the IEPs for a 21-year old student with Down syndrome and other disabilities having difficulties with her transitioning program. The IEPs ran from January of one school year through January of the next. The hearing officer held that nothing in the IDEA or its regulations prohibited such a procedure. The soundness of the approach from an educational perspective was a matter of methodology within the discretion of the school district unless the parents could demonstrate its relatedness to a denial of FAPE. No allegations to that effect were discussed in the opinion.

12. Must the annual review of the IEP be conducted on or around the same time each year?

No, as indicated in Question 11 above, annual review can occur at any time within the year. Further, according to OSEP in its *Letter to Sheridan,* 20 IDELR 1163 (OSEP 1993), a school district is not required to conduct its annual review on or around the anniversary date of the last review or establishment of the IEP, as long as the requirement for review at least annually (34 C.F.R. § 300.343(d)) is met.

13. Is a school district obligated to continue to provide a service that was included in a prior year's IEP?

Not according to two courts who considered this issue—the South Dakota Supreme Court in *Sioux Falls School District v. Koupal,* 22 IDELR 26 (S.D. 1994), and the District Court for the Northern District of Illinois in *Board of Education of Downer's Grove Grade School District No. 58 v. Steven L. & Christine L.,* 23 IDELR 36 (N.D. Ill. 1995). Both held that a service provided in one year's IEP need not continue to be provided in succeeding years' IEPs if the IEP team determines, during its required periodic review, that the service is no longer required to provide FAPE. Further, a service should not be presumed to be a necessary element of a given year's IEP simply because it had been included in the IEP for a previous year.

In *Koupal,* the earlier case, the school district had included teacher training in the TEACCH program[7] in the student's IEP for two years before proposing to eliminate it. Entertaining the parent's due process claim to continue the training, the hearing officer, contrary to usual procedure, placed the burden to demonstrate that teacher training was not necessary to provide FAPE, and then found that the district had not met its burden. In reversing, the court held that the district had no greater burden in proposing to delete a service previously provided under an IEP than it would have if the parent were bringing a due process claim demanding provision of that service for the first time. The court further found the contents of a student's prior IEP to be irrelevant. To hold otherwise, it held, would make meaningless the requirement for review and revision, if necessary, at least annually as mandated by 34 C.F.R. § 300.343(d).

The school district in *Koupal,* premised its removal of the services at issue on the fact that teacher training was not a related service in the first instance. In *Downer's Grove,* the issue was whether consultative services could be substituted for the direct instructional services previously provided to a learning-disabled student who evidenced the potential to continue his high achievement. The court found that the school district's proposed IEP provided FAPE and further found that it had no greater burden in demonstrating appropriateness because it proposed to reduce the amount and intensity of services provided under a previous IEP.

The parents in *Downer's Grove* filed for due process because of the school district's proposal to provide consultative, rather than direct instructional, services to their son, a highly intelligent student with a learning disability who was expected to continue his outstanding record of academic achievement even with the reduction. The court held for the school district, finding, as did the court in *Koupal,* that the school district had no greater burden when it proposed to reduce services that it had provided to a student under the prior year's IEP than it would otherwise have. In all cases, the school district was simply required to show that the proposed IEP provided FAPE.

The annual review requirement of 34 C.F.R. § 300.343(d) also supported the decision of the court in *Tanya v. Cincinnati Board of Education,* 21 IDELR 1120 (Ohio Ct. App. 1995). In that instance the court held that a lower state court exceeded its authority under the IDEA when it ordered a school district to provide an inclusive placement, with an aide to provide tracheotomy care, to an eight-year-old student with spina bifida for the remainder of her school career.

---

[7] The Treatment and Education of Autistic and Related Communications Handicapped Children (TEACCH) program is an intensive intervention program for young children with autism and related conditions developed at the University of North Carolina in Chapel Hill. It is offered by public agencies throughout the country that incorporate its strategies and modifications in self-contained classes with low teacher-student ratios. It is often supplemented by similar strategies provided by parents in the home setting.

14. Is a school district's revision of an IEP to provide services not previously provided evidence that the previous IEP was inadequate?

It does not have to be. Following the reasoning of the courts in *Sioux Falls School District v. Koupal,* 22 IDELR 26 (S.D. 1994) and *Board of Education of Downer's Grove Grade School District No. 58 v. Steven L. & Christine L.,* 23 IDELR 36 (N.D. Ill. 1995), the appropriateness of each IEP must be determined independently and judged on its own merits. Adding additional services does not create the inference that a previous IEP failed to provide FAPE.

The district court for the District of Rhode Island held in *Scituate School Committee v. Robert B.,* 1985-86 EHLR 557:207 (D.R.I. 1985), that a district's addition of services to a proposed IEP after parents had rejected it, but prior to due process, is not prima facie evidence that the originally proposed IEP was inadequate, no matter whether the change was motivated by concern for the student or fear of impending litigation. *Accord Edmonds Sch. Dist.,* 16 EHLR 1049 (SEA Wash. 1990). Similarly, the hearing officer in *Gaston School District,* 24 IDELR 1052 (SEA Or. 1996), found that a school district's amendment of the IEP for a 15-year-old student with a learning disability to provide additional services was not evidence of any prior shortcomings on the part of the district. Rather the additional services were "adds-ons" to satisfy the parents, offering the student more than the legal requirement.

Implementing the IEP

15. Must the school district implement an agreed-upon IEP in its entirety?

Clearly the school district must implement an agreed-upon IEP in its entirety.[8] 34 C.F.R. § 300.342(b). Nevertheless, the school district in *Hillsborough County School Board,* 21 IDELR 191 (SEA Fla. 1994), violated the IDEA by intentionally failing to provide individual speech and language services to a multidisabled six-year-old student despite those services being included in an IEP developed with the parents' consent. In this case the district deceptively modified the IEP to delete the service without notice to or input from the parents.[9]

In the more typical case, deliberate non-implementation is not the issue; incomplete or incorrect implementation is. In these cases, though, a denial of FAPE still may be

---

[8] If the parents do not agree to all or parts of the IEP, then different rules apply. *See* Question 6, *supra,* and Questions 12 and 13 in chapter 12, *infra.*

[9] *See* Question 11 in chapter 1, *supra,* for further discussion of this case.

the result. For example, the school district in *Ocean View (CA) Elementary School District,* 23 IDELR 896 (OCR 1995), denied FAPE to a developmentally disabled kindergartener because the behavioral aspects of his IEP were not completely or consistently applied. The student's regular teacher was granted a stress-related leave after the student bit her. In her absence, the staff was confused about what services to provide the student, and the substitute was reluctant to implement consistently some aspects of the behavioral programming.

Further, impossibility does not excuse implementation of the agreed-upon IEP, according to OSEP in *Letter to Williams,* 25 IDELR 634 (OSEP 1996). The inquirer raised an issue confronting school districts in many growing locales: unanticipated growth in enrollment. The particular question she posed concerned the remedy available to parents when the IEP of a student with a disability identifies a need for placement in a small class when resource limitations compel placement in large classes (35-40 students). OSEP did not provide a specific response to the question, but it did confirm that "to the extent that the particular class size impacts on the provision of FAPE to a child, the public agency must ensure that the child receives the special education and related services as specified on the IEP."

16. May a school district refuse to implement an IEP if the parents refuse to consent to its contents?

No. Lack of agreement does not excuse a school district from providing all appropriate programming and services that have not been rejected by the parent, as long as the student remains publicly enrolled.

At all stages of a disabled student's IEP development, parents must be given the opportunity to bring due process complaints concerning "any matter relating to the identification, evaluation, or educational placement of the child or the provision of a free appropriate public education." 20 U.S.C. § 1415(b)(1)(E). As a result, if there is a particular issue relating to the provision of FAPE over which a parent and a school district cannot agree, a school district may not unilaterally refuse to implement a student's IEP based on the parent's refusal to consent to the contents of the IEP. Rather, in such a situation, the parents must be notified of their right to an impartial due process hearing on the issue.

During the pendency of the due process hearing, the school district must implement those portions of the IEP upon which the parties are, or were, in agreement. As explained by OSEP in the Notice of Interpretation on IEP Requirements, steps must be taken to ensure that there is an interim course of action for serving the student pending resolution of the areas of disagreement. Appendix C to 34 C.F.R. Part 300, Question 35. The better course would be for the parties to reach an agreement about what programming and placement will be provided pending resolution of the dispute.

If such agreement is not possible, the IDEA mandates that the student's last agreed placement remain in effect in the areas of disagreement. This is the stay-put provision of 20 U.S.C. § 1415(e)(3). Operation of the stay-put, also called an IDEA automatic injunction, is a topic largely beyond the scope of this publication, but see Question 12 in chapter 12 for further discussion of this issue in connection with disputes.

17. How soon after an IEP is formulated must it be implemented?

"As soon as possible" following the IEP meeting, directs Part B regulations at 34 C.F.R. § 300.342(b)(2). In contrast to the specific 30-day timeline established for convening an IEP once a preplacement evaluation is completed (34 C.F.R. § 300.343(c)), neither the regulations nor the IDEA itself impose specific time limits for implementation of IEPs. *Letter to Anonymous,* 18 IDELR 627 (OSEP 1991).

"As soon as possible" is not the most precise of terms. To clarify the matter somewhat, the Note to section 300.342 suggests that, in the normal course, "the IEP of a child with a disability will be implemented immediately following the [IEP meeting]," although immediate implementation would not be required under the two specific circumstances described in the Note.[10] Even when such circumstances excuse immediate implementation, the Note concludes that "there can be no undue delay in providing special education and related services to the child."

The Notice of Interpretation on IEP Requirements confirms that the immediate implementation directive of the Note is generally the rule. In response to the question "[h]ow much of a delay is permissible between the time an IEP of a child with a disability is finalized and when special education is provided?" the Notice provides:

> In general, no delay is permissible. It is expected that the special education and related services set out in a child's IEP will be provided by the agency immediately after the IEP is finalized. The Note following § 300.342 identifies some exceptions (1) when the meetings occur during the summer or other vacation period, or when there are circumstances that require a short delay, such as working out transportation arrangements. However, unless otherwise specified in the IEP, the IEP services must be provided as soon as possible following the meeting.

Appendix C to 34 C.F.R. Part 300, Question 4.

18. Are the two circumstances specified in the Note to § 300.342 the only exceptions for delay in IEP implementation?

There is limited case law addressing this issue, but the District Court for the Northern District of Indiana in *Evans v. Evans,* 19 IDELR 1005 (N.D. Ind. 1993),

---

[10] The two exceptions are: (1) when the meetings take place during the summer vacation period and (2) when a short delay is needed to complete arrangements.

suggested that few, if any other circumstances, would excuse delay. That state had established an additional application and review process for students whose IEPs called for residential placement that resulted in average delays of 160 to 200 days between development of the IEP and the actual placement. In ruling that the state procedure violated the IDEA the court held that "[t]he only exceptions for delay are specified in § 300.342 and the answer to question No. 4. . . . The regulations did not contemplate a systematic delay, and in any event allow room for only short delays. . . ." 19 IDELR at 1008.

While circumstances beyond the school district's control, such as those which might be considered "acts of God," would likely justify a short delay, a school district's lack of resources, such as budgetary or personnel constraints, are not valid grounds for delay. In the administrative decision *In re Child with Disabilities,* 21 IDELR 624 (SEA Conn. 1994), the school district tried unsuccessfully to attribute its delay in implementing the work-study program called for in the student's IEP to factors beyond its control, claiming it was unable to identify a suitable placement in the community. The school district failed to provide the work-study experience called for in the IEP altogether; in fact, it claimed that the parents were responsible for finding a suitable work site.

That may be an extreme case, though, because of the school district's overall record of severe procedural and substantive violations. A more mild example of "benign" bureaucratic delay was considered by OCR in *Mt. Pleasant Township (IN) Community School Corp.,* 20 IDELR 1256 (OCR 1993). In that case OCR found that the school district's 17-day delay in implementing the IEP of a student with a learning disability due to the need to hold meetings regarding its implementation had only a minimal impact on the student. Thus, the school district was not obligated to provide additional services, despite the student's failing grades in science.

In some cases, intransigent parents may interfere with the timely implementation of the IEP. However, unless the parent's interference rises to the level of bad faith, it is not likely that failure to cooperate will excuse a delay in implementation. *See, e.g., Franklin #5 Sch. Dist.,* 1984-85 EHLR 506:387 (SEA Wis. 1985).

In the world of special education, though, even seemingly universal rules may have to bend to meet the unique needs of a child with a disability. Thus, the Fifth Circuit Court of Appeals affirmed the decision of the district court in *Bonnie Ann F. v. Calallen Independent School District,* 20 IDELR 736 (S.D. Tex. 1993), in a brief *per curiam* opinion, 22 IDELR 615 (5th Cir. 1994). In that case, the lower court ruled that the school district had not violated its duty to implement a student's new IEP as soon as possible when it agreed at a meeting in February that an aural/oral program best met the needs of the student, but provided instruction in both that method and the previously approved signing method from February to August to serve the best interests of the student by allowing her to make a gradual transition.

19.   When is an IEP considered "finalized," triggering the implementation requirement?

While the Notice of Interpretation states that "[i]t is expected that the special education and related services set out in a child's IEP will be provided by the agency immediately after the IEP is finalized" (Appendix C to 34 C.F.R. Part 300, Question 4), it does not further define what it means to finalize the IEP. Presumably, a plain-meaning interpretation is appropriate, such that the IEP is finalized when the IEP meetings are completed and the parties have agreed to the provision of the program specified in the written IEP document (or the parents have indicated that they will not agree to the district's final proposal).

This was the view taken by the district court in *Evans v. Evans,* 19 IDELR 1005 (N.D. Ind. 1993). The district argued that an IEP providing residential placement was not finalized until the state agency completed its post-IEP meeting review of the placement through its own procedures, thus making the term synonymous with the term "in effect" in 34 C.F.R. § 300.342(b)(1). The court found otherwise, reasoning that the use of term "meetings" meant IEP meeting, as that term is used in 34 C.F.R. § 300.343.

20.   Must an IEP be in effect at the beginning of each school year?

Yes. Once a child with a disability has been identified as IDEA-eligible, there must be an IEP in effect for that child at the beginning of each school year. 34 C.F.R. § 300.342(a). *See Fort Zumwalt Sch. Dist. v. Missouri State Bd. of Educ.,* 24 IDELR 222 (E.D. Mo. 1996) (school district's failure to have an IEP developed until October entitled the parents to tuition reimbursement for the entire year when they had already signed a contract that did not allow refunds in the case of withdrawals). Accordingly, a district's annual review (required under 34 C.F.R. § 300.343(d)) should be conducted so that, in the ordinary course, the IEP that is to be the basis of the upcoming school year's programming is finalized by the end of the prior school year. While atypical circumstances may result in a child starting the school year without an IEP in effect, generally the IDEA does not permit exceptions to this requirement.

This is particularly true when the violation of this requirement is not an isolated incidence of noncompliance with regard to a particular student. For example, the school district in *Evans v. Board of Education of Rhinebeck Central School District,* 24 IDELR 338 (S.D.N.Y. 1996), was ordered to reimburse the parents' for private school tuition because it committed the following procedural violations in addition to not having an IEP in effect at the start of the school year: failure to convene an impartial due process hearing within 45 days of the parent's request (34 C.F.R. § 300.512); failure to include in the IEP a statement of present levels of educational functioning and strategies to evaluate progress (34 C.F.R. § 300.346(a)); and failure to follow all the evaluation procedures for determining the existence of a specific learning disability (34 C.F.R. § 300.540).

Administrative convenience, for example, does not excuse compliance. Thus, if an IEP has not been finalized by the end of the prior school year, then the school district must meet with parents during the summer. *Myles S. v. Montgomery County Bd. of Educ.*, 20 IDELR 237 (M.D. Ala. 1993); *accord Norton Pub. Schs.*, 16 EHLR 832 (SEA Mass. 1990). Further, so-called administrative hardship does not excuse compliance. In *Franklin #5 School District*, 1984-85 EHLR 506:387 (SEA Wis. 1985), a school district whose responsible special education official was physically incapacitated in August was not excused from not having an IEP in effect for a student at the beginning of that school year.

Failure to agree on a placement does not excuse compliance. For example, in *Los Angeles Unified School District*, 24 IDELR 503 (SEA Cal. 1996), the school district convened two IEP meetings concerning a six-year-old child with orthopedic and hearing impairments in June 1995 to design a program for the upcoming school year. At the first meeting, an IEP was written with the contemplated placement being a special day class (SDC). The IEP included present levels of performance, annual goals with short-term objectives, special education and related services. The possibility of full inclusion in a regular education kindergarten class was mentioned only in passing. The meeting was adjourned at the parents request so they could visit the alternative SDCs in which their daughter could be placed.

When the second meeting was held, the parents requested a fully inclusive placement. This time the district members proposed adjournment—stating that the participation of an inclusion placement expert was necessary to complete the IEP by including a full inclusion component (required modifications of regular education). All parties agreed that the IEP was thus not complete. After the meeting, the parents became concerned about how well their child would do in her neighborhood school's kindergarten class because of the large class size. A district representative offered to have the parent observe, but stated that they would not be able to visit the class until summer vacation was over. No date to reconvene the IEP meeting was proposed. That appears to be how things were left, until mid-August, when the parents enrolled the student in a private school and filed a request for due process. The parents did observe the kindergarten class in September, but were not pleased with the class size and now expressed other concerns as well. They were pleased with the private school and did not indicate that they wished to enroll their child publicly. As a result, the school district did not reconvene the IEP team to complete the IEP.

Big mistake! The hearing officer concluded that the district's failure to reconvene the IEP meeting to complete the student's IEP resulted in a denial of FAPE. In so holding, the hearing officer relied on 34 C.F.R. § 300.342, requiring that an appropriate IEP be in effect at the beginning of the school year. In this instance, it was undisputed that the IEP was never completed.

Failure to agree about programming also was the complicating factor in *Delaware County Intermediate Unit #25 v. Martin and Melinda K.*, 20 IDELR 363 (E.D. Pa. 1993), in which the school district was ordered to reimburse the parents of a preschooler diagnosed as having pervasive development disorder-not otherwise specified.[11] The child turned three in October 1991, becoming eligible for Part B services. The child was receiving services under Part H and in September and October 1991 the parents met with the responsible agency to develop an IEP. The parents recommended 40 hours of at-home Lovaas programming plus a mainstream component, but the agency was in favor of a continuation of the much more limited programming the child was then receiving. No agreement was reached at the IEP meetings and the agency promised that an IEP would be forthcoming on or before November 1, 1991. No IEP was produced and on January 25, 1992, the parents filed for due process. Six days later the agency issued the IEP. Not surprisingly, the programming offered did not adopt the parent's recommendations. Thus, the dispute continued, leading to judicial resolution.

A substantial period of time did elapse between when the IEP team met and the IEP was proposed. But in what specific way did that violate the IDEA? (The child was receiving services and there is no specific timeline for completing the IEP process.) The hearing officer held that the agency violated 34 C.F.R. § 300.342(a), requiring that an IEP be in effect at the beginning of the school year. Because the child was a preschooler in 1991, the author questions the applicability of this requirement, but the court agreed with the hearing officer. Both also cited a state requirement establishing a timeline of 30 days from completion of multidisciplinary evaluation to IEP creation; this seems better support for the holding. In our view, a better federal law rationale would have been reliance on the requirement that FAPE be available to a child on his or her third birthday. 34 C.F.R. § 300.300; *Northshore Sch. Dist.*, 20 IDELR 121 (SEA Wash. 1993) (the school district violated the IDEA by failing to provide an eligible child with FAPE by the required age of three).[12]

A troubling case involving both a serious rift with parents and summer vacation is the state review panel decision in *Cape Henlopen School District*, 24 IDELR 1087 (SEA Del. 1996). The student in that case was a 12-year-old boy identified as having a learning disability, ADHD and a mild-to-moderate oppositional defiant disorder. The school district first proposed an IEP in March 1995 to be effective for the student's next school year. The parent disagreed with the proposed IEP and the school district thus scheduled another IEP meeting for May 1995 to reconsider. The parent, having filed for due process, declined to attend. The school district then scheduled another meeting for June 1995, but that meeting was postponed when a settlement agreement

---

[11] A developmental disorder less severe than autism.

[12] *See also* Questions 5 through 11 in chapter 11, *infra*, concerning children transitioning from Part H to Part B.

reached at the due process hearing resulted in the district funding a summer placement at a special school for children with learning disabilities.

The summer passed without another meeting being scheduled, even though the student was discharged from the summer program due to behavioral problems. The parent received a letter the day before the start of the school year advising where the student would be placed, an issue of contention. The school then offered to schedule a meeting promptly, but the parent instead filed for due process for a second time. A meeting was held in late September to discuss interim proceedings until resolution of due process. Another meeting was scheduled for November but the parent did not attend.

To make a long story short, for the entire school year the student did not attend school, although he did receive a limited amount of homebound instruction. In seeking private placement the parent charged that the student was denied FAPE because, among other things, the school district did not have an IEP in place at the start of the school year.

The school district claimed that summer vacations and changing assignments prevented completion of the IEP before the start of school. The review officer concluded that this was no excuse and was, in fact, particularly unacceptable in this circumstance. "Too much time, effort and resources had been devoted to [the student] by that point, and his needs were too great, to permit him to fall through the cracks in this fashion." 24 IDELR at 1094. Despite the blatancy of the violation and the duration of the delay in completion of the IEP, the parent was not awarded private placement. The IEP eventually proposed was substantively appropriate and compensatory education services would provide adequate remediation.

Further, the parents also were to blame for the student not attending school. The review officer found their "passivity" in the face of district inaction over the summer "remarkable" and their decision to allow the student to remain at home irresponsible. "Even though the [parent's] anger at the District's not completing [the student's] IEP prior to the start of the year is understandable and justified, their overriding obligation was to act in [the student's] best interests." 24 IDELR 1087.

On the opposite end of the spectrum, slight delays in having an IEP in effect at the start of the school year may be excusable, at least from a Section 504 perspective. In *Robertson County (TN) School District*, 22 IDELR 1147 (OCR 1995), for example, OCR found that there was insufficient evidence to support the parent's allegation that the school district discriminated against her daughter by failing to implement her IEP on a timely basis. While there were start-up problems with the student's resource classroom at the beginning of the school year, the student's IEP was being fully implemented by the first week in September.

21. Can a school district provide special education and related services prior to having an IEP in effect?

In theory, no. IDEA regulations at 34 C.F.R. § 300.342(b) make it clear that an IEP must "be in effect before special education and related services are provided to a child." To protect the rights of parents and children, districts must follow a sequence—evaluation, IEP design, placement prior to implementation of services—no matter how well intended its efforts to provide needed services as soon as possible. To do otherwise puts the cart before the horse. As OSEP affirmed in *Letter to Donnelly,* EHLR 211:349 (OSEP 1984), placing a student in a special education program without a written IEP violates the IDEA.

That being said, courts have recognized circumstances in which the student was well-served by receiving needed programming and services before the IEP was formulated and finalized. In each of these cases, the student received FAPE as a substantive matter, notwithstanding the school district's violation of this most central IEP procedural requirement. For example, in *Doe v. Alabama State Department of Education,* 17 EHLR 41 (11th Cir. 1990), the Eleventh Circuit Court of Appeals held that a district complied with the IDEA when it provided special education and related services, including in-home tutoring, to a youth with a serious emotional disturbance even though there was no written IEP. Central to the court's decision were three factors: (1) the delay in formalizing the IEP resulted from the active participation of the parents in the IEP process, such participation making it impossible to conclude the meetings; (2) the school district made diligent efforts to reach agreement with the parents; and (3) the youth received educational benefit from the services.

More typical though, is the decision of the district court in *P.J. v. Connecticut Board of Education,* 18 IDELR 1010 (D. Conn. 1992). In that case the court found the district violated the IDEA when it attempted to enroll a four-year-old child with Down syndrome in a preschool program before it had formulated an IEP (or even conducted an evaluation).

22. What does it mean for an IEP to be considered to "be in effect"?

According to the district court in *Evans v. Evans,* 19 IDELR 1005 (N.D. Ind. 1993), the term "in effect," when used in 34 C.F.R. § 300.342(a) means something more than the term "finalized" when used in connection with 34 C.F.R. § 300.342(b)(2). As interpreted in the Department of Education's Notice of Interpretation on IEP Requirements the term "be in effect" means that the IEP "(1) has been developed properly (i.e., at a meeting(s) involving all of the participants specified in the Act. . . . ; (2) is regarded by both the parents and the agency as appropriate in terms of the child's needs; and (3) will be implemented as written." Appendix C to 34 C.F.R. Part 300, Question 3.

Because the term "in effect" implicates parental agreement, questions arise about how an IEP may be implemented to comply with the requirement of this section when the parties disagree about what services should be provided where. *See* Question 12 in chapter 12, *infra* for further discussion.

23. Does a school district comply with the requirement that an IEP be in effect when it provides services under an interim IEP?

While the IDEA generally requires completion of an evaluation and formulation of an IEP prior to placing and providing services to a student with a disability, OSEP has recognized limited circumstances under which a student may receive services under an interim IEP prior to completion of the normal process. In *Letter to Saperstone,* 21 IDELR 1127 (OSEP 1993), OSEP acknowledged that in certain cases of initial eligibility determinations, a student may require a temporary placement in a program as part of the evaluation process to help determine the most appropriate placement. In such cases, the school district must implement an interim IEP, and the district is considered to have complied with the prohibition on provisions of services prior to having an IEP be in effect.

The Notice of Interpretation on IEP Requirements, approving the use of interim IEPs in connection with the evaluation process, cautions against permitting the temporary placement to become the final placement before the IEP is finalized. Appendix C to 34 C.F.R. Part 300, Question 5. To forestall such an occurrence, it suggests that school districts follow this four-step procedure:

1. Develop an interim IEP for the child that sets out the specific conditions and timelines for the trial placement.

2. Ensure that the parents agree to the interim placement before it is carried out, and that they are involved throughout the process of developing, reviewing, and revising the child's IEP.

3. Set a specific timeline (e.g. 30 days) for completing the evaluation and making judgments about the most appropriate placement for the child.

4. Conduct the IEP meeting at the end of the trial period in order to finalize the child's IEP.

Interim placements typically come into play in connection with interstate transfers or analogous circumstances, such as when a youth enters a mental health facility for health-related reasons or becomes a pretrial detainee in the custody of the state's penal authority. According to OSEP in *Letter to Boney,* 18 IDELR 537 (OSEP 1991), interim IEPs should be used only in such special circumstances. They should not be a tool permitting a school district to circumvent IDEA requirements. Following OSEP's reasoning, the court in *Myles S. v. Montgomery County Board of Education,* 20 IDELR 237 (M.D. Ala. 1993), ruled that the school district's use of an interim IEP (what it termed a "preparatory IEP") for the first two weeks of a student's first-grade year, while harmless in this case, violated the IDEA because the district should have held the required IEP meeting within a time frame permitting an IEP to be in effect when the student started the school year.

There are always exceptions. Because the parents themselves prevented the school district from complying with the IDEA requirements for developing and implementing final IEPs, the extended use of an interim IEP was justified, according to the review officer in *Nenana City Public Schools,* 18 IDELR 489 (SEA Alaska 1991). In that case, the parents requested that changes be made to their son's IEP and an interim IEP was informally framed in September pending a formal IEP meeting to determine a new long-term IEP. The school district intended to use the interim IEP to gather additional data on which to base the formal IEP. The interim IEP was implemented for a few weeks at the beginning of the school year, until the parents, dissatisfied with the program, withdrew the student and formally requested that an IEP meeting be convened.

Prior to that request, the school district had proceeded with what the review officer termed a not surprising, given the size of the community, "excess of informality." But once the parents sounded the alarm, the district played by all the rules. In fact, four IEP meetings were held in October and November. But it became clear by the final meeting that no consensus was going to be reached. For one thing, the parents' attorney was contentious.

In ruling on the parents' claims, the review officer acknowledged that the school district had committed "procedural irregularities"[13] in its timely formulation of an IEP. Nonetheless, the parents were not entitled to any relief on this basis. The student's right to FAPE was not compromised by the school district's lapses. It was the parents who had to be repeatedly urged to attend IEP meetings and who sabotaged and disrupted the IEP process.

24. Is the provision of special education and related services under a "transitional" IEP consistent with the IDEA?

"Transitional" IEPs, a variation on interim IEPs, are not consistent with the IDEA, according to the district court in *Briere v. Fair Haven Grade School District,* 25 IDELR 55 (D. Vt. 1996). They inhibit coordination and planning and vitiate "the spirit" of the IDEA. In *Briere,* the parent of a student with a severe learning disability and borderline mental retardation unilaterally placed her daughter at a residential facility for three years, beginning in the ninth grade. Each of those years the school district proposed an IEP that the parent believed did not provide FAPE. The court agreed on the basis of procedural defects, finding that in each of the three years at issue the school district committed a variety of procedural violations that were *per se* violations of the law.

---

[13] The author suspects that the use of this term is a tip-off that the decision-maker is going to find that the school district's actions did not result in a denial of FAPE. Were it otherwise, the term "procedural violations" might more likely be used.

A particular violation occurring in connection with the IEP intended for the student's first year of attendance at the regular high school was the promulgation of a so-called transitional IEP. The IEP lacked annual goals and short-term objectives in critical academic areas, even in the area of the student's most profound disability. Further, no special education programming was identified in four critical skill areas. That was on purpose, the school district claimed. The IEP was intended to be "vague and rudimentary" so that educators at the high school could complete it after the student enrolled and had attended for an adjustment period. A school district representative testified that a transitional IEP had been prepared for the student and such a type of IEP was common in the district.

Not anymore! The court made it clear that the IEP must be complete and capable of describing all aspects of an educational program that provides FAPE before the student receives services. Further, the IEP team has the sole responsibility for designing the IEP. It cannot delegate any aspect of it to other school officials. Being incomplete, the IEP unquestionably failed to provide FAPE.

25. Must the school district provide a copy of the IEP to the regular education teachers who instruct a student with a disability?

No, but if copies are not provided, the school district must assure that the teachers are otherwise informed about the contents of the IEP. As stated in the Notice of Interpretation on IEP Requirements: "If the regular teacher does not attend [the IEP meeting] the agency should either provide the regular teacher with a copy of the IEP or inform the regular teacher of its contents." Appendix C to 34 C.F.R. Part 300, Question 16; *accord Letter to Ellis*, 24 IDELR 176 (OSEP 1995) (if the school district does not provide a copy, the method adopted to inform the regular education teacher of the IEP contents must be sufficient to allow the teacher to provide FAPE in accordance with the IEP). One such possibly compliant method, according to *Letter to Ellis*, is requiring the teacher to "sign out" for review only a copy of the IEP from the office of the building administrator.

When a school district does not ensure that all concerned personnel are familiar with the contents of a student's IEP, the student may not receive a FAPE. *See, e.g., Ocean View (CA) Elementary Sch. Dist.*, 23 IDELR 896 (OCR 1995) (evidence presented showed that the school district failed to consistently implement the child's IEP because there was confusion about its contents among the student's teacher, aide and other district personnel).

Because the 1997 Amendments require the attendance of at least one education teacher whenever the student with a disability either participates or may participate in the regular education environment (Section 614(d)(1)(B)(ii)), this issue may be of less concern, at least on the elementary school level.

26. Can a teacher refuse to provide a service the school district agrees to provide in the IEP?

No. OSEP made clear in its 1994 *Letter to Williams,* 21 IDELR 73 (OSEP 1994), that the determination of what special education and related services should be provided to a child with a disability, where it should be provided, and who should provide it, are educational issues, not labor-management issues. In that response, OSEP stated that the provisions of a collective bargaining agreement cannot justify a school district's failure to provide students with the rights and protections guaranteed under the IDEA. Following from that premise, OSEP opined that a regular education classroom teacher cannot refuse to perform an accommodation for an ADD student because the union contract does not require teachers to do so. Teachers who refuse to perform an accommodation may find themselves in the position of the defendant teacher in *Doe v. Withers,* 20 IDELR 422 (W. Va. 1993). A jury found him liable under Section 1983 for $5,000 in compensatory damages and $10,000 in punitive damages because he refused to provide oral testing for a student with a disability.

27. Should the placement decision be made before or after an IEP is developed?

To act consistently with the individualization policies of the IDEA, a school district should formulate an IEP *before* it makes a placement decision. IDEA regulations at 34 C.F.R. § 300.552(a)(2) provide that placement decisions can be made only after the development of an IEP and in accordance with its terms. Only after the IEP has been developed does a school district have an informed basis for determining where the student's needs can best be served.

As further explained by the Department of Education in its Notice of Interpretation on IEP Requirements:

> The appropriate placement for a given child with a disability cannot be determined until after decisions have been made about what the child's needs are and what will be provided. Since these decisions are made at the IEP meeting, it would not be permissible to first place the child and then develop the IEP. Therefore the IEP must be developed before placement.

Appendix C to 34 C.F.R Part 300, Question 5.

Deciding the placement before finalizing the IEP usually is considered a serious substantive violation of the IDEA. At its worst, the process, called "shoehorning," involves the school district deciding where it will place a student with a disability and then designing his or her IEP by identifying only those needs or objectives that can be met in that setting.

Shoehorning can become an issue when a school district is considering the placement of a hard-to-place severely disabled child. In such a case, the incentive to place the child in an already existing program or a less costly placement may be strong. This may have happened in the often-cited decision in *Speilberg v. Henrico County Public School*, 1988-89 EHLR 441:178 (4th Cir. 1988), *aff'g* 1986-87 EHLR 558:202 (E.D. Va. 1987).

In that case, the court found that the school district first formed the intent to change the placement for a 19-year-old student with autism and profound mental retardation from an out-of-state private residential placement to an in-state public day program. Having decided to transfer the student, the district then conducted a special reevaluation (less than one year after it had conducted the student's triennial reevaluation) that—surprise!—supported its proposed change of placement. The school district then convened an IEP meeting for the purpose of revising the IEP consistently. All these actions took place just months after the parents and the district agreed to an annual IEP confirming the student's need for residential placement.

The district court found, and the appeals court confirmed, that the IDEA forbids such a maneuver because the proposed change in placement was made without regard to the student's individual needs. It was, in the court's view, either a prohibited categorical approach to programming, at best, or a prohibited attempt to reduce the costs necessarily incurred in educating the student, at worst.

Determining placement before finalizing the IEP is not always nefarious. But it still may be a substantial violation of the IDEA, entitling the parents to tuition reimbursement.

In a thoughtful administrative decision, *In Student with a Disability*, 24 IDELR 612 (SEA Ver. 1996), the hearing officer recognized that educators may blur the distinction between programming and placement decisions when the totality of the student's circumstances strongly suggests that the student attend a particular facility. He observed that:

> [t]he distinction between the IEP itself and placement is not, in practice, so easily maintained. In fact, in *Burlington School Committee v. Department of Education* . . . the Supreme Court seems to equate or at least confuse the two. The Court states the question before it as whether the lower court had the authority to order reimbursement for a private school placement by the parents "if the court ultimately determines that such placement, rather than the proposed IEP, is proper under the Act," and it refers to an IEP calling for placement in a public school. . . . The key question becomes whether the violation is a mere technical one or whether there has been . . . a violation of the "spirit and intent" of the Act.

24 IDELR at 617.

In *Student with a Disability*, the hearing officer found that the multidisciplinary team convened to evaluate the educational needs of a 12-year-old student with a learning disability also determined the placement before the IEP meeting was held. Despite holding an IEP meeting and making the "official" placement decision after the IEP meeting was completed, testimony and review of minutes of the meetings made it clear that the IEP team merely rubberstamped the foregone conclusion of the preceding MDT meeting. The IEP meeting was, in effect, an artifice that did not disguise or defeat the reality of the school district's "inexorable march to its predetermined destination."

Significantly, the hearing officer refused to entertain the district's argument that the proposed placement was appropriate and would have been the same even had the district complied with the IEP procedural requirements. "Whether or not the result would have been different cannot be determined and is not relevant: the violation here was sufficient to subvert the underlying assumption of the IDEA." 24 IDELR at 618.

The hearing officer's decision in *In Re Bryan S.,* 22 IDELR 65 (SEA Ver. 1994), illustrates the same point even more powerfully. (And is also a compelling illustration of how sometimes educators do not take advantage of the body of published administrative decisions. Even if not precedential, they certainly can be food for thought. Nevertheless, neither the Vermont school district nor the hearing officer in *In re Student with a Disability* appeared to consider this thoughtful decision.)

Bryan S. was (at the time of the decision) a 16-year-old with high intellectual ability and a mild learning disability whose educational needs included college preparation. His school district had just established a program for such college-bound students, called the academic learning disabled (ALD) program. The educator (Mr. McDonnell) involved in designing Bryan's IEP had been hired mainly to complete the many years' development of the ALD program and launch it. Thus, as recounted by the hearing officer:

> It is difficult to imagine how Mr. McDonnell could resist or why he would even try to resist envisioning certain [school district] students fitting into the ALD program. While he clearly drew on research done by, and acted upon, at [other institutions and schools], it was surely appropriate for him to factor in the profiles and needs of specific [school district] students as he was finalizing the design of the ALD program.

> The [student] is among those who seemed to be a likely candidate for the program which had as its primary objective the preparation of higher functioning LD students for college. Unfortunately, the imaginary line between [the student] as an example of the kind of student being targeted by the ALD program, and [the student] as a specific student with legal rights to a free and appropriate public education developed pursuant to a stringent set of regulations, was crossed by the district.

22 IDELR at 67.

Thus, while the hearing officer acknowledged that the ALD program was well-constructed to meet the general needs of college-bound students with learning disabilities, the district's IEP was nonetheless fatally defective because it was drafted for the student to fit the ALD program and was therefore a predetermined placement. *See also Greenport Union Free Sch. Dist.,* 21 IDELR 269 (SEA N.Y. 1994) (a school district could not change the placement of a student with a learning disability because it did not first prepare an IEP reflecting the proposed change); and *Mount Horeb Area Sch. Dist.*, 25 IDELR 286 (SEA Wis. 1997) (school district violated the IDEA when it made a placement offer concurrent with a draft IEP, entitling the parents to one year of compensatory education in spite of the appropriateness of the IEP rejected by the parents).

In an interesting twist, the District Court for the District of Maryland found in *Kutin v. Anne Arundel County Board of Education*, 24 IDELR 666 (D. Md. 1996), that the state administrative decision-makers themselves violated the IDEA by ordering relief that created, in effect, a predetermined placement. In that case, the parents of a nine-year-old student with a language impairment filed for due process, claiming that the district's proposed IEP failed to provide sufficient special instruction and related services (speech and language therapy) to constitute a FAPE. The hearing officer (affirmed by the review panel) agreed with the parents and made substantial changes to the IEP, identifying additional needs and goals and objectives, as well as adding additional related services. He then directed the school district to implement the new IEP in the placement it had originally proposed for the less intensive program of the original IEP. This violated the IDEA by seeking to develop an IEP retrospectively to fit an already made placement, the court held, citing *Speilberg v. Henrico County Public School.*

28. If a parent signs the IEP, does his or her signature indicate consent to the placement proposed by the school district?

It could. The IDEA compels school districts to obtain the consent of parents to initial placements. (34 C.F.R. § 300.504(b)). For a consent to be effective under the IDEA it must meet the requirements at 34 C.F.R. § 300.500(a), which generally establish that consent must be both informed and voluntary.

Typically, the IEP document itself may not contain the requisite disclosures that would permit it to serve as memorializing consent. This should not be understood as a deficit in the document. Rather, it is a logical consequence of that fact that placement and programming are two distinct issues, with the programming issue the proper subject of the IEP meeting. There are many instances, in fact, in which parents agree to the school district's proposed programming but object to the proposed placement.

However, assuming the IEP includes a statement on initial placement that meets the definition of consent in § 300.500, the parent's signature on the IEP would satisfy the consent requirement. Appendix C to 34 C.F.R. Part 300, Question 30.

Chapter 4

Conducting IEP Meetings

This chapter addresses the general conduct of the IEP meeting. Chapter 5 discusses in greater detail the required—and permitted—attendees of such a meeting, and chapter 6 explores the role of parents at IEP meetings, particularly in those instances in which there is no agreement among the parties.

The IEP meeting provides a forum for the parents and the school district to jointly determine the needs of the child with a disability and to develop a program that will provide that child with an appropriate education. Collaboration among the parties most interested in and knowledgeable about the child is vital to the design of a program of appropriate services.

As a collaboration, development of the IEP must be a deliberative step-by-step process that starts with the basics—defining the child's deficit areas. From there, the team should progress through the next logical steps—setting goals and objectives, deciding what related services are needed to help the child meet those goals and, finally, determining the appropriate setting for the child.

The IEP team should start with the regular classroom with appropriate supplementary aids and services, and consider whether an appropriate IEP could be implemented in that setting. If not, the team must continually progress along the continuum of options until the team agrees where an appropriate program, reasonably calculated to provide educational benefit, can be implemented.

At least, that's the theory. The practice may be something else, at least in some cases, according to a 1995 report prepared by the National Association of State Directors of Special Education.[1] In interviews with the authors of the report, special education

---

[1] M. MCLAUGHLIN & S. WARREN, INDIVIDUAL EDUCATIONAL PROGRAMS: ISSUES AND OPTIONS FOR CHANGE (NASDE 1995). This report was prepared for the U.S. Department of Education's Office of Special Education Programs.

administrators observed that IEP meetings can be "episodic," "ritualistic" and "pro forma."

The report's thoughtful critique included these analyses of why IEP meetings may have turned out to be less meaningful than envisioned by Congress in 1975:

• Often the real crafting of the IEP is done before and after—not during—the IEP meeting, thus marginalizing the role of parents. Individuals interviewed attributed this not to resistance to the principle that parents have a legitimate role in IEP design, but to systemic time and resource limitations. According to one administrator who was interviewed, if the IEP team were to sit down to draft the entire IEP document in one meeting, the process would take several hours. Given the number of students who have IEPs (roughly 12 percent of the school population, according to the Department of Education) teachers do not have that kind of time available for this effort.

• Regrettably, the need to demonstrate compliance with the procedural requirements of the IDEA shifts the focus from true brainstorming to "dotting the i's and crossing the t's." Along the same lines, the awareness that what is said and done during the meeting may be fodder for evidence in later overtly adversarial proceedings may limit true candor and collaboration.

• For a variety of reasons, discussed in more detail in the introduction to chapter 6, parental participation may contribute little of substance to the IEP meeting deliberations.

A truly regrettable trend discerned by some educators is the increasing view of some IEP team participants—whether they be parents or school officials—that the IEP meeting is just the first step in an adversarial process. People may come into the meeting to state their case for the record, not really to try to fashion an appropriate IEP in the student's LRE. All too often participants come to the meeting with a predetermined direction they want the meeting results to take. The meeting starts at the end, instead of at the beginning.

Format of Meeting

1. How long should an IEP meeting be?

The IDEA prescribes no specific length for an IEP meeting. As a practical matter, initial IEP meetings generally take more time than meetings to review existing IEPs, assuming the child is making satisfactory progress on his or her IEP goals and no difficulties have arisen since the last meeting. Similarly, the amount of time required to adequately address the educational needs of students will be a function of how complex those needs are. Appendix C to 34 C.F.R. Part 300, Question 10.

In all events, as a legal matter, a school district must schedule sufficient meeting time to allow the parents to meaningfully participate, but it also has the right to adjourn the meeting after a reasonable time, even if the parents object. For example, the hearing officer in *Grapevine-Colleyville Independent School District*, 21 IDELR 875 (SEA Tex. 1994), found that the school district's Admission, Review, and Dismissal (ARD) Committee's refusal to continue discussions of topics raised by the parent did not violate the procedural requirements of the IDEA. The Committee already had met twice before to arrive at a consensus on the IEP, then met a third time to review the parent's itemized points of objection. This being done, they adjourned, despite the parent wanting to discuss arguably peripheral issues. Because the parent had a chance to participate in the IEP process, the Committee acted reasonably in adjourning.

As a matter of establishing and maintaining cordial relations, a school district should make every reasonable effort to not make parents feel rushed. When a meeting is taking longer than anticipated as a result of parents' questions or concerns, resulting in some attendees having to leave to meet previously scheduled commitments, the meeting should be continued at a later time. Parents who feel they have been given short shrift are more likely to believe they must assume an adversarial position with the school district.

2.   Must IEP meetings be held in person?

Not always, but the extent of deviation from conducting the IEP meeting face-to-face depends on who requests the meeting.

According to OSEP, the requirement in IDEA regulations at 34 C.F.R. § 300.343 that each school district (or public agency) initiate and conduct IEP meetings to develop, review or revise an IEP means that the child's parents have a right to meet face-to-face with the other participants. *Letter to Soffer,* EHLR 213:187 (OSEP 1989). 34 C.F.R. § 300.345(c) does authorize the school district to use "other methods, including individual or conference telephone calls" to conduct the meeting when the parents are unable to attend.

But does a reasonable interpretation of those two provisions mean the school district cannot hold an IEP meeting by alternative means when the parents can attend in person? No, according to *Soffer.* Parents may waive their right to an in-person meeting and, assuming all other required participants (as identified in 34 C.F.R. § 300.344) are mutually agreeable to meeting by alternative methods, they may do so.

An exception that allows IEP meetings by telephone at the option of other than the parents is found in 34 C.F.R. § 300.348 concerning IEP procedures for students publicly placed in private schools or facilities. Subsection 300.348(a)(2) provides that if a required representative of the private placement cannot attend in person, he or she may participate by other methods.[2]

---

[2] *See* Question 5 in chapter 9, *infra.*

With regard to what types of alternative methods of conducting the IEP meeting pass muster, the inquirer in *Soffer* was perhaps ahead of his time when he asked if computer conferencing was permissible alternative to meeting face-to-face. While OSEP responded that computer-conferencing would be acceptable if mutually agreeable to all parties, including the parents, it suggested that school districts proceed cautiously in considering this option. Many parents may not have access to the necessary equipment. Even if they do, using it in these circumstances could be "uncomfortable."

3. When the parent's native language is other than English, must the school district provide a translator at the IEP meeting?

Generally, yes. IDEA regulations at 34 C.F.R. § 300.345 state that "[the school district] shall take whatever action is necessary to ensure that the parent understand the proceedings at [an IEP] meeting, including arranging for an interpreter for parents with deafness or whose native language[3] is other than English." *See E.H. v. Tirozzi*, 16 EHLR 787 (D. Conn. 1990). For example, the school district in *Michael I.*, 1985-86 EHLR 507:222 (SEA Mass. 1985), provided a translator for a parent whose native language was Portuguese.

OCR interprets the procedural safeguard of Section 504 (at 34 C.F.R. § 104.36) as mandating that the school district provide a translator at IEP meetings for parents whose native language is other than English. *E.g., DeKalb (GA) Sch. Dist.*, 18 IDELR 921 (OCR 1991).

What if both parents attend, only one of whom wishes to have the IEP conducted in their native language? In one such case OCR found that the school district did not violate Section 504 when it conducted the IEP meeting in English. In *West Las Vegas (NM) School District*, 20 IDELR 1409 (OCR 1993), the rights and procedural safeguards of the parents were not abridged by the use of the English language at their son's IEP meetings. Although the parents' native language was Spanish, the student's mother expressed her preference for the use of English in conversation, and said she preferred to conduct the IEP meetings in that language. Because the parents attended together and the school district had several staff members available to speak Spanish had it been requested, the school district complied with the requirements of 34 C.F.R. § 104.36.

4. Must a school district make accommodations necessary to enable a parent with a disability to meaningfully participate in an IEP meeting?

Yes, there is support for imposition of such a requirement in both IDEA and Section 504/Americans with Disabilities Act regulations.

---

[3] Native language is defined in IDEA regulations at 34 C.F.R. § 300.12 as "when used with reference to an individual of limited English proficiency, . . . the language normally used by that individual."

IDEA regulations at 34 C.F.R. § 300.345(e), requiring that school districts take "whatever action is necessary to ensure that the parent understand the proceedings at [an IEP] meeting," would seem to apply to accommodating disabilities, both physical and cognitive, as well as providing interpreters for parents with deafness or whose native language is other than English.

In addition, to the extent the parent has a qualifying disability, he or she is entitled to accommodations under Section 504 or the ADA. 34 C.F.R. §§ 104.4, 104.3(k)(4); 28 C.F.R. § 35.130. In *Grapevine-Colleyville (TX) Independent School District*, 24 IDELR 574 (OCR 1996), OCR found that the school district provided sufficient accommodations to enable a parent with a learning disability to meaningfully participate in her son's Admissions, Review, and Dismissal (ARD) meetings. The district adequately addressed the parent's disability by: providing a teacher to read the ARD minutes to her, providing her with a written copy of the minutes and audiotaping the meeting.

5. May a school district open an IEP meeting by presenting a completed IEP?

No. While a school district may prepare and present a draft IEP, it may not present a completed IEP to parents at the commencement of an IEP meeting. *Letter to Helmuth*, 16 EHLR 503 (OSEP 1990). Even if the school district's intent is to use the IEP document simply as a basis for discussion, presenting a completed IEP has the appearance of trying to marginalize the contribution of the parents to the IEP process. This undercuts the essential principle of parental participation that infuses the IDEA.

Unquestionably, school districts should prepare for IEP meetings. As stated in the Notice of Interpretation on IEP Requirements, school district staff would do well to come prepared with evaluation findings and statements of present levels of educational performance. Appendix C to 34 C.F.R. Part 300, Question 55. They also should have recommendations to raise with the parents regarding annual goals, short-term objectives, and the kind of special education and related services the child should receive.

Typically, school districts consolidate these recommendations and findings in what is termed a "draft IEP." According to OSEP, school districts may present such a draft IEP to parents at an IEP meeting, provided it is "made clear to the parents at the outset of the meeting that the services proposed by the agency are only recommendations for review and discussion with the parents." Appendix C to 34 C.F.R. Part 300, Question 55; *Letter to Helmuth, supra*.

As a related matter, it is vital that school officials do not become invested in the draft IEP to such an extent that they discount, or give the appearance of discounting, any proposals for change made by the parents at the meeting, or in other ways make the parents feel as if the truly meaningful discussion about the child already has taken place. This includes forwarding a draft IEP to other agencies in advance of the actual IEP meeting. This was what happened in the administrative review decision *In re Child with Disabilities,* 23 IDELR 654 (SEA Del. 1995). The school district in that case was ordered to fund the residential placement advocated by the parents because, among other things, it had forwarded its draft IEP to the district's funding committee prior to the IEP meeting with the parents, leading the review panel to conclude that it had already committed itself to a particular program before receiving any input from the parents. The panel found this was a substantive, rather than a mere technical, violation of the IEP.

The Third Circuit's decision in *Fuhrmann v. East Hanover Board of Education,* 19 IDELR 1065 (3d Cir. 1993), is a good example of how a school district can pass IDEA muster when presenting a draft IEP at the IEP meeting. In that case the school district's draft IEP was discussed, all the parent's suggestions were considered, and some were incorporated. Similarly the school districts in *Hudson v. Wilson,* 1986-87 EHLR 558:186 (W.D. Va. 1986), *aff'd,* 1987-88 EHLR 559:139 (4th Cir. 1987) and *Scituate School Committee v. Robert B.,* 1985-86 EHLR 557:207 (D.R.I. 1985), *aff'd,* 795 F.2d 77 (1st Cir. 1986), passed muster despite having drafted the IEP before the meeting. In *Hudson,* the court overruled the parents' objection to an IEP "proposal" that was drafted three weeks earlier, without the participation of the parents. The court reasoned that the school district did not violate the regulations because it could have modified the proposal at the meeting it held with the parents to finalize the IEP. In *Scituate,* the court held that the parents' post-IEP meeting actions clearly demonstrated that the school district's presentation of a draft IEP was not intended to, and did not have the effect of, short-circuiting the parents' right to participate in the development of the IEP. The parents, accompanied by their attorney, failed to participate in the IEP meeting. Writing to the school district three days after the meeting, the parents, through their attorney, advised that they needed more time to evaluate the IEP, would respond with their comments concerning needed revisions, and were, accordingly, deferring their decision on whether or not to accept the IEP until the school district had responded to their input.

6. Must a school district convene an IEP meeting to review the results of an independent educational evaluation?

Yes. If the independent educational evaluation (IEE) relates to decisions about programming, then the IEP team must reconvene to review the results.

An IEE is an evaluation conducted by a qualified examiner not employed by the school district or other public agency responsible for the education of the student in question. 34 C.F.R. § 300.503(a)(3). Parents have the right to obtain an IEE at any time during their child's education and to have the IEE "considered by the public agency with respect to the provision of FAPE to the child." 34 C.F.R. § 503(c).

IDEA regulations do not specify who precisely is required to consider the IEE.[4] But it is clear that when the IEE concerns programming (see *Letter to Anonymous,* 23 IDELR 563 (OSEP 1995)), rather than identification or placement, the IEP team is the appropriate body for review.

7. What actions must the IEP team take at the meeting to meet the requirement to consider the independent educational evaluation?

While it is clear that a school district's obligation to consider the IEE does not translate into an obligation to adopt the IEE or accept its recommendations, it is not so clear what the process of consideration entails.

The IDEA includes neither a statutory nor regulatory definition of what it means to "consider" a privately funded IEE; nor are there any requirements specifying the weight it must be accorded. In *Letter to Anonymous,* 23 IDELR 563 (OSEP 1995), OSEP states that the IEP team (or the MDT) must review the IEE, discuss its results and, to the extent it is not adopted, discuss the basis for any disagreement.

In the case of *T.S. v. Board of Education of the Town of Ridgefield,* 20 IDELR 889 (2d Cir. 1993), the Second Circuit Court of Appeals ruled that, in the absence of a statutory or regulatory definition, the plain meaning of "consider"—to reflect on or think about with some degree of care or caution—was appropriate. Using that standard, the court found that the school district had properly considered the IEE at issue, despite the fact that a copy of the full report was not distributed to every team member, when: (1) the report was read in full by the director of special education; (2) portions of the report were read in full at the IEP meetings, with the balance summarized; and (3) the minutes of the meeting reflected some subsequent discussion of the issues raised by the IEE.

8. Must the IEP team document its consideration of the independent educational evaluation at the IEP meeting?

No, there is no requirement in the IDEA that anything other than the information specified in 34 C.F.R. § 300.346 be included in the IEP. Further, there is no requirement for production of minutes or other documentation of the proceedings of the IEP meeting over and above the IEP document itself. OSEP amplified the regulations in *Letter to Anonymous,* 20 IDELR 1460 (OSEP 1994), when it stated that recommendations submitted or discussed by participants at the IEP meeting, including the parents, did not have to be memorialized in the IEP document.

---

[4] State law may, though. Massachusetts, for example, requires that an IEP meeting be convened to consider the results of the IEE. Sharon Pub. Sch., 21 IDELR 339 (SEA Mass. 1994).

The author notes that one hearing officer disagrees with this interpretation. In *Des Moines Public School,* 16 EHLR 1166 (SEA Iowa 1990), the officer stated that "a reasonable interpretation of the 'must consider' [requirement of 34 C.F.R. § 300.503(c)] is that the school district should document how the results of the IEE were considered and the reasons, if any, for disagreeing with the IEE results." 16 EHLR at 1169.

The Second Circuit's decision in *T.S. v. Board of Education of the Town of Ridgefield,* 20 IDELR 889 (2d Cir. 1993), illustrates how important it is, from the viewpoint of effective advocacy, for a district to document its consideration of an IEE, including: (1) how the report was made available to MDT/IEP team members; (2) the forum in which the report was reviewed and discussed by the team members; and (3) to the extent the school district disagrees with the IEE, the reasons why the findings and recommendations of the IEP are not accepted.

Documentation of Proceedings

9. *May a school district tape-record an IEP meeting?*

Surprisingly, the issue is unresolved as a matter of federal law, although OSEP's informal interpretation of the IDEA generally would permit tape-recording.

The use of tape recorders at IEP meetings is neither required nor prohibited by either the IDEA or its regulations. In its 1981 Notice of Interpretation on IEP Requirements, the Department of Education (DOE) opined that, while taping is not required, it is permissible at the option of either the parents or the public agency. Appendix C to 34 C.F.R. Part 300, Question 12. However, for the very reason that tape-recording is not specifically addressed one way or the other in the IDEA, DOE considers that section of the Notice as "non-binding suggestions and guidance" rather than legal interpretation used by the agency in evaluating compliance.

The district court in *E.H. v. Tirozzi,* 16 EHLR 787 (D. Conn. 1990), explains well the implications of that distinction in connection with the school district's (or a parent's) right to tape-record IEP meetings:

> Since this language [of Question 12 of Appendix C] is not mandatory or binding, it has prompted several inquiries regarding the status of tape recording at [IEP] meetings. Unfortunately, the response has been somewhat equivocal. Initially, the OSEP's informal opinion was that taping should be allowed if either the parents or school officials requested it. The OSEP noted, however, that it did not have authority to require or prohibit recordings; this would require an amendment to the regulations. Later, in response to a similar inquiry, the OSEP changed its position to state that the language of Question 12 "at the option of either party" meant that either party could tape record the [IEP meeting] without permission of the other. Most recently, the OSEP has determined that this interpretation was inconsistent with the intent and background of Question 12 and was therefore incorrect. Although the OSEP's

informal opinion would still permit taping, it did not have the authority to require or prohibit taping at [IEP] meetings. *Letter to Doerr*, EHLR 213:127 (OSEP 1988).

16 EHLR at 790 (some citations omitted).

Thus, the question of whether a school district may tape-record an IEP meeting without parental consent has not been addressed head-on by OSEP. And the issue of consent has come up in reported decisions more in connection with school district opposition to parental taping. Nevertheless, a credible argument could be made that, if taping makes parents uncomfortable, it inhibits their ability to participate fully in the IEP meeting and thus violates their rights under the IDEA.

School districts should be aware, though, that any tape recording it does make is considered an education record, subject to access by the parents as a right. *Letter to Baugh*, EHLR 211:479 (OSERS 1987); *see also* Question 10, *infra*.

10. Must a school district provide a transcript of the IEP meeting to the parents?

No. While parents do have the right to a "written or electronic transcript" of a due process hearing or administrative review (34 C.F.R. § 300.508(a)(4)), that entitlement, more appropriate to an adversarial proceeding, does not extend to IEP meetings. Under the IDEA, the school district is not required to make a verbatim recording of the IEP meeting. Appendix C to 34 C.F.R. Part 300, Question 12; *Letter to Baugh*, EHLR 211:479 (OSERS 1987).

On the other hand, if a school district does elect to record and prepare a transcript of an IEP meeting (Appendix C to 34 C.F.R. Part 300, Question 12), that transcript becomes an "education record" as that term is defined for purposes of the Family Educational Rights and Privacy Act (FERPA), codified at 20 U.S.C. § 1232g, and the parents are entitled to inspect and review it in accordance with the statute. (Under FERPA, a school district must comply with a parental request to examine an education record "without unnecessary delay . . . and in no case more than 45 days after the request has been made." 34 C.F.R. § 300.562(b)(2).)

A school district may want to tape-record an IEP meeting when it anticipates that a due process hearing is in the offing, both to aid in preparation and to present as evidence. However, even if the district plans to introduce the tape as evidence at the hearing, the transcript retains its character as an education record. In *Letter to Baugh*, EHLR 211:479 (OSERS 1987), an inquirer posed the situation of a school district attorney who advised that the school district could deny a parent who had requested a due process hearing access to a tape recording of the IEP meeting more expansive than that granted under the "five-day rule" for disclosure of evidence that applies to due process hearings. 34 C.F.R. § 300.508(a)(3).

11. *Do parents have the right to tape-record an IEP meeting?*

As discussed in Question 9 above, OSEP's informal interpretation of the IDEA generally would permit parents to tape-record, or otherwise commission the recording of, IEP meetings. Generally, state law determines if a parent may tape-record an IEP meeting.[5]

Nevertheless, published decisions show that some school districts have made this issue a point of contention, adding complications to already difficult situations. As a distressing example of how the stakes can be raised over what should be a non-issue, consider the situation reported in a 1990 OCR Letter of Findings, *Farmington (MI) Public School District,* 16 EHLR 1403 (OCR 1990).

Trouble started when, several days prior to a scheduled IEP meeting, the district's special education director was told that the parent might bring a court reporter to the IEP meeting. When the parent arrived for the meeting with the court reporter, the district initially refused to convene the meeting because it objected to recording. After discussion, the district agreed to record the meeting, but only by means of its own tape recorder. The parent agreed to the use of a tape recorder, but only the one used by the court reporter, claiming that the district's recorder was not sophisticated enough to record all persons seated in the room. The IEP meeting was never held; the parties proceeded straight to due process.

Disputes over tape-recording have made their way even into the courts in two 1990 cases in Connecticut. (Two different school districts were involved; there was no state law involved.) In each case, the parents claimed tape-recording was necessary for meaningful participation in the IEP process, thus implicating the requirement of 34 C.F.R. § 300.345(e) that school districts take "whatever action is necessary to ensure that the parent understands the proceedings at a meeting."

In the first case, *E.H. v. Tirozzi,* 16 EHLR 787 (D. Conn. 1990), a parent whose native language was Danish wanted to record the IEP meeting, claiming she needed to review the proceedings at home with a dictionary to surmount the language barrier and fully participate. The child's teacher refused to be tape-recorded, claiming she would be uncomfortable being taped and had a right not to be taped. At first the district refused to allow the mother to tape the meeting, then allowed her to tape all but the teacher's remarks, which were summarized in written notes. The mother requested due process and the district then raised two additional objections to tape-recording, claiming it was inconsistent with the goals of the IEP meeting because—borrowing from principles recognized in labor law—it inhibited full and free discussion among the participants and also hindered the mother in her ability to participate.

First acknowledging that the IDEA did not address the issue, the district court said that OSEP's informal view permitting taping was entitled to great deference. It

---

[5] *See, e.g.,* Question 15, *infra.*

then treated the particular dispute as a weighing of competing interests—the parent's interest in maximizing her ability to participate in the IEP process as against the teacher's "right" not to be recorded. The parent's interest outweighed the teacher's, the court found. The district's other arguments also were rejected rather handily.

The school district in *V.W. v. Faloise,* 16 EHLR 1070 (D. Conn. 1990), tried the inhibits-free-discussion and limits-parental-participation tack, with the same lack of success. The court upheld the parent's right to tape-record IEP meetings. The mother in this case wanted to tape-record the meetings because she had a partial disability in her hand that made note-taking difficult. She also wanted to let her husband, who had to work, know what had happened during the meetings. The school district claimed tape-recording would have a chilling effect on the free exchange of ideas. More to the point, perhaps, it claimed that the recording of disagreements among school personnel might be used against it in litigation.

If it is a question of competing interests, the court ruled, then the parent's interests prevail. The court held that the district violated the IDEA by, in effect, conditioning the parent's participation in the IEP meeting on her relinquishing the right to tape-record. Under the IDEA, it stated, "participation means something more than mere presence" and the parent's right to effective participation necessarily encompassed the right to tape-record IEP meetings.

12. May either parents or the school district videotape an IEP meeting?

In *Letter to Conley,* 16 EHLR 1080 (OSEP 1990), OSEP considered the use of tape recorders as including use of videotape recorders. Thus, the same considerations discussed in Questions 9 and 11, concerning audio tape-recording, should apply.

13. Must a school district provide a copy of the IEP to the parents?

Yes. While school districts generally are not obligated to provide copies of education records to parents (34 C.F.R. § 300.562),[6] IDEA regulations at 34 C.F.R. § 300.345(f) state that a public agency shall give the parents, upon their request, a copy of the IEP. The Notice of Interpretation provides further guidance by recommending that school districts inform parents of their right to request a copy at the IEP meeting or send them a copy of the IEP itself "within a reasonable amount of time following the meeting" or both. Appendix C to 34 C.F.R. Part 300, Question 31.

---

[6] *See* Question 10, *supra,* concerning education records.

14. Does the IDEA require that the school district prepare minutes of IEP meetings?

No, the minutes of an IEP meeting are not technically part of the IEP document, nor does the IDEA require their preparation. *See, e.g,* 34 C.F.R. § 300.346; *Grapevine-Colleyville Indep. Sch. Dist.,* 21 IDELR 875 (SEA Tex. 1994) (the Admission, Review, and Dismissal (ARD) Committee's failure to prepare written reports of its meeting did not violate the procedural requirements of the IDEA).

Nevertheless, there are many good reasons why minutes should be prepared. For one thing, they can be used to document who attended the meeting, as required. Appendix C to 34 C.F.R. Part 300, Question 29. Another reason minutes may be kept is to better ensure that what is agreed to at the IEP meeting is clear and incorporated into the IEP. The hearing officer in *In re Child with Disabilities,* 21 IDELR 624 (SEA Conn. 1994), found the minutes of an IEP meeting crucial for just that reason. In that case, the hearing officer found that the minutes established the school district's failure to, among other things, follow through with the actions it said it would take to secure the work opportunities included in the IEPs for two learning disabled twins.

A good example of why detailed minutes are needed is seen in *Gorham School Department,* 20 IDELR 862 (SEA Maine. 1993):

> The [IEP team] determination to provide diagnostic testing is less clear. The school insists that it was always of the understanding that the parties had agreed to conduct diagnostic testing at the same time as the psychological testing: in November when [the student] was home on Thanksgiving break. The parent stated that she was of the opinion that the diagnostic testing would occur during the summer and had made that clear through a follow-up letter to the school. . . . The partial transcript of the [IEP meeting] has a brief exchange noted during the discussion of testing where [the student's] mother states ". . . I was just concerned about the reading and thought it should be done in the summer." To which the Director of Special Education answered, "Yep." The next couple of sentences clearly indicate that the parent was discussing summer reading and math diagnostic testing.
>
> The school may have genuinely felt that the [IEP team] had agreed on completing all testing in the fall, but it is clear that the parent did at least express a wish to have the diagnostic testing done in the summer. The transcript ends abruptly, and the minutes of the meeting do not assign a date to the diagnostic testing separate from the psychological testing so it's not possible to determine whose memory is correct.

20 IDELR at 864-64.

Minutes of an IEP meeting are education records parents are entitled to review. And, as can be seen by the recitation of cases above, meeting minutes can be evidence in an adversarial proceeding. Either party may introduce them as evidence at a due process hearing. In some disputes with parents, the minutes can be crucial support for the school district.

A review of published administrative decisions illustrates various reasons a party may opt to introduce IEP meeting minutes. Here are some additional examples, by no means intended to be exhaustive, from administrative decisions and OCR complaint investigations.

- In *DeKalb County School District*, 21 IDELR 426 (SEA Ga. 1994), the school district introduced the meeting minutes to show that two members of the IEP team disagreed with the recommendation to provide additional services wanted by the parents.

- The school district in the same case, *DeKalb County School District*, also used the minutes to, in effect, prove a negative. The parents claimed that the IEP team had agreed that a majority vote would prevail at the meeting. The minutes made no mention of any such agreement. The hearing officer found the school district more credible.

- To counter a complainant's testimony that school district officials did not actively participate in the development of IEPs for hospitalized students who were wards of the state, the IEP minutes showed that district officials contributed to the development at IEP meeting, rather than let the hospital staff make all the decisions. *Georgia Dep't of Educ.*, 20 IDELR 29 (OCR 1993).

- Minutes can be a persuasive counter to parents' claim that they were not permitted to be equal participants in IEP meetings.[7] According to OCR: "When a local education agency is aware that the parents of a child are in disagreement with a proposed placement, some care should be taken to document the alternative placements considered in order to establish that there was serious consideration of the alternatives." *DeKalb County Bd. of Educ.*, 17 EHLR 1206, 1212 n.13 (OCR 1991); *see also In the Matter of a Child with Disabilities*, 19 IDELR 203 (SEA Conn. 1992).

- Minutes also can show meaningful parental participation by documenting that the parents posed questions to the school district and that the school district considered the results of an IEE and possible alternative placements. *Board of Educ. of Waterford-Halfmoon Union Free Sch. Dist.*, 20 IDELR 1092 (SEA N.Y. 1994).

Naturally, due to the scope of review in civil actions, particular pieces of evidence are not discussed as extensively in court opinions. Nevertheless, evaluation of meeting

---

[7] *See* Question 1 in chapter 6, *infra,* discussing in more detail what it means for a parent to be an equal participant.

minutes played a part in two notable judicial decisions: *Greer v. Rome City School District,* 18 IDELR 412 (11th Cir. 1991) (minutes of MDT meeting showed that placement in a regular education classroom was never considered) and *G.D. v. Westmoreland School District,* 17 EHLR 751 (5th Cir. 1991) (minutes of IEP meeting showed that placement was not determined prior to development of the IEP; to the contrary, the minutes show that the parent raised the issue of placement at the meeting, but the district team members informed her that placement would be discussed at a later meeting).

State statutes or decisional law may, in fact, require that information concerning parents' viewpoints or recommendations be included in the minutes. For example, the court in *Reusch v. Fountain,* 21 IDELR 1107 (D. Md. 1994), required as a matter of state law that, if decisions at IEP meetings are made by voting and neither parents nor teachers have a vote, then their positions should be otherwise recorded in the records of the proceedings. Similarly, New York has a statutory requirement that the school district document the reasons it chooses not to provide a program or service recommended by the parent or a different program or service than those so recommended. *See Board of Educ. of North Cent. Collins Sch. Dist.,* 24 IDELR 897 (SEA N.Y. 1996).

The 1997 Amendments do not establish a requirement for minutes. They do specify items that must be discussed at IEP meetings but that are not identified among the items that must be included in the IEP document. Pending further guidance, the wise course would be preparation of minutes memorializing discussion of the mandated items.

Section 614(d)(3)(B), for example, provides in relevant part:
The IEP Team shall—

(i) in the case of a child whose behavior impedes his or her learning or that of others, consider, when appropriate, strategies, including positive behavioral interventions, strategies, and supports to address that behavior;

(ii) in the case of a child with limited English proficiency, consider the language needs of the child as such needs relate to the child's IEP;

(iii) in the case of a child who is blind or visually impaired, provide for instruction in Braille and the use of Braille unless the IEP Team determines, after an evaluation of the child's reading and writing skills, needs, and appropriate reading and writing media (including an evaluation of the child's future needs for instruction in Braille or use of Braille), that instruction in Braille or the use of Braille is not appropriate for the child;

(iv) consider the communication needs of the child, and in the case of a child who is deaf or hard of hearing, consider the child's language and communication mode, academic level, and full range of needs, including opportunities for direct instruction in the child's language and communication mode; and

(v) consider whether the child requires assistive technology devices and services.

15. May a party introduce a tape recording of an IEP meeting as evidence at a due process hearing?

While the rules of evidence of a particular state will determine the answer, there is nothing in the IDEA itself to prohibit such use of a tape recording. In fact, in the case of a dispute about what was said at the meeting, use of the recording as evidence may be a prime purpose for recording the meeting in the first instance. In this sense, a tape recording serves the same purpose as minutes or a transcript, but, in the case of parents in particular, saves the expense of transcription.

There is one interesting administrative decision that seems to hold, albeit unclearly, that intent to use tape recording as evidence in a legal proceeding is not a legitimate reason to tape-record the IEP meeting. In *Warrensburg Central School District,* 17 EHLR 371 (SEA N.Y. 1990), the state Commissioner on Education determined that both parents and school districts generally have a right to tape-record IEP meetings (called committee on special education or CSE). However, it held that such right is limited by the use intended to be made of the tape. The right to tape-record, it opined, can be exercised by a parent only to promote understanding of the IEP process and to make informed decisions; it may be forfeited by a parent who attempts to use the tape as "a weapon or shield."

Even more interesting, and showing the regrettable contentiousness that can infect the relationship between parents and school district officials, is the dispute over submission of tape recordings as evidence in *Santa Monica-Malibu Unified School District,* 2 ECLPR ¶ 112 (SEA Cal. 1995). Both the parents and the school officials tape-recorded the IEP meeting and submitted a tape as evidence. One would think they would be identical, but guess again! The parents' tape contained several gaps. They, for their part, accused the school district of tampering with its own tape submission. The hearing officer observed: "Obviously, there were omissions in the tape recordings submitted by both parties. These irregularities created the appearance that neither party was being fully candid with the Hearing Officer." 2 ECLPR § 112 at 453 n.2.

16. Must the school district document who attended the IEP meeting?

Yes, according to the Notice of Interpretation. In addressing whether IEPs must be signed by the parents, it stated, "A signed IEP is one way to document who attended the meeting. If signatures are not used, the agency must document attendance in some other way." Appendix C to 34 C.F.R. Part 300, Question 29.

Chapter 5

IEP Meeting Participants

Parents, teachers and attorneys: those are the three groups of participants whose attendance at IEP meetings have received the most analysis. Parental participation is covered in greater detail in chapter 6. But as an introduction to this chapter, which examines the law and legal pronouncements concerning who must, or may, attend IEP meetings, the focus is on the roles of teachers and attorneys representing parents.

The presence of a child's teacher at an IEP meeting ensures that the type of person who will most likely implement the IEP is involved in its development. The teacher's particular knowledge provides essential information concerning the placement, programs and services that could or should be employed to meet the goals of the IEP. The child's current teacher is in a unique position to provide input for development of the new IEP and for setting proper goals, because he or she is familiar with the child's needs and learning style and can provide insight on the particular instructional methods that have been most effective.

But who is the child's current teacher? This year's teacher or next year's teacher? Since annual IEP review meetings often are held at the end of the school year the current teacher—who is required to attend the meeting—may not actually be the child's teacher the following year. The IDEA does not, however, require the presence of the child's new teacher at the annual review, probably because the identity of the subsequent year's teacher often is unknown at the time of the IEP meeting.

Actually, the new teacher's identity could not be known since the IDEA prohibits predetermined placements. Since the next year's placement is decided at the IEP meeting, the next year's teacher cannot, as a technical—if not practical matter—be invited *before* the meeting. Notwithstanding the above, when the IEP team members, including the parents, have previously discussed a likely placement for the child in the next school year and have reached a general consensus, it is advisable for that new teacher to attend the IEP meeting.

Another teacher selection dilemma involves students who divide their school days between special and regular education classrooms. Which teacher should attend? Prior to the 1997 Amendments, either could attend, with the selection being left to the discretion of involved officials. Ideally, both should attend in some instances.

Nonetheless, despite the largely successful efforts undertaken to include students with disabilities in the regular classroom and pursue the regular curriculum, appropriately modified, there was still an inclination to view a student's special education programming as the more important aspect of his or her education and his or her special education teacher as the more appropriate individual to attend the IEP meeting as the child's teacher.

This mindset is a relic of the early days of the IDEA, no longer serving to further the goals of the Act. As explained by the Department of Education in its summary and explanation of the proposed Individuals with Disabilities Education Act Amendments of 1995 (Reauthorization):

> IEPs often fail to include meaningful educational goals designed to provide students with access to the general curriculum and the special education and related services to enable them to achieve much more. . . . [T]he annual review of the student's progress at the IEP meeting often fails to take a hard look at the results of ongoing classroom assessment to determine whether a revision of the child's program is necessary or the student continues to need special education and related services.
>
> Experience offers insight into why this is the case: IEP meetings too frequently focus only on the time each day or each week the child is "in" special education and on the detailed short-term objectives that bear little relation to how children learn or their parents' aspirations for them. And, because the law does not require regular education classroom teachers to attend IEP meetings, for those students who spend much of their day in the regular classroom, the discussion of what instructional approaches and services are necessary to enable the student to achieve to high standards often takes place without the teacher with whom the student spends most of his or her time. In effect, the IEP meetings focus on access to special education rather than on access to an overall high-quality education.[1]

Based on this reasoning, that the permitted selection of the child's special education teacher for IEP meetings contributed to diminishing the effectivity of the IEP process, the 1997 Amendments close off that option. At least one regular education teacher, in addition to the special education teacher, must be a member of the IEP team if the student is or may be eligible to participate in the regular education environment.

In light of the elimination of attorneys' fees to prevailing parties for attorney representation at IEP meetings, the author feels compelled to include here a brief word about the claimed increasing presence and deleterious impact of attorneys representing parents at IEPs meetings. The presence of an attorney *can* make an IEP meeting more

---

[1] Accessed by the author at <http://www.ed.gov/IDEA/amend95/prin2.html>, p. 3 of 6.

contentious. Some parents' attorneys, in fact, are difficult to deal with. Like all people, some have better interpersonal skills, others worse. Some are well-trained and self-possessed, others inexperienced or unprepared.

But with all the lamenting about their negative influence, what is rarely explored is why parents retain attorneys in the first place. Even in today's litigious times, most people do not hire an attorney without a perceived need for legal representation. And, most parents do not see their child's disability and resulting educational needs primarily as a legal issue. So the reader is urged to consider: Why has this parent felt the need to bring an attorney to this IEP meeting? What occurred in the course of prior dealings to make the parent think representation is necessary to be treated fairly and to receive all the services to which his or her child is entitled under the law? If there is nothing amiss in the prior personal relationship, consider whether other parents have complained about school district actions—and whether they had reason to do so. Consider also the general reputation of your school district, for even bad press of a general nature may put a parent on guard.

In sum, the likely unpopular view of the author is this: Involvement of parents' attorneys early in the IEP process does not create problems. Those problems were already there, and elimination of attorneys' fees for IEP meetings will not resolve them.

Mandatory School District Participants

1. Who is required to participate in IEP meetings?

IDEA regulations at 34 C.F.R. § 300.344 identify mandatory attendees at IEP meetings. The designated attendees are those individuals deemed essential to any determination regarding the special education program of a student with a disability.

When an IEP meeting is improperly constituted, both the meeting itself and any resulting IEP may be considered fatally defective. *See, e.g., W.G. v. Board of Trustees of Target Range School District No. 23,* 18 IDELR 1019 (9th Cir. 1992) (because the school district failed to ensure the attendance of all necessary parties, the resulting IEP was incomplete and insufficient).

Further, tardy attendance may be treated the same as absence. For example, in *Board of Education of the City School District of the City of New York,* 24 IDELR 199 (SEA N.Y. 1996), the student's teacher was substantially late, causing the parent to leave before her arrival. The school district did not adjourn the meeting, however, and when the teacher arrived, the team completed the meeting and prepared an IEP the parent challenged in due process. The hearing officer held that the IEP was a nullity because the meeting at which the contested decision was reached was not validly composed due to the teacher's lateness and should have been adjourned. The IEP team was ordered to meet again to revise the student's IEP to include appropriate annual goals.

Section 300.344(a) identifies the school district personnel whose attendance at the IEP meeting the school district (or other responsible public agency) must ensure.

In every instance IEP meeting attendees must include:

(1) a representative of the school district (or other public agency charged with providing FAPE to the child) (34 C.F.R. § 300.344(a)(1)) and

(2) the child's teacher (34 C.F.R. § 300.344(a)(2)).

When the meeting concerns a child with a disability who has been evaluated for the first time, the IEP meeting also must include evaluation personnel. 34 C.F.R. § 300.344(b).[2]

One or both of the child's parents also are required participants. 34 C.F.R. § 300.344(a)(3). Clearly the school district has no police power to compel their attendance. What it is required to do, though, is to schedule a meeting at a time that makes the parents' attendance reasonably convenient and to provide adequate notice.[3]

Similarly, 34 C.F.R. § 300.344(a)(4) requires attendance of the child in all cases, "if appropriate," although the decision about whether the child should attend is made by the parents. Appendix C to 34 C.F.R. Part 300, Question 21. In addition, when transition services are to be addressed at the IEP meeting, the school district is encouraged to "invite the student." 34 C.F.R. § 300.344(c)(i).

The concept of inviting participants to an IEP meeting to discuss transition services also is extended to include "representatives of any other agency likely to be responsible for providing or paying for transition services." 34 C.F.R. § 300.344(c)(ii).[4]

Somewhat different requirements for attendees, set out in 34 C.F.R. § 300.348, apply when the child is proposed to be placed or has been placed by the public agency in a private school or facility.[5]

The individuals who staff IEP meetings are dubbed the "individualized education program team" or "IEP Team" in the 1997 Amendments. Section 614(d)(1)(B). As in the IDEA itself, mandatory attendees under the Amendments include a representative of the school district, the child's teacher, and the child's parents. In addition, an individual competent to "interpret the instructional implications of evaluation results" (Section 614(d)(1)(B)(v)) also must be a part of the IEP Team. We identify the more specific statutory requirements about the mandatory district participants in the following questions in this chapter:

District representative—Question 2

---

[2] *See* Question 4 in chapter 3, *supra.*

[3] *See* Question 25 in this chapter, *infra.*

[4] *See* chapter 10 regarding IEP meetings addressing transition services.

[5] *See* chapter 9, *infra.*

Child's teacher—Question 4

Evaluation interpreter—Question 9

The impact of the 1997 Amendments on requirements for IEP Team members for transition services and private school students are addressed in chapters 10 and 9, respectively.

2. Who is authorized to serve as the representative of the school district (or other public agency) at an IEP meeting?

Generally, federal IDEA requirements mandate that the representative must be in a position of knowledge and power with respect to both designing and implementing the IEP for that particular child. The IEP meeting must be, in effect, "one-stop shopping" for all the resources needed to provide FAPE. Beyond that, the choice is largely left to the discretion of state and local officials, provided the representative is someone in authority who can commit the resources of the district.

The one specific federal requirement is actually a prohibition. 34 C.F.R. § 300.344(a)(1) states that the representative must be someone other than the child's teacher (a required attendee under 34 C.F.R. § 300.344(a)(2)).

Otherwise, 34 C.F.R. § 300.344(a)(1) simply mandates that the representative be "qualified to provide, or supervise the provision of" special education. The Notice of Interpretation on IEP Requirements gives clearer guidance:

> The representative of the public agency could be any member of the school staff, other than the child's teacher, who is qualified to provide, or supervise the provision of, specially designed instruction to meet the unique needs of children with disabilities. Thus, the agency representative could be (1) a qualified special education administrator, supervisor or teacher (including a speech-language pathologist), or (2) a school principal or other administrator—if the person is qualified to provide, or supervise the provision of, special education.

> Each State or local agency may determine which specific staff member will serve as the agency representative. However, the representative should be able to ensure that whatever services are set out in the IEP will not be vetoed at a higher administrative level within the agency. Thus, the person selected should have the authority to commit agency resources (i.e., to make decisions about the specific special education and related services that the agency will provide to a particular child.)

> For a child with a disability who requires only a limited amount of special education, the agency representative able to commit appropriate resources could be a special education teacher, or a speech-language pathologist, other than the child's teacher. For a child who requires extensive special education and related services, the agency representative might need to be a key administrator in the agency.

Appendix C to 34 C.F.R. Part 300, Question 13.

The requirement that the IEP team contain an agency official follows necessarily from the directive that an IEP be implemented as soon as possible after the IEP meeting. 34 C.F.R. § 300.342(a)(2). Thus, the court in *Bray v. Hobert City School Corp.,* 19 IDELR 1011 (N.D. Ind. 1993), held that Indiana violated the IDEA when its school districts established a separate post-IEP meeting review for recommended residential placements rather than having an individual empowered to authorize such placements serve as the public agency representative at IEP meetings.

The parents in *Richardson Independent School District,* 21 IDELR 333 (SEA Tex. 1994), had less success with that argument, though. In that instance the school district was excused from having as the agency representative someone authorized to approve a residential placement. While the meeting was convened at the parent's specific request, they refused to disclose beforehand that they wanted to discuss that topic.

The 1997 Amendments emphasize the need for the public agency representative to have expertise with regard to both special education and general education. Section 614(d)(1)(B)(iv) states that such individual must be:

(I) . . . qualified to provide or supervise the provision of, specially designed instruction to meet the unique needs of children with disabilities;

(II) . . . knowledgeable about the general curriculum; and

(III) . . . knowledgeable about the availability of resources of the local educational agency.

3. Does a school board have the authority to overrule the IEP agreed to by the IEP team at its meeting?

No, once the determination has been made by the IEP team, a school board has no authority under Part B to unilaterally change the IEP. *Letter to Anonymous,* 18 IDELR 969 (OSEP 1991). This insulation of the IEP team may in some instances be necessary, as the inquirer in *Letter to Anonymous,* points out. School boards may inject concerns about school district finances and taxes into a determination of what a student with a disability requires to receive an appropriate education.

The necessity of finality of decisions made by the IEP team is, in fact, the reasoning behind the regulatory requirement that an official with the authority to commit the resources of the school district is a required IEP meeting participant. Appendix C to 34 C.F.R. Part 300, Question 13; *Letter to Williams,* 25 IDELR 634 (OSEP 1996).

4. Which teacher should attend the IEP meeting as the child's teacher?

As a threshold matter, administrative and judicial decisions almost uniformly hold that an IEP meeting that does *not* include the child's teacher violates the IDEA. *See, e.g. New York City Sch. Dist. Bd. of Educ.,* 18 IDELR 501 (SEA N.Y. 1992) (an IEP developed without the participation of the child's teacher was invalidated). An exception was the decision of the Sixth Circuit Court of Appeals in *Cordrey v. Euckert,* 17 EHLR 104 (6th Cir. 1990). In that case, the parents, accompanied by counsel, objected to the absence of the child's teacher at a scheduled IEP meeting, but refused the school's good faith offer to reschedule. Thus, the court held that the parents knowingly and voluntarily waived their right to a procedurally correct IEP meeting.

The individual attending the meeting as the child's teacher must be able to assess how the proposed IEP will be implemented in the child's classroom. Generally, that individual will be a teacher who has worked directly with the child, although that need not always be the case. If there is no other public agency representative at the meeting who is knowledgeable about the child's disability, then the designated teacher must be. 34 C.F.R. § 300.344 note 1.

Overall, consistent with the individualization requirement of the IDEA, there is no universally correct answer to this question, as different situations make different individuals appropriate for the particular child. *But see* below in connection with the 1997 Amendments.

This potential for variability is recognized in the recommendations made in both Note 1 to 34 C.F.R. § 300.344 and various questions and answers in the Notice of Interpretation. Following their lead, we pose various scenarios in Questions 5 through 8, below.

No matter who is the appropriate teacher to serve as the "child's teacher" for purposes of compliant IEP meeting composition, OSEP makes it clear that the designated individual must, in fact, be employed as a teacher. In *Letter to Anonymous,* 18 IDELR 1036 (OSEP 1992), OSEP opined that an administrator who is qualified to supervise special education may not attend an IEP meeting in place of the child's teacher.

One of the more significant changes in the 1997 Amendments was the narrowing of the discretion of states and local authorities to select the teacher designated to serve as the "child's teacher" on the IEP Team. The new law essentially requires both a special education teacher and regular education teacher to serve as members of the IEP Team for an as yet undetermined range of eligible children with disabilities.

The new statutory requirements identify the teacher contingent of the IEP Team as follows:

(ii) at least one regular education teacher of such child (if the child is, *or may be,* participating in the regular education environment);

(iii) at least one special education teacher, or where appropriate, at least one special education provider of such child.

Section 614(d)(1)(B)(ii) and (iii) (emphasis added).

These provisions raise immediate questions about when regular education teachers are required to be IEP Team members. Seemingly, most children with disabilities have at least the potential for some participation in a regular education environment. One hopes that new regulations will address this issue forthwith.

Assuming regular education teachers are properly members of a substantial percentage of most IEP Teams, the administrative burden imposed on the teachers could be crushing unless their obligations as team members are limited. Establishing such limitations is the purpose of the rather unclear language of Section 614(d)(3)(C), entitled "Requirement with respect to regular education teacher." As explained in the Committee Report to accompany the Senate's Reauthorization bill:

> [T]he bill provides that regular education teachers participate on the IEP Team but this provision is to be construed in light of the bill's proviso that the regular education teacher, to the extent appropriate, participate in the development of the IEP of the child. The committee recognizes the reasonable concern that the provision including the regular education teacher might create an obligation that the teacher participate in all aspects of the IEP team's work. The committee does not intend that to be the case and only intends it to be to the extent appropriate.

S. Rep. No. 105-17, at 23 (1997).

5. Which teacher should attend the IEP meeting as the child's teacher when the IEP meeting is convened for initial programming?

If the child is not in school yet, selection is left to the discretion of the school district, provided that either the individual selected as the child's teacher or the agency representative is qualified in the child's area of suspected disability. 34 C.F.R. § 300.344 note 1(c).

Assuming the child has been a regular education student, there may be no individual teacher who is both knowledgeable about the child and his or her area of disability. In that case, the district may select either the child's regular education teacher or a teacher qualified to provide education in the child's area of suspected disability, or both. Again, there must be one individual at the IEP meeting who is qualified in the child's area of suspected disability. 34 C.F.R. § 300.344 note 1; Appendix C to 34 C.F.R. Part 300, Question 15.

State law may be less flexible in this regard. For example, California state education law requires that the student's classroom teacher be present at the IEP meeting as the child's teacher unless he or she is "unavailable," in which case a special education teacher qualified to teach the student may substitute. According to the Ninth Circuit Court of Appeals in *United States of America v. Anton,* 24 IDELR 569 (9th Cir. 1996), a school district's policy of allowing routine substitution when the regular classroom teacher was not absent due to illness or similar problems violated state law.

See Question 4 of this chapter with regard to the 1997 Amendments.

6. Which teacher should attend the IEP meeting as the child's teacher when the IEP meeting is convened to consider a special education placement?

Note 1(b) to 34 C.F.R. § 300.344 suggests the school district consider either the child's regular education teacher, a teacher "qualified to provide education in the type of program in which the child may be placed or both."

In *Ryan K. v. Puyallup School District,* 21 IDELR 664 (9th Cir. 1994), the parents of a disruptive adolescent with Tourette's syndrome and ADHD claimed that both the student's regular classroom teacher, and a teacher from the proposed self-contained placement (the STARS program) were required to attend the IEP meeting relating to the new placement. The court found otherwise; only one teacher was required for the meeting to comply with the IDEA.

A close reading of the opinion discloses that the STARS program teacher had some familiarity with the student, as well as knowledge of the program, as the student had already been placed there for a 45-day interim placement. The court, however, failed to suggest that the result would have been otherwise if that teacher had not known the student at all. But, the court in *Brimmer v. Traverse City Area Public Schools,* 22 IDELR 5 (W.D. Mich. 1994), did invalidate the school district's IEP because the IEP meeting included a teacher who was qualified to provide educational services in the type of program the district was proposing, rather than a teacher who knew the two hearing-impaired siblings whose placements were at issue.

Because the school district in *Brimmer* intended to propose changing the student's placement from the State school for the deaf to a less restrictive placement in the community, it should have offered to schedule the IEP meeting so that the student's current teacher at the State school could attend. When the teacher responded that the proposed date was inconvenient, the school district should have advised her that it planned to propose a change in placement at the meetings and should have made reasonable efforts to accommodate her schedule.

See Question 4 of this chapter with regard to the 1997 Amendments.

7. Which teacher should attend the IEP meeting as the child's teacher when the student is enrolled in both regular and special education classes?

According to the Notice of Interpretation, generally the student's special education teacher should attend. Appendix C to 34 C.F.R. Part 300, Question 16.

This answer appears at first glance to be completely different under the 1997 Amendments: Both teachers should attend. With a second look, it is uncertain under what circumstances it would be appropriate to have a special education provider, rather than a regular education teacher, serve as a member of the IEP team. *See* Question 4 of this chapter in this regard.

8. If the student with a disability is a high school student who attends several regular education classes, must all of his or her teachers attend the IEP meeting?

Generally no. Consistent with 34 C.F.R. § 300.344, only one teacher need attend, although there may be circumstances when the attendance of additional teachers may be beneficial. The Notice of Interpretation expands on this:

> [T]here may be specific circumstances, where the participation of additional staff would be beneficial. When the participation of the regular teachers is considered by the agency or the parents to be beneficial to the child's success in school (e.g., in terms of the participation in the regular education program), it would be appropriate for them to attend the meeting.

Appendix C to 34 C.F.R. Part 300, Question 17.

9. Must an individual who performed the preplacement evaluation attend the IEP meeting?

No under both the IDEA and the 1997 Amendments.

Personnel knowledgeable about the preplacement evaluation need attend only in the case of initial IEPs. Even in such circumstances, 34 C.F.R. § 300.344(b) gives two options for satisfying the requirement that evaluation personnel attend:

> (1) That a member of the evaluation team participates in the meetings; or (2) That the representative of the public agency [34 C.F.R. § 300.344(a)(1)], the child's teacher [34 C.F.R. § 300.344(a)(2)], or some other person present at the meeting, is knowledgeable about the evaluation procedures used with the child and is familiar with the results of the evaluation.

Courts have supported the right of the school district to convene a properly constituted IEP without the attendance of the individuals who actually performed the evaluation in *T.S. v. Board of Education of Town of Ridgefield,* 20 IDELR 889 (2d Cir. 1993) and *Holland v. District of Columbia,* 23 IDELR 552 (D.C. Cir. 1995), both in connection with independent educational evaluations (IEEs).

The IEP Team requirements of the 1997 Amendments include the participation of "an individual who can interpret the instructional implications of evaluation results" at all proceedings of the IEP Team. Section 614(d)(1)(B)(v). Thus, the requirement to have someone with that expertise attend has been expanded from the initial IEP meeting only requirement of the IDEA.

Under both the old and new law, however, the person performing the evaluation need not be the designated IEP Team member. In fact, under Section 614(d)(1)(B)(v) any of the following individuals, otherwise members of the IEP Team, may be considered to meet this requirement assuming the requisite competence: regular education teacher, special education teacher, representative of the local educational agency, or an individual who is an invited (permissive) member of the IEP Team under Section 614(d)(1)(B)(vi). *See* Question 11 of this chapter with regard to the 1997 Amendments' take on permissive IEP Team members.

10. Must evaluation personnel attend the IEP meeting when the student has been reevaluated?

No. The requirement set out in 34 C.F.R. § 300.344(b) is, by its terms, expressly limited to children who have been evaluated for the first time. As a result, the court in *Rebecca S. v. Clarke County School District*, 22 IDELR 884 (M.D. Ga. 1995), rejected the claims of the parents of an adolescent girl with moderate autism, whose behaviors at home had become significantly more challenging, that the IEP meeting was procedurally flawed by the absence of a psychologist.

As discussed in Question 9 of this chapter, the 1997 Amendments require that "an individual who can interpret the instructional implications of evaluation results" be part of the IEP Team and attend all IEP meetings.

Permitted Participants

11. Is attendance at IEP meetings restricted to the mandatory attendees?

No. 34 C.F.R. § 300.344(a)(5) states that other individuals (in addition to those listed in 34 C.F.R. § 300.344(a)(1)-(4) may attend "at the discretion of the parent or agency."

This may seem like an open invitation for either party to invite *anyone*, but certain standards have evolved. As enunciated in administrative decisions and policy letters, these standards serve to limit attendance to individuals who have something of value to offer and who attend to contribute their expertise.[6] According to the Department of Education's Notice of Interpretation on IEP Requirements the legislative history of the IDEA clearly indicates that attendance at IEP meetings should be limited to "those who have an intense interest in the child." Appendix C to 34 C.F.R. Part 300, Question 20.

---

[6] Questions 12 through 18, *infra*, review issues concerning the attendance by invitation of various individuals.

Appearing to codify the Notice of Interpretation in this regard, the 1997 Amendments specify that either the parents or the school district may invite other individuals "who have knowledge or special expertise regarding the child" to serve as additional members of the IEP Team. Section 614(d)(1)(B)(vi).

As a related consideration, another section of the Notice of Interpretation suggests that a school district would be well-advised to limit its invitees in the interest of conducting an effective meeting. "Generally, the number of participants at IEP meetings should be small. Small meetings have several advantages over large ones. For example, they (1) allow for more open, active parent involvement, (2) are less costly, (3) are easier to arrange and conduct, and (4) are usually more productive." Appendix C to 34 C.F.R. Part 300, Question 17.

In connection with inhibiting parental participation, it is indeed possible that a parent could be uncomfortable attending an IEP meeting with a large number of school district officials. In 1995 a parent filed a complaint with OCR, going so far as to allege that the school district packed the student's IEP meeting with an "excessive" number of attendees as part of a campaign to harass and intimidate her in order to interfere with her efforts to secure FAPE for her children. OCR investigated, but found no evidence to cause concern. There is no regulation limiting the number of attendees; no evidence suggested unlawful discriminatory intent. *Milford (NH) Pub. Sch.*, 24 IDELR 181 (OCR 1995).

12. Can a school district ever violate the IDEA by not inviting individuals who are not mandatory attendees to attend the IEP meeting?

Generally no, although the decision of the District Court for the Northern District of New York in *Taylor v. Board of Education*, 1986-87 EHLR 558:243 (N.D.N.Y. 1986), shows how general rules must always bend to individual circumstances when the IDEA is concerned. That case shows that a district acts at its peril when it complies with the requirements of 34 C.F.R. § 300.346(a), but nonetheless fails to invite professionals with knowledge of the child's disability to participate in developing a program.

In *Taylor* the school district did not bring the doctors and teachers from the child's then-current placement outside the school system into the IEP process. As a result, the district proposed a set of services that was totally inadequate for the needs of the child, who had cerebral palsy, mental retardation, spastic quadriplegia, blindness, a hearing impairment and a seizure disorder. The court found that the school district violated the procedural requirements of the IDEA by failing to give sufficient consideration to the opinions of the individuals who knew the child best. By the court's reasoning, inviting those persons to the IEP meetings would have prevented the district from making an inadequate proposal.

A more typical result is found in *Alexandria City Public School*, 20 IDELR 840 (SEA Va. 1993), concerning a young child with developmental disabilities. In that case the hearing officer rejected the parents' contention that the school district was required to include the student's preschool teacher and experts engaged by the parents as IEP meeting participants. He held that the meetings, without the attendance of those individuals, were convened in accordance with 34 C.F.R. § 300.344 and no provision within either the IDEA or state law requires experts to be present.

Reaching the same result, the review panel in *Sunman-Dearborn Community School Corp.,* 23 IDELR 1159 (SEA Ind. 1996), held that not having school psychologists present at IEP meetings did not violate either federal or state special education law. Thus, an administrative hearing officer acted *ultra vires* in ordering that licensed psychologists be present at all IEP meetings where triennial evaluations were discussed or questions of continuing eligibility considered.

13. Are school districts permitted to be represented by attorneys at IEP meetings?

Yes. As OSEP acknowledged in *Letter to Diehl,* 22 IDELR 734 (OSEP 1995), nothing in either the IDEA or its regulations expressly prohibits a school district from exercising its discretion under 34 C.F.R. § 300.344 to bring an attorney to an IEP meeting, even in those circumstances when the parents themselves attend unrepresented or give no indication that they intend to pursue due process.

Notwithstanding the above, OSEP went on to state its position: "OSEP discourages public agencies from bringing their attorneys to IEP meetings. The participation of a school district's attorneys could potentially create an adversarial atmosphere at the meeting, which could interfere with the development of the child's IEP in accordance with the requirements of Part B." 22 IDELR at 736. As one review officer put it, "Unfortunately, attorneys are not generally good at assisting in a consensus-building process." *Nenana City Public Schools,* 18 IDELR 489, 490 (SEA Alaska 1991) (conduct of parents' attorney at IEP meetings made it impossible for parents and school officials to reach consensus).

The inquirer in *Letter to Diehl* describes how the presence of a school district attorney at an IEP meeting could be counterproductive.

> On several occasions, parents have reported that the school's attorney has acted as an "[IEP team] Chairperson" and conducted the meeting much like a due process hearing would be held. In fact, one of the attorneys involved in this new practice is one of our former due process hearing officers for the state. He, in particular, is conducting meetings like hearings. Another attorney . . . has advised some Special Education Directors to conduct the meeting like a hearing with only the "school representative" and the "parent representative" permitted to talk at the meeting. These meetings have been known to run for two six-hour days to develop one child's IEP (with up to 25 persons in attendance).

22 IDELR at 535.

Of course, it's not only school attorneys who may create problems at IEP meetings. Parents' attorneys can be difficult as well. One such attorney's representation at an IEP meeting even became immortalized in a footnote in the Ninth Circuit Court of Appeals' celebrated opinion in *Clyde K. v. Puyallup School District,* 21 IDELR 664, 667 n.5 (OSEP 1994).

> Though Ryan's parents were frustrated by the absence of [the student's regular education] teachers at the May 1 meeting, this did not justify the singularly counter-productive stance taken by their attorney, [Mr. M.]. Instead of at least initiating discussions with the school, he abruptly ended the meeting, declaring that further negotiations would be pointless. He then announced that Ryan would be returning to [his regular school] on the next school day, May 4. When school officials pleaded with the parents to stay and help prepare for Ryan's return to [the regular school], Mr. M. insisted they leave the meeting with him at once.
>
> Judge Bryan, who remained composed and patient throughout the proceedings in the district court, cogently asked "[w]hat happened there? All we know is that [the parent] did not participate very actively. Their participation was through Mr. M. Mr. M.'s approach was rigid, it was one way, 'my way or the highway,' so to speak. It was not realistic."
>
> If Mr. M. was concerned that the parents might be waiving their statutory rights by staying, he surely knew how to make a record indicating that the parents were staying under protest. But it is difficult to imagine what interests of Ryan's were served by thrusting him back into school environment where he was having significant difficulty and then refusing even to discuss how these problems might be ameliorated. Such hardball tactics are seldom productive even in ordinary civil litigation, and are particularly ill-advised in this context.

21 IDELR at 667 n.5.

OSEP further noted that school districts considering bringing an attorney to an IEP meeting should be mindful that, to act consistently with the IDEA, the focus of all IEP meeting participants must be the child.[7] Appendix C to 34 C.F.R. Part 300, Question 20.

14. Should related services personnel be invited to attend the IEP meeting?

While they are not required attendees under 34 C.F.R. § 300.344 of the IDEA or the 1997 Amendments, it may be appropriate to either include them in the IEP meeting or to have them otherwise be involved in development of the IEP, such as submitting for consideration at the IEP meeting a written recommendation concerning the nature,

---

[7] *See* Question 16 in this chapter, *infra,* for discussion of attendance of school board members.

frequency and amount of the specific service. Appendix C to 34 C.F.R. Part 300, Question 23. This holds true even when, as posited in *Letter to Butler,* EHLR 213:118 (OSERS 1988), the student has cerebral palsy and the main components of the special education and related services contained in the IEP are physical therapy and occupational therapy.

While not precisely an exception, Question 18 of the Notice of Interpretation recognizes that special circumstances may apply to the attendance of specialists providing speech-language pathology services.[8] According to the Notice, when a child's primary impairment is a speech impairment, then a speech-language pathologist usually would serve as the child's teacher for purposes of attendance at the IEP meeting. In that case, the speech-language pathologist would be a required attendee.

The 1997 Amendments do not mandate the participation of related services providers on the IEP team in all instances in which the IEP includes related services. Nonetheless, the Committee Report accompanying the Senate's Reauthorization bill recognizes the importance of their participation and encourages inclusion of professionals that perhaps are not ordinarily considered for IEP team membership.

> [Related services] personnel can include personnel knowledgeable about services that are not strictly speaking special education services, such as specialists in curriculum content areas such as reading. Furthermore, the committee recognizes that there are situations that merit the presence of a licensed registered school nurse on the IEP team. The committee also recognizes that schools sometimes are assumed to be responsible for all health-care costs connected to a child's participation in school. The committee wishes to encourage, to the greatest extent practicable and when appropriate, the participation of a licensed registered school nurse on the IEP team to help define and make decisions about how to safely address a child's educationally related health needs.

S. Rep. No. 105-17, at 23 (1997).

15. If a school district invites related service providers who are not employees to participate in the IEP meeting, must it pay for their attendance?

No. As opined in *Letter to Butler,* EHLR 213:118 (OSERS 1988), even if the participation of the service providers at the IEP meeting would be beneficial, it is not appropriate for the school district to pay expenses associated with securing attendance.

A hearing officer reached the same conclusion in *Brian F. v. Mesquite (TX) Independent School District,* 1988-89 EHLR 401:229 (SEA Tex. 1988). When personnel who provide related services are employed by the school district, the district may take

---

[8] Under 34 C.F.R. § 300.17(a)(2) a state may elect to consider speech pathology as special education, rather than as a related service.

steps to ensure their participation in IEP meetings, including paying for attendance. However, if such personnel are not employed by the school district, it would not be appropriate for the district to take steps to ensure participation. Even when the parents so request, the school district is not required to provide reimbursement for attendance.

16. May the school district invite members of the school board to attend an IEP meeting?

Yes. In theory, a school district may invite members of the school board to attend an IEP meeting. Nevertheless, a school district should exercise caution in so doing. The right to invite attendees under 34 C.F.R. § 300.344(a)(5) generally extends to the school district inviting school board members. *Letter to Anonymous,* 18 IDELR 969 (OSEP 1992). However, two concerns limit the circumstances under which such invitations should be extended.

First, the school district and any invited school board members must keep in mind their obligations as IEP meeting participants to design an appropriate individualized educational plan for the child. As was the case in the inquiry, school district members could have a different agenda—limiting costs. Thus, not only does the school district member lack the required intense interest in the child (Appendix C to 34 C.F.R. Part 300, Question 20), but he or she may try to steer the meeting toward making decisions on the sole basis of costs, regardless of the child's individual needs. Second, the presence of school board members may raise concerns of privacy rights.[9]

It is not clear whether a state law prohibiting attendance of school board members violates the rights of the parties under 34 C.F.R. § 300.344(a)(5). Certainly, a parent's right to attend cannot be abrogated even if he or she is a school board member. *Letter to Anonymous,* 20 IDELR 629 (OSEP 1993). While it would seem more problematic to exclude school board members who are invited by parents, that is apparently just what New York law did, according to the administrative decision in *Corning City School District,* 1986-87 EHLR 508:196 (SEA N.Y. 1986). That decision rejected claims of violation of federal rights in upholding a state law forbidding school board members from attending IEPs.

17. May representatives of teacher organizations attend IEP meetings?

No, although organizations may try to negotiate with school districts on this point. The issue arises because some teacher organizations have advocated for teachers who believe they should not be required to perform some of the related services or individualized instruction called for in an individual child's IEP. DOE made clear in its Notice

---

[9] *See* Question 19 in this chapter, *infra.*

of Interpretation on IEP Requirements that organization representatives have no legitimate place at IEP meetings.

> [P]art B does not provide for the participation of representatives of teacher organizations at IEP meetings. The legislative history of the Act makes it clear that attendance at IEP meetings should be limited to those who have an intense interest in the child. . . . Since a representative of a teacher organization would be concerned with the interests of the teacher rather than the interests of the child, it would be inappropriate for such an official to attend an IEP meeting.

Appendix C to 34 C.F.R. Part 300, Question 20.

The parents' privacy rights under the Family Educational Rights and Privacy Act (FERPA) also are implicated by the attendance of individuals who are neither school district employees nor agents.[10] The parent in *Doe v. Alfred,* 23 IDELR 623 (S.D. W. Va. 1995), for instance, filed a Section 1983 claim alleging, among other things, that her rights under FERPA were violated by the school district allowing a representative of the federation of teachers to attend the student's IEP meeting. The court, without explanation, rejected the school district's motion to dismiss.

18.   May the school district invite law enforcement officials to attend IEP meetings?

There is little authority discussing this issue in connection with students who are not incarcerated and who are attending public school. One administrative decision, *Garrison Independent School District,* 16 EHLR 262 (SEA Tex. 1989), did find that the school district improperly invited the local constable, justice of the peace and juvenile probation officer to the IEP meeting for a student with mental retardation who had assaulted the school principal in a classroom. The hearing officer held that the law enforcement officials should not have been invited because they had no interest in the student's education and inhibited the parents' full participation. In addition, while not discussed in *Garrison,* the parents could have asserted their privacy rights under FERPA to bar attendance of those individuals without their consent.

19.   How do the confidentiality provisions of the Family Educational Rights and Privacy Act apply to attendance at IEP meetings?

An IEP is an education record, as that term is used in FERPA (20 U.S.C. § 1232g) and its implementing regulations (at 34 C.F.R. § 99.3), both of which are incorporated

---

[10] *See* Question 19 *infra,* for a fuller discussion of FERPA in relation to IEP meeting attendance.

into the IDEA regulations at 34 C.F.R. § 300.560(b). Thus, parents may assert rights to privacy and confidentially with respect to personnel invited by the school district to attend IEP meetings under the permissive attendance regulations at 34 C.F.R. § 300.344.

FERPA generally protects students' and parents' privacy interests in education records. Under FERPA regulations an education record is defined as "those records that are: directly related to a student; and maintained by an educational agency or institution or by a party acting for the agency or institution." An IEP is therefore an education record. Appendix C to 34 C.F.R. Part 300, Question 58.

Where applicable, FERPA generally requires that a parent consent before an educational agency or institution may disclose personally identifiable information from such records to third parties, generally understood to be non-school district employees or agents. *See, e.g., Letter to Diehl,* 22 IDELR 734 (OSEP 1995).

Personally identifiable information is, in turn, defined in Part B regulations at 34 C.F.R. § 300.500(c) as including:

> (1) The name of the child, the child's parent, or other family member; (2) The address of the child; (3) A personal identifier, such as the child's social security number or student number; or (4) A list of personal characteristics or other information that would make it possible to identify the child with reasonable certainty.

A number of exceptions do apply. For example, under 34 C.F.R. § 99.31(a)(1), a school district may disclose personally identifiable information without the consent of the parents to other school officials whom the district has determined have legitimate educational interests. Under 34 C.F.R. § 99.6(a)(4), each school district must adopt a policy which includes a statement indicating whether it has a policy of disclosing personally identifiable information under 34 C.F.R. § 99.31(a)(1), and if so, a specification of the criteria for determining which parties are school officials and what the agency considers to be a legitimate educational interest. Therefore, the determination of whether other individuals or representatives of other agencies should be permitted to attend without parental consent must be made on a case-by-case basis.

20. May parents be represented at IEP meetings?

It is well settled that under 34 C.F.R. § 300.344(a)(5) parents may be represented by counsel or lay advocates at IEP meetings. Whether the presence of attorneys is a good or a bad thing is another question, of course, and one not answered here.[11]

And, while the concern about attorney participation centers on the potential for *too much* attorney participation usurping the proper roles of the actual participants, the opinion in *Johnson v. Bismarck Public School District,* 18 IDELR 571 (8th Cir. 1991),

---

[11] Question 13 in this chapter *supra,* discusses how attorneys may create an adversarial atmosphere at IEP meetings.

suggests that *too little* participation also can be a problem. In that appeal of denial of attorneys' fees for representation at a due process hearing to parents who achieved their objectives through a consent agreement, the school district argued successfully that the parents unreasonably prolonged the dispute by refusing to meaningfully cooperate with the school district. One of the points it made to support their argument: rather than advocating for the parents at the IEP meeting, their attorney said nothing.

21. Can parents recover attorneys' fees for their attorney's presence at an IEP meeting?

Neither the IDEA statute nor its regulations provide a clear answer, although limited judicial authority has found both for and against recovery of attorneys' fees for representation at IEP meetings. The 1997 Amendments take a firmer stand, prohibiting recovery in most instances. Section 615(i)(3)(D)(II) provides: "Attorneys' fees may not be awarded relating to any meeting of the IEP Team unless such meeting is convened as a result of an administrative proceeding or judicial action. . . ."

The IDEA, at 20 U.S.C. § 1415(e)(4)(B), provides that "[i]n any action or proceeding brought under this subsection, the court, in its discretion, may award reasonable attorneys' fees as part of the costs to parents or guardians of a [disabled] child or youth who is the prevailing party."

Under the IDEA, when the parents have prevailed at a due process hearing or civil action, the issue often is framed as whether the scope of reimbursable services includes participation in the IEP process. When the parents have not needed to proceed to due process to get the result they wished, the issue, alternatively, typically is framed as whether the IEP meeting itself is a "proceeding" under the statute.

Decisions holding attorneys' fees are recoverable for participation at IEP meetings include: *Medford v. District of Columbia,* 1987-88 EHLR 559:468 (D.D.C. 1988) (attorneys' fees awarded for time spent at IEP meeting because such attendance contributes to the parents' success in the case); and *Ian E. v. Board of Education, United School District No. 501,* 21 IDELR 980 (D. Kan. 1994) (attorneys' fees awarded for attorney's attendance at IEP meeting, when attendance at meeting was part of a course of representation that ended when the school district agreed to provide the requested services one day after the parents' filing for due process).

Decisions denying attorneys' fees for IEP meeting attendance include: *Kletzelman v. Capistrano Unified School District,* 20 IDELR 1064 (C.D. Cal. 1994) (where issues were ultimately resolved without a request for a due process hearing being made, attorneys' fees not recoverable for advice rendered at IEP meeting); and *Fenneman v. Town of Gorsham,* 19 IDELR 155 (D. Me. 1992) (the scope of covered actions and proceedings does not permit reimbursement for attorneys' fees arising from participation in IEP meetings held before a request for a hearing).

While the *Fenneman* court based its position on what it claimed is the "plain language" of the IDEA's attorneys' fees provision, it concluded its argument against attorneys' fees on a more philosophical note: "Treating [IEP meetings] as part of the administrative hearing/legislative process will encourage adversarial conduct, a result out of keeping with their purpose." 19 IDELR at 157.

The *Kletzelman* court similarly sought to make a distinction between activities involved in resolving a disagreement between the parents and the school district—a proceeding, in other words—and activities that are part of the IDEA statutorily established process of designing a child's educational program. No matter how one defines a "proceeding," an activity that is undertaken in the ordinary course of complying with the statute is not a proceeding.

There also must be a dispute between the parties. Thus, even though the attorney representing the parents of a child with a serious emotional disturbance participated in two IEP meetings and the parents were satisfied with the resulting residential placement, the parents in *Kletzelman* were not entitled to receive an award of attorneys' fees for their legal representation at those proceedings. The court rejected the parents' fees petition because they failed to establish that any dispute existed between the parties before the district agreed to place the student; the two IEP meetings did not give rise to a dispute for purposes of 20 U.S.C. § 1415(e)(4)(B).

As the court reasoned, the school district did not immediately agree with the parents about the need for their proposed placement. But lack of immediate acceptance is not the same as a dispute. By deciding to conduct further evaluation and deferring the placement decision pending completion of the evaluation, the school district did not create a dispute.

The Committee Report accompanying the Senate's Reauthorization bill does not get philosophical about the 1997 Amendments' denial of attorneys' fees for attorney representation at IEP meetings. Instead, the report succinctly states that "[t]he committee believes that the IEP process should be devoted to determining the needs of the child and planning for the child's education with parents and school personnel." S. Rep. No. 105-17, at 26 (1997).

22. May a school district conduct an IEP meeting without a parent of the child with a disability in attendance?

Yes, in exceptional circumstances. While the philosophy of the IDEA makes active parental participation crucial, the business of education must go on in all events, even when the parents decline to become involved. Thus, IDEA regulations at 34 C.F.R. § 300.345(d) make it clear that if the school district takes all required steps to urge the parents to attend, but is "unable to convince the parents that they should attend" then it must conduct the meeting without a parent.[12]

---

[12] *See* Question 8 in chapter 3, *supra,* with regard to the IDEA requirements to conduct IEP meetings and to review the IEP annually in the absence of parental participation.

23. May a parent waive the right to have the school district convene an IEP meeting?

Generally no. Even if the parents decline to attend and state that they do not require the school district to convene an IEP meeting, the district must do so if the IDEA so requires.

A leading case making this point is *Jackson v. Franklin County School Board*, 1986-87 EHLR 558:195 (5th Cir. 1986). In that case, an adolescent with behavioral difficulties was charged with delinquency in county Youth Court and, with his mother's consent, was sent to the state hospital for evaluation and treatment. He was discharged in the spring. Therefore, an IEP meeting should have been convened to review the programming and placement that would be appropriate for him upon his return to school.

What actually happened next was disputed by the parties. The school district claimed the mother had decided that, since the school year was almost over, the student would not return until the next school year. The mother claimed she never said that. In any event, no IEP meeting was convened upon the student's release.

When the mother brought an action charging failure to provide FAPE during that period, the school district raised the defense of waiver to no avail. The court held that failure to convene an IEP meeting upon the student's return to school following release from the state hospital was a denial of FAPE.

Most published opinions addressing circumstances in which parents decline to attend IEP meetings arise when there is an on-going dispute about the appropriateness of a program already offered by the school district. Generally, the parents have unilaterally enrolled the student in a private school as a result.[13]

24. What steps must a school district take prior to convening an IEP meeting without a parent in attendance?

Parents have an absolute right to attend and participate in IEP meetings. 34 C.F.R. § 300.345. This is true even when it is clear that the parents intend to reject the IEP and unilaterally place the student. *E.g., Norton Pub. Schs.*, 16 EHLR 832 (SEA Mass. 1990). Thus, school districts must take three steps—two to make sure parents have an opportunity to attend the meeting and one more in those instances in which a parent is unable or unwilling to attend a meeting—in order to comply with the IDEA in holding an IEP meeting without a parent in attendance.

1. A school district must notify the parents of the IEP meeting "early enough to ensure that they will have an opportunity to attend." 34 C.F.R. § 300.345(a)(1).

---

[13] *See* Question 8 in chapter 3, *supra,* for a further discussion of preparing IEPs in this particular problem situation.

2. A school district must schedule the IEP meeting at a "mutually agreed on time and place." 34 C.F.R. § 300.345(a)(2).

3. Assuming neither parent can attend an IEP meeting in person and assuming compliant notice and attempts to schedule, the school district "shall use other methods to ensure parental participation, including individual or conference telephone calls." 34 C.F.R. § 300.345(c).

Parents must be notified of all planned IEP meetings, and a district's failure to so notify is a substantial violation of the IDEA. That there are no exceptions was the lesson learned by the school district in *Norton Public Schools,* 16 EHLR 832 (SEA Mass. 1990). That district violated the IDEA when it failed to invite the parents of a unilaterally placed student to an IEP meeting. Parents have an absolute right to attend their child's IEP meeting, even in those circumstances when the appropriateness of the previous year's IEP is pending review and the district knows to an absolute certainty that the parents will reject the IEP to be proposed.[14]

Nonetheless, a failure to give written notice may not result in a denial of FAPE if the parents were not prejudiced thereby. For example, the parents in *Carroll County Public School,* 23 IDELR 157 (SEA Va. 1995), presented evidence to support their contention that they did not receive notice of the IEP causality meeting held to determine the relationship between the student's learning disability and his misconduct. The parents, however, received verbal notice and participated in the meeting without objection. Thus, the hearing officer found that such a lack of written notice was a technical violation that did not amount to a substantive violation of the IDEA.

25. How far in advance must a school district notify parents about a proposed IEP meeting?

No specific timelines are imposed in connection with the IEP meeting notice requirement of 34 C.F.R. § 300.345(a)(1). Rather, that subsection simply requires school districts to notify parents "early enough to ensure that they will have an opportunity to attend."

So what is "early enough?" It is adequate time to make whatever arrangements may be required for a parent to make an alteration in his or her typical daily schedule, whether that includes working, child care or other commitments. Ten school days is a customary period, given no emergent circumstances. Consistent with other requirements of the IDEA that are not regulated by specific timelines (for example, implementation of formulated IEPs and completion of evaluations), a standard of reasonableness is

---

[14] *See also* Question 8 in chapter 3, *supra,* concerning the district's obligation to propose IEPs at all in these circumstances.

applied in determining whether a notice is timely. *Letter to Constantian,* 17 EHLR 118 (OSEP 1990).

26. Must a school district schedule an IEP meeting on an evening or weekend if a parent so requests?

No, not in every instance; arguably not in most. But there could be circumstances when a school district should accede such a request.

34 C.F.R. § 300.345(a)(2) requires a school district to schedule the IEP meeting at a mutually agreeable time and place. In interpreting this requirement, the recurring standard of reasonableness comes into play and governs the expectations placed on a district in satisfying a parent's demands. OSEP weighed in with its take on the standard of reasonableness in this context in *Letter to Anonymous,* 18 IDELR 1303 (OSEP 1992). It opined that, in considering a parent's request that an IEP meeting be held in the late afternoon or evening, or on a weekend, the school district should make a good faith effort to find a mutually agreeable time, but is not precluded from considering the scheduling needs of its own personnel.

Jefferson County School District R-1, 19 IDELR 1112 (SEA Col. 1993), shows how school districts can have an obligation to schedule IEP meetings during non-business hours in special circumstances. In that case, the school district proposed convening an IEP meeting to review transition services needs for a 17-year-old student with severe mental retardation (and the mental age of a toddler). The parents told school officials that due to their recently acquired jobs neither would be able to miss work to attend an IEP meeting during the day. The district convened the meeting without trying to accommodate the parents' schedule or secure their participation by alternate means.

As it turned out, the resulting IEP failed to provide FAPE as a substantive matter, according to the hearing officer. In ordering that a new IEP be convened, he ordered the school district to schedule the meeting on a weekend or evening if those were still the only times the parents could attend.[15]

27. What information must the school district include in its notice to parents about the IEP meeting?

The IDEA makes a distinction between the basic information requirements of the notice that must be sent to parents advising them of the planned IEP meeting (set out in 34 C.F.R. § 300.345) and the more detailed disclosures of the notice of procedural safeguards that must be sent under 34 C.F.R. § 300.504 (as set out in 34 C.F.R.

---

[15] The case made it all the way to the Tenth Circuit Court of Appeals, which ultimately held for the school district. *See* a discussion of that decision, Urban v. Jefferson County School District R-1, 24 IDELR 465 (10th Cir. 1996), in connection with the provision of transition services in Question 18 in chapter 10, *infra.*

§ 300.505). In the 1997 Amendments Congress opted to require full notice of procedural rights upon each notice of an IEP meeting. Section 615(d)(1)(B).

Under the IDEA, the notice to parents, sometimes also referred to as the invitation to parents, should contain, as a matter of federal law:

- date, time and location (34 C.F.R. § 300.345 (b)(1));

- purpose of meeting (34 C.F.R. § 300.345 (b)(1)); and

- identity of individuals who will be attending (34 C.F.R. § 300.345 (b)(1)).[16]

According to OSEP, the notice need not meet the more detailed content requirements of 34 C.F.R. § 300.504/505 (notice required when a change—or refusal to accede to a request for a change in—identification, evaluation, placement or provision of FAPE is at issue).[17] *Letter to Evans,* 17 EHLR 1105 (OSEP 1991).

This distinction may still cause some confusion as is shown in the decision of the hearing officer in *Allamakee Community School District and Keystone AEA1,* 24 IDELR 516 (SEA Iowa 1996).

In that case the hearing officer found a five-year-old with autism was denied FAPE because the notice parent received about the IEP meeting scheduled to consider her son's need for ESY services was inadequate. For one thing, it failed to identify the participants, clearly an omission that violates 34 C.F.R. § 345(b)(1). But, the notice also was significantly defective because it failed to provide the information required by the notice requirement of 34 C.F.R. § 300.505. In particular, it failed to include the following: information relating to applicable procedural safeguards, a description of the proposed program, and evaluation procedures.

Courts may be inclined to view a partially compliant notice as a technical violation only, if the parent cannot demonstrate that the defect significantly impaired meaningful participation. For example, the IEP meeting notice the school district sent to the parents of a 20-year-old young man with Duchenne muscular dystrophy in *Chuhran v. Walled Lake Consolidated Schools,* 20 IDELR 1035 (E.D. Mich. 1993), indicated that the purpose of the meeting was to consider a change in status, but did not indicate that the particular change the school district had in mind was graduation. Nevertheless, the court refused to hold that the school district failed to provide FAPE on that basis. The parents were aware that the school district had been proposing graduation for the past two years. Thus they had no reasonable basis for surprise that the issue of graduation was again going to be raised.

As another example, the school district's notice to the parent in *Scituate School Committee v. Robert B.,* 1985-86 EHLR 557:207 (D.R.I. 1985), failed to comply with

---

[16] *See also* Question 26 in chapter 4, *supra.*

[17] *See* Question 5 in chapter 12, *infra,* regarding the notice requirements of 34 C.F.R. § 300.504.

federal (and state) requirements because it did not: (1) specify who would be attending; (2) mention that other individuals may attend; or (3) indicate the purpose of the meeting. Nevertheless, the district court reversed the review officer's invalidation of the IEP resulting from that meeting on the basis of the deficiencies in the notice:

> The facts of this case are such that the spirit of the regulation was satisfied and the procedural inadequacies are not fatal. [The student's] mother had attended a previous IEP meeting . . . and was in fact aware of the purpose of such meetings. While the notice did not state who would be in attendance, the people who actually did attend were the same MDT members that had met with [the mother] on September 15. There were no surprise participants and no one that the parents expected to attend were absent. While a list of the names and positions of those expected to attend could easily and should have been supplied, the school's failure to do so did not in any way prejudice the parents. . . . [The parents] were not actually prejudiced by the technical omissions in the October 8 notice, and the school did not act in bad faith or deliberately set out to provide inadequate notice.

1985-86 EHLR at 557:21.

Thus, best practice suggests that under the IDEA the invitation should include, or be accompanied by, at least the following:

- an explanation of parental rights;
- an invitation to bring their child (Appendix C to 34 C.F.R. Part 300, Question 21); and
- a statement of the right of parents to bring other participants (Appendix C to 34 C.F.R. Part 300, Question 28).

Starting on July 1, 1998 the 1997 Amendments will make transmission of a procedural safeguards notice mandatory upon, among other things, "each notification of an individualized education program meeting." Section 615(d)(1)(B). As set out in 615(d)(2), that notice must meet the following requirements and contain the following information:

(2) Contents—The procedural safeguards notice shall include a full explanation of the procedural safeguards, written in the native language of the parents, unless it clearly is not feasible to do so, and written in an easily understood manner, available under this section and under regulations promulgated by the Secretary relating to—

(A) independent educational evaluation;

(B) prior written notice;

(C) parental consent;

(D) access to educational records;

(E) opportunity to present complaints;

(F) the child's placement during pendency of the due process proceedings;

(G) procedures for students who are subject to placement in an interim alternative educational setting;

(H) requirements for unilateral placement by parents of children in private schools at public expense;

(I) mediation;

(J) due process hearings, including requirements for disclosure of evaluation results and recommendations;

(K) State-level appeals (if applicable in that State);

(L) civil actions; and

(M) attorneys' fees.

As to how the required information is presented, the school district should assure, as it does in other notices to parents, that the notice is written in language understandable to the public and, if the parents' native language is other than English, that it is written in such other language, to the extent reasonably possible.

When transition services are to be discussed at the IEP meeting, then the additional notice and scheduling requirements of 34 C.F.R. § 300.345(b)(2) also apply.[18]

28. Must the school district's notice to parents identify by name individuals who will be attending the IEP meeting?

No, assuming the individuals are identified by position. That is the opinion of OSEP, as expressed in *Letter to Livingston*, 21 IDELR 1060 (OSEP 1994).

34 C.F.R. § 300.345(b)(1) directs school districts to notify parents about the purpose, time and place of the IEP meeting and also "who will be in attendance." Seeking to clarify the requirement, the Department of Education stated in its Notice of Interpretation on IEP Requirements that "[i]f possible, the agency should give the name and position of each person who will attend." Appendix C to 34 C.F.R. Part 300, Question 28.

The key words are "if possible." In *Livingston*, OSEP stated that a school district complies with the law if it identifies attendees only by position. "While public agencies could elect to indicate in the notice the names, as well as the positions of the individuals who will be in attendance, there is no requirement for public agencies to do so." 21 IDELR at 1061.

All right, but what is an individual's "position" for purposes of the notice? That was the follow-up question raised by Ms. Livingston in *Letter to Livingston*, 23 IDELR

---

[18] *See* Question 9 in chapter 10, *infra*.

564 (OSEP 1995). She queried if an IEP notice that identified participants as including "your child's teacher(s) and at least one other staff member of the school district" was compliant? No, said OSEP, that disclosure contains no "meaningful information." "Position" means position within the school district, not within the IEP team.

29. How does a school district effectively document that it was unable to convince the parents to attend the IEP meeting?

Failure to document efforts to convince parents to attend could place the school district in a vulnerable position if the adequacy of those efforts becomes an issue. IDEA regulations set out suggested documentation requirements:

[T]he public agency must have a record of its attempts to arrange a mutually agreed on time and place such as—

(1) Detailed records of telephone calls made or attempted and the results of those calls;

(2) Copies of correspondence sent to the parents and any responses received; and

(3) Detailed records of visits made to the parent's home or place of employment and the results of those visits.

34 C.F.R § 300.345(d).

However, as seen in connection with other procedural requirements, technical compliance sometimes is excused when failure to comply does not impede a parent's ability to participate. Thus, a district's failure to document its inability to arrange a mutually agreeable time and place was "insubstantial," not justifying tuition reimbursement, when the record as a whole clearly showed the parents' unwillingness to participate at any time, no matter how convenient. *Cordrey v. Euckert,* 17 EHLR 104 (6th Cir. 1990).

30. Can a failure to give appropriate notice result in a denial of FAPE?

Maybe, although parents would have to establish that they were prejudiced by the lack of appropriate notice. There are few published decisions in which failure to disclose the purpose of the meeting or identify the attendees resulted in a finding that the student had been denied FAPE.

Nevertheless, such a failure to disclose a specific purpose for convening the meeting was the major problem leading to the result in *Brimmer v. Traverse City Area Public Schools,* 22 IDELR 5 (W.D. Mich. 1994) (school district's failure to disclose that it proposed changing placement from State school for the deaf to community program resulted in teacher at current placement failing to request rescheduling so she could attend).

To the opposite effect, the court in *E.H. v. Tirozzi,* 16 EHLR 787 (D. Conn. 1990), held that it was not required to invalidate the student's IEP despite the fact that the notice of the meeting did not disclose the purpose of the meeting or who would be attending. The parent knew about the IEP process through attending previous years' meetings, she came to the meeting represented by counsel and was not surprised by the lack of adequate notice.

Similarly, the hearing officer in *In re Student with a Disability,* 24 IDELR 612 (SEA Ver. 1996), held that the district's failure to properly disclose the purpose of the meeting on the notice was not a "substantial" violation. In that instance the parent, while surprised, was not "unprepared" and had sufficient familiarity with the process and her rights to have requested a postponement, if she wished. In addition, the notice violation paled in comparison to other major procedural violations which of themselves justified the award of tuition reimbursement by the hearing officer.

31. Must the school district appoint a surrogate parent when the child's parents refuse to attend an IEP meeting?

No. Under IDEA regulations at 34 C.F.R. § 300.514 a school district must appoint a surrogate parent for a child with a disability only when his or her parents cannot be located. If the parents' whereabouts are known, the district cannot appoint a surrogate parent even if the parent refuses to participate in the educational planning process. *Letter to Perryman,* EHLR 211:438 (OSEP 1987).

Further, as recognized by the administrative decision-maker in *Dundee Central School District,* 1987-88 EHLR 509:191 (SEA N.Y. 1987), the IDEA does not permit appointment of a surrogate parent even when the parent acts in a manner that is opposed to or inconsistent with the best interests of his or her child.

32. When parents are divorced, are both parents entitled to participate in the IEP meeting?

Clearly, a custodial parent is entitled to participate in the IEP. Whether the noncustodial parent also has such rights is a matter of state law and the terms of the divorce agreement between the parents or court order.

As a threshold matter, keep in mind that under the IDEA school districts are required to ensure that at least one parent participates in IEP meetings. 34 C.F.R. § 300.344(a)(3). There is no requirement that both parents participate.

Neither the IDEA nor its regulations specifically address the rights of divorced noncustodial parents. OSEP stated in *Letter to Dunlap,* EHLR 211:462 (OSEP 1987), that state and local law control the extent to which a divorced noncustodial parent[19] may exercise parental rights of courts and state family law. "OSEP would not seek to create a rule intruding on the jurisdiction under the IDEA." EHLR at 211:463.

Following OSEP's guidance and deferring to local court decisions, due process hearing and review officers generally have refused to permit divorced parents who had neither legal nor physical custody to participate in the IEP process. *See, e.g., Tustin Unified Sch. Dist.,* 1985-86 EHLR 507:120 (SEA Cal. 1985), *Randolph Sch. Dist.,* 1987-88 EHLR 509:183 (SEA Va. 1987).

One federal court, though, has found that the IDEA creates a preemptive right of a noncustodial parent to be involved in his or her child's educational program. In *Doe v. Anrig,* 1986-87 EHLR 558:278 (D. Mass. 1987), the student's mother had been awarded sole legal custody, but the father was responsible for the student's educational expenses. While the school district considered the mother to be the sole parent entitled to the procedural safeguards of the IDEA, the court found otherwise.

Specifically, the court found that the father was entitled to receive notice of the meeting to develop his son's IEP. Because he did not receive such notice, the mother's consent to the IEP was legally insufficient and the IEP she had approved invalid. The court ruled that a divorced parent's right to be involved in his or her child's educational planning and progress is basic and the IDEA favors extensive parental involvement. Thus, in the absence of a court order to the contrary, school districts should allow both parents to participate in development of their child's IEP.

33. Why are school districts required to take steps to ensure parents attend IEP meetings?

The U.S. Supreme Court has long recognized that the IEP is the centerpiece of the IDEA and parental participation is a central principle of the IEP process. Because Congress was reluctant to impose detailed pedagogical rules on states and local school districts, it opted to devise an elaborate procedural system that, in effect, gives parents the means to enforce the substantive educational standards implicated in the provision of an appropriate individualized educational program for their children. Thus, federal law in this instance (34 C.F.R. § 300.345(d)) established the type of detailed internal documentation requirement otherwise absent from the statutory scheme.

In *Board of Education of the Hendrick Hudson Central School District v. Rowley,* 1981-82 EHLR 553:656 (1982), the Court stated:

> When the elaborate and highly specific procedural safeguards embodied in [the Act] are contrasted with the general and somewhat imprecise substantive admonitions

---

[19] Many states distinguish between legal custody and physical custody and recognize that either or both can be shared by the parents. Legal custody is the right to make major decisions concerning, among other things, the child's education.

contained in the Act, we think the importance Congress attached to these procedural safeguards cannot be gainsaid. It seems to us no exaggeration to say that Congress placed every bit as much emphasis upon compliance with procedures giving parents and guardians a large measure of participation at every stage of the administrative process . . . as it did upon the measurement of the resulting IEP against a substantive standard.

1981-82 EHLR at 553:669-70.

Similarly, the Court observed in *Honig v. Doe*, 1987-88 EHLR 559:231 (1988):

[A]ware that schools had all too often denied [disabled] children appropriate educations without in any way consulting their parents, Congress repeatedly emphasized throughout the Act the importance . . . of parental participation . . . and establishe[d] various procedural safeguards that guarantee parents both an opportunity for meaningful input into all decisions affecting their child's education and the right to seek review of any decisions they think inappropriate.

1987-88 EHLR at 559:233.

That's the high-minded statement of principles. On a more work-a-day level, the administrative law judge in *Howard County Public Schools*, 24 IDELR 719 (SEA Va. 1996), explained why school districts are well-advised to take all necessary steps to involve parents in the IEP process.

No definitive analysis yet exists as to the impact of parental participation on the ultimate quality and effectiveness of the educational program provided students with disabilities. However, administrative decisions reflect the costly and time consuming battles that arise when the parents do not believe they are true participants in the IEP process.

24 IDELR at 723; *see* Question 6 in Chapter 6, *infra,* for further discussion of the importance of parental participation.

34. Can a court find that parents were not permitted to participate in the IEP process even if they attended the IEP meeting?

Yes, if the parent can establish that the school district independently developed the IEP before the meeting and then made it plain to the parents at the meeting that their input was not welcome.

One way a school district can cook its own goose is to present a completed IEP at the IEP meeting.[20] Another way is to determine the placement first and then "shoehorn" the student's program.[21]

---

[20] *See* Question 5 in chapter 4, *supra.*

[21] *See* Question 27 in chapter 3, *supra.*

The school district involved in the Ninth Circuit's opinion in *W.G. v. Board of Trustees of Target Range School District No. 23,* 18 IDELR 1019 (9th Cir. 1992), for example, did not present a completed IEP to the parents of a student with a significant learning disability at the IEP meeting. Nonetheless, the court awarded reimbursement for the parents' unilateral placement because, among other substantial procedural violations, the court affirmed the lower court's finding that the district had prepared the IEP prior to the meeting.

In particular, the court found from the evidence that: (1) school district representatives had agreed among themselves and prepared the IEP before the IEP meeting; and (2) at the meeting no alternatives to that program were proposed, despite the objections voiced by the parents. The parents testified credibly that "the district assumed a 'take it or leave it' position at the meeting." 18 IDELR at 1021.

Parental claims of denial of meaningful participation are among the most serious a school district can face in a dispute over a student's IEP. Accordingly, we discuss the issue in more detail in chapter 6.

35. When is it appropriate for a student to attend an IEP meeting?

According to the Notice of Interpretation on IEP Requirements, generally, the student should attend when his or her attendance will be helpful in developing the IEP or will directly benefit the child. Appendix C to 34 C.F.R. Part 300, Question 21. This is more likely to be the case with older students. A student who participates in IEP meetings may be more motivated to accept accountability for his or her role in benefiting from the IEP because the student becomes invested in the process. *Id.*

Educators support the position taken by the Department of Education in the Notice as a matter of educational concern. The consensus view is that a child should be present only when his or her attendance would be helpful in developing the IEP or would be beneficial to the child. Otherwise the student should not attend the meeting. Generally, application of these guidelines results in only older children—such as those in secondary schools—being encouraged to attend meetings. When such children do attend, they may be able to provide insight not available from others. They also may benefit from participation as a step toward more independence.

Student attendance is regarded differently, as a legal matter, when transition services are to be discussed. *See* Chapter 10.

The 1997 Amendments emphasize the determinative role state law plays in determining when it is appropriate for a student to become a member of the IEP Team and attend IEP meetings. For a further brief discussion *see* Question 35 of this chapter.

36. Do the parents of a student with a disability retain the right to attend an IEP meeting when the student reaches the age of majority?

While the issue is not explicitly addressed in the IDEA, it appears that the IDEA contemplates the co-existence of procedural rights for both parents and their adult children. Thus, when a student acquires procedural rights upon reaching the age of majority, his or her parents continue to retain their rights on his or her behalf.

In the Notice of Interpretation, the Department of Education states that: "The Act is silent concerning any modification of the rights of the parents of a student with a disability when the student reaches the age of majority." Appendix C to 34 C.F.R. Part 300, Question 22.

The 1997 Amendments broke the silence, but only to confirm that the issue was, for the most part, one that should continue to be left to the states. It appears that if state law so provides, parents may lose the right to attend IEP meetings when the student reaches the age of majority, assuming he or she is considered to be competent under state law. Section 615(m), regarding procedural safeguards, is entitled "Transfer of Parental Rights at Age of Majority" and states in pertinent part:

(1) In general.—A State that receives amounts from a grant under [new Part B] *may* provide that, when a child with a disability reaches the age of majority under State law (except for a child with a disability who has been determined to be incompetent under State law)—

(A) the public agency shall provide any notice required by this section to both the individual and the parents;

(B) all other rights accorded to parents under this part transfer to the child. . . .

(2) Special rule.—If, under State law, a child with a disability who has reached the age of majority under State law, who has not been determined to be incompetent, but who is determined not to have the ability to provide informed consent with respect to the educational program of the child, the State shall establish procedures for appointing the parent of the child, or if the parent is not available, another appropriate individual, to represent the educational interests of the child throughout the period of eligibility of the child under this part.

Section 615(m) (emphasis added).

There may be a variety of results under state law. For example, as stated in *Unified School District of De Pere,* 21 IDELR 1206 (SEA Wis. 1994), state law in Wisconsin provides that when a student with a disability reaches the age of 18, he or she has all the educational rights previously granted to his or her parents. (Although in that case the parents retained the right to seek tuition reimbursement.)

Chapter 6

More on Parental Participation

One of the main objectives of the Department of Education's Individuals with Disabilities Education Act Amendments of 1995 was to increase parental participation in the IEP process. The Department cited worrying research that indicated that about one-fourth of all parents do not participate at all in their child's IEP meeting, with higher levels of nonparticipation noted among students of low-income levels and culturally and linguistically diverse backgrounds.[1]

A 1989 study cited by an inquirer to OSEP in 1991 suggested that actual parental participation in the IEP process is not always the meaningful exchange of ideas it is clearly intended to be.

> [A]fter 15 years of implementation of [the IDEA] parents are involved to a significantly greater degree in the special education process than they were prior to 1975. However, the degree of their involvement in the decision-making partnerships remains less than the legislative intent and less than what many professionals and parents would like. [The study] found that: The average IEP meetings lasted 36 minutes; professionals did 75-80% of the talking and made 80-90% of the decisions; 90% of all IEPs were written before the parents arrived; only 50% of the parents raised questions when asked if they had any; and parents (and revealingly, professionals also) said they hated IEP meetings. The study also revealed that 76% of the professionals surveyed believed that parents are incapable of setting adequate goals for their children.

Letter to Bina, 18 IDELR 582, 584 (OSEP 1991).

Increasing participation is not the solution to all the problems that plague the relationships between school districts and parents. Serious challenges to the IDEA's vision of collaborative teams of parents and school officials may increase when parents

---

[1] Accessed by the author at <http://www.ed.gov/IDEA/amend95/iep.html>.

do participate. There appears to be a thin line between active, informed participation and what school districts view as intransigent, confrontational opposition—or a desire to micromanage all aspects of the educational process. (For a good example of parents who admit they are too intense and, despite the best intentions, have a negative impact on their son's education, see the articulate opinion of the hearing officer in *Board of Education of Portage Public School,* 25 IDELR 372 (SEA Mich. 1996)).

We recognize that educators and school attorneys well understand the dynamics of educational programming, including how to build and maintain successful relationships with parents. Nevertheless, these groups may not be able to appreciate fully parents' concerns, hopes and fears unless they have walked a mile in the parents' shoes. Most of us have not.

Thus we introduce this chapter with brief, informal and from-the-heart tips for dealing more effectively with the parents of children with disabilities.

First, recognize that all parents—just like their children with disabilities—are unique. Some may rise to the challenge of caring for their child. Others may not be able to conquer their anxiety or frustration, or they may be truly disagreeable. Thought needs to be given to how to build a relationship with an edgy or depressed parent.

Second, acknowledge that some parents may know more than you do about their child's disability and needs. Many make their children their life's focus. Do not discount the value of what they have to offer; do not try to one-up them.

Third and finally, even parents who have not steeped themselves in a study of their child's disability have an intense interest in their child's welfare. The author acknowledges that educators cannot—and should not—have the same level of emotional involvement. But even the well-meaning educator risks ill-will if he or she gives the appearance that it's all in a day's work. Similar to physicians, educators need to master projecting the appropriate level of concern and individual regard.

1. What does it mean for a parent to be an "equal participant" in the IEP meeting?

DOE's Notice of Interpretation of IEP Requirements describes parents as "equal participants" in developing, reviewing and revising their child's IEP. According to the Notice, being an equal participant involves two things:

1. participating in the discussion of the child's need for special education and related services; and

2. joining with the other members of the IEP team to decide what services the school district must deliver to provide FAPE.

Appendix C to 34 C.F.R. Part 300, Question 26.

Being an equal participant does not involve having a "vote" equal to that of the school personnel who are the other members of the IEP team. This is implied in *Doe v. Maher,* 1985-86 EHLR 557:353 (9th Cir. 1986)[2] and made explicit in *Buser v. Corpus Christi Independent School District,* 20 IDELR 981 (S.D. Tex. 1994), *aff'd,* 22 IDELR 626 (5th Cir. 1995).

The district court in *Buser* rejected the parents' "equal vote" interpretation of the IDEA, finding it a misstatement of the law for which there was no supporting authority. Equal participation does not mean equal voting power, the court opined. To the contrary, citing *Honig v. Doe,* 1987-88 EHLR 559:231 (1988), the court held that the IDEA required that parents be given an opportunity for meaningful input and the right to seek review of decisions with which they do not agree. "To adopt [the parent's] argument would allow parents to prevent the implementation of an IEP anytime there is a disagreement. This is not the intent of the IDEA." 20 IDELR at 984.

On appeal, the Fifth Circuit explained why the parents had been treated as equal participants, notwithstanding the fact that they had no legal right to an equal vote. The parents were notified of scheduled IEP meetings, given the opportunity to compare previous IEPs with the new proposed IEP and given the opportunity to participate in the development of the new IEP.

While the parents in *Buser* may not have made a good argument, as a legal matter, in claiming that they believed their participation was futile, they raised an issue that bears exploring. According to DOE, parents should be "active" participants in the IEP process.[3] Thus, when parents feel marginalized, questions of compliance with the IDEA procedural requirements may be lurking.

2. What actions must a school district take to ensure that parents participate meaningfully in IEP meetings?

Two cases illustrate what a school district should do to demonstrate that parents have an opportunity for meaningful participation at IEP meetings:

- *Consider the parents' suggestions and, to the extent appropriate, incorporate them in the IEP.* Although the school district did not agree to provide the programming and placement advocated by the parents, the Third Circuit Court of Appeals in *Fuhrmann v. East Hanover Board of Education,* 19 IDELR 1065 (3d Cir. 1993), held that the parents had an opportunity to participate in the IEP formulation process in a meaningful way. At the IEP meeting the school district team members presented a draft IEP for discussion. The parents made several suggestions for changes that should be made. The team considered those suggestions and incorporated some, resulting in changes to the draft IEP.[4]

---

[2] *See* Question 7 in this chapter, *infra.*

[3] *See* Question 2 in this chapter, *infra.*

[4] *See* Question 5 in chapter 4, *supra,* concerning presenting draft IEPs at meetings.

- *Consider the results of any IEE, discuss placement options and answer parents' questions.* The parents of an eight-year-old with disabilities in reading and writing claimed in *Board of Education of Waterford-Halfmoon Union Free School District,* 20 IDELR 1092 (SEA N.Y. 1994), that they were not treated as equal participants because the IEP team did not answer their questions about the nature of their child's learning disability, did not consider the results of the independent evaluation and did not consider placement options other than the one proposed by the school district. But the review officer, basing her decision on testimony and minutes of the IEP meeting, found that the school district had given the parents their rightful opportunity for meaningful participation. The minutes showed that the IEE was considered and placement options discussed. They also showed that the parents questioned the etiology of their child's learning disability and the school district team members responded accurately and appropriately that there could be many causes, no one on the team could really know, and it wasn't particularly pertinent to the design of an appropriate educational program. "The fact that the [IEP team] did not answer the [parents'] questions to their satisfaction does not afford a basis for concluding that [they] were denied the opportunity to participate in developing the child's IEP." 20 IDELR at 1096.

Other cases show school districts violating the IDEA by failing to accord parents the meaningful participation to which they are entitled, for example:

- *Refuse to discuss options proposed by parents.* The school district in *Briere v. Fair Haven Grade School District,* 25 IDELR 55 (D. Vt. 1996), took various actions that denied the parent of a middle-school age girl with serious learning disabilities and borderline mild mental retardation the right to equal participation in the IEP process. Among them: school district personnel met to develop tentative educational plans for the student without her mother in attendance. As a result, the district came to the scheduled IEP meeting with a particular program and placement—the local high school—in mind. At the IEP meeting the mother asked that a residential placement be considered, but the school district personnel refused to discuss the option or explain the reasons for their refusal. According to the court, their actions "inhibited meaningful parental involvement and contravened the letter and spirit of the statute." 25 IDELR at 61.

Finally, while the hearing officer in *Le Mars Community School District,* 19 IDELR 284 (SEA Iowa 1992), found that the school district did not deny the parents of a 16-year-old student with autism an opportunity to participate equally in the IEP team, he did highlight inappropriate conduct toward the parents that could not be "condoned." In that case notes taken from the meetings with the parents contained side comments by school district representatives that were highly inappropriate and had the effect of making the parents feel they had unequal status. (The hearing officer does not detail what those comments were.)

3. Why is meaningful parental participation in the IEP process so important?

In an effort to maximize the likelihood of providing an appropriate education for each child with a disability, the IDEA requires special educators and administrators to encourage parental participation. 20 U.S.C. § 1415(b)(1)(A). Ideally, these parties act as partners in a good faith effort designed to meet the needs of each child with a disability. Almost always, no one has a greater interest in a child's welfare than his or her parents. They are supremely motivated to enforce their child's entitlement to the educational benefits guaranteed by the IDEA.

In *Board of Education of Hendrick Hudson Central School District v. Rowley*, 1981-82 EHLR 553:656 (1982), the U.S. Supreme Court established the paramount importance of meaningful parental participation in formulating and implementing a child's IEP. Emphasizing the importance of that decision to achieving the objectives of the IDEA, the Fourth Circuit Court of Appeals in *Hall v. Vance County Board of Education*, 1985-86 EHLR 557:155 (4th Cir. 1985), stated:

> *Rowley* recognizes that parental participation is an important means of ensuring state compliance with the Act. Unless school systems apprise parents of their procedural protections, however, parental participation will rarely amount to anything more than parental acquiescence, because parents will presume they have no real say, and the participatory function envisioned by *Rowley* will go unfulfilled.

1985-86 EHLR at 557:159.

4. What specific provisions of the IDEA are intended to maximize parental participation in the development of an IEP?

The IDEA statute and its regulations mandate a range of specific procedural requirements intended to compel the school district to give parents a genuine opportunity to participate in the design of the educational program for their children with disabilities. While many significant aspects of the IEP process are left to the discretion of state and local authorities, federal regulations do establish several detailed administrative procedures.

While all of these provisions are discussed in more detail in other sections of this publication, the following summary of the provisions—from initial evaluation through agreement on program and placement—gives an overview of this aspect of the IEP legal landscape.

- School districts have an affirmative obligation to seek an evaluation of any child suspected of having a disability. 34 C.F.R. § 300.128.

- The school district must provide a detailed notice to the child's parents and then seek to obtain consent from the parents to conduct an evaluation of the child. 34 C.F.R. § 300.504.

- After identification, a meeting must be held to determine whether the child should be classified as disabled and, if so, what placement and services should be provided to furnish the child with FAPE. 34 C.F.R. §§ 300.343, 300.532.

- Before a school district may propose to initiate or change the identification, evaluation or educational placement of a child—or refuse to accept a parent's request for same—the school district must first provide a detailed notice, in writing, to the child's parents. 34 C.F.R. § 300.504(a).

- After the evaluation is concluded, the school district must hold a meeting attended by certain mandated participants, including the parents. 34 C.F.R. § 300.343.

- Other individuals invited by the parents may attend the meeting. 34 C.F.R. § 300.344.

- The school district must ensure that one or both parents are afforded an opportunity to participate in the meeting. 34 C.F.R. § 300.345.

- Sufficient notice must be provided to the parents to allow them to arrange to be present. 34 C.F.R. § 300.345.

- The meeting must be scheduled at a mutually agreeable time and place. 34 C.F.R. § 300.345.

- In the event that the parents cannot otherwise participate in the meeting, telephone conference calls are permissible. 34 C.F.R. § 300.345.

- The school district may conduct the meeting without the parents in attendance only if it has made and recorded its unsuccessful attempts to arrange a mutually agreeable time and place for the meeting. 34 C.F.R. § 300.345.

- The IEP determination is final, not subject to veto by either the Board of Education of the school district or the state educational agency. *See, e.g., Letter to Tucker,* 18 IDELR 965 (OSERS 1992).

The most notable changes in the 1997 Amendments are intended to maximize parental participation in the development of the IEP. These changes relate more to mandating parental involvement in both eligibility (Section 614(a)(4)) and placement determinations (Section 614(f)) rather than to the development of the IEP document itself. While Section 614(d)(3) does add new statutory language requiring IEP teams to consider "the concerns of the parents for enhancing the education of their child," this amendment seems merely a codification of existing law and best practice.

5. If a school district infringes on a parent's rights to participate in the IEP process, has it denied FAPE to the student with a disability?

It may well have, even if the IEP offers an appropriate education as a substantive matter.

The U.S. Supreme Court in *Board of Education of Hendrick Hudson Central School District v. Rowley,* 1981-82 EHLR 553:656 (1982), clearly established the principle that failure of an educational agency to comply with the procedures set forth in the IDEA may constitute sufficient reason to rule that a child with a disability has been denied a FAPE. If those procedural violations are found to be "mere technical violations" that have not harmed the student, however, then a court or administrative reviewer may decline to intervene,[5] but if those violations interfere with a parent's right to participate in the IEP formulation process, they are likely to be considered violations of the IDEA that are not merely technical. *W.G. v. Board of Trustees of Target Range Sch. Dist. No. 23,* 18 IDELR 1019 (9th Cir. 1991).

Courts are likely to hold serious infringements on parental participation *per se* violations of the Act, so grave that substantial remedies such as tuition reimbursement for private placements are warranted without consideration of the merits of the school district's defectively formulated proffered program.

There is a fair amount of litigation, including one oft-quoted federal circuit court opinion, in which the issue before the court is whether the school district interfered with the parent's ability to participate in the IEP process, and, if so, what remedy should be ordered. Consistent with the IEP process itself, the litigated cases involve individualized analysis of a unique amalgamation of circumstances. These illuminating cases are summarized below.

W.G. v. Board of Trustees of Target Range School District No. 23, 18 IDELR 1019 (9th Cir. 1991)

Student: Student with a significant specific learning disability, unilaterally placed by his parents in a private school

Procedural inadequacies: The court found many. Failure to invite teachers from the private school the student was attending is discussed in Question 11 in chapter 9. With regard to parental participation, the court found the IEP meeting was a sham; district

---

[5] *See* Question 10 in chapter 12, *infra,* for a more detailed discussion of court cases finding that a school district's violations of the IEP procedural safeguards were only technical in nature.

representatives had prepared an IEP before the meeting without the participation of the parents and presented it as a *fait accompli*. Although the parents objected, no alternatives were considered. One parent testified that the district assumed a "take it or leave it" position at the meeting.

Remedy: Tuition reimbursement

Briere v. Fair Haven Grade School District, 25 IDELR 55 (D. Vt. 1996)

Student: High school student with a serious learning disability, borderline mental retardation, a severe language disorder, a visual impairment and a heart murmur, unilaterally placed by her mother in a private school

Procedural inadequacies: The IEP document itself was significantly defective. In addition, the school district committed the following violations involving limitation of the parent's right to participate in IEP formulation: refused to discuss the placement proposed by the mother, delayed scheduling an IEP meeting for 23 months and failed to finalize the resulting IEP for another year. The court summarized the school district's conduct: "The violations committed by the District over the three year period go to the heart of parental participation. The Court finds that such violations constitute a denial of a free appropriate public education per se." 25 IDELR at 62.

Remedy: Tuition reimbursement for three years of private school, at a cost of $80,700.

Jefferson County School District R-1, 19 IDELR 1112 (SEA Col. 1993)

Student: 17-year-old student with multiple disabilities attending a self-contained program in a public school

Procedural inadequacies: The issue that ultimately made its way to the Tenth Circuit Court of Appeals (*Urban v. Jefferson County School District R-1,* 24 IDELR 465 (10th Cir. 1996)), was whether the school district denied the student FAPE by failing to include a statement of transition services in the IEP and failing to place him in his neighborhood school. The parental participation issue involved the district's refusal to schedule the IEP meeting on a weekend or evening so the parents could attend and failure to urge more strenuously that they take off work to attend during the day.

Remedy: The school district was ordered to convene an IEP meeting on a weekend or evening if necessary to accommodate the parents.

Frederick County Public School, 2 ECLPR ¶ 145 (SEA Md. 1995)

Student: Four-year-old with autism

Procedural inadequacies: At the IEP meeting the parents expressed dissatisfaction with the proposed IEP. The school district did not convene another IEP meeting, but amended the IEP without notice to the parents or parental participation once the parents filed for due process. The first the parents heard of the new IEP, which was responsive to their objections at the IEP meeting, was when the school district presented it in discovery under the five-day rule.

Remedy: Reimbursement for home-based Lovaas program and other services provided by the parents.

In the administrative decision in *Bloomfield Board of Education,* 18 IDELR 1147 (SEA N.J. 1992), the administrative law judge (ALJ) found that the school district had committed procedural violations significantly inhibiting parental participation, but declined to end the inquiry there. While the parents of an autistic student seeking continued funding for an out-of-state placement at the Boston Higachi school failed to attend the IEP meetings, the school district also failed to take necessary action to involve the parents or the private school in its deliberations. Borrowing principles of equity, the ALJ found that neither party could prevail on a claim of procedural violations.

> In this case, however, there was an abject lack of cooperation and furnishing of data to the CST [Child Study Team] by the parents and by Higachi. The parents acknowledge that they intentionally declined to attend the IEP meeting, claiming that the process had become a farce, and that placement was already a foregone conclusion. That opinion on the part of the parents did not relieve their obligation to cooperate and to offer their best efforts, meaningful data, and participation, including input from Higachi. On the other hand, the CST did not make sufficient attempts to secure this cooperation and data, but it certainly was not forthcoming from [the parents] or from Higachi. The *Rowley* tests contemplate mutual compliance. The parents' lack of participation and refusal to cooperate negates any claim that the Board failed to follow appropriate procedures by acting without sufficient parental input. No exclusion of blame for the lack of communication can be attributed to either party.

18 IDELR at 1159.

6. Do parents have an obligation to act in good faith in participating in the IEP process?

Yes, parents do have an obligation to act in good faith, although enforcement of that obligation is difficult, as a disabled child's right to FAPE cannot be forfeited as a sanction for parental misconduct. Further, the extent to which the school district also has conducted itself inappropriately, committed procedural violations of the IDEA and offered a program that provides FAPE as a substantive matter are all variables that enter into how a parent's failure to participate in good faith should be factored into the resolution of the dispute between the parties.

Because the IDEA makes parental participation a central tenet of the IDEA process, parents are in a position to truly foul things up if they behave obstructively. One example, of many found in published opinions, concerns the parents of a child with cerebral palsy, severe language, motor, mobility and visual disabilities and a gastrostomy stomate button. The parents and the school district were poles apart on placement—neither was appropriate, according to the hearing officer—but contention between the parties resulted in the student being withdrawn from the public school and losing a year's worth of programming that both parties essentially agreed would provide educational benefit. The hearing officer concluded, as a matter of law, that the parents consistently acted hostilely and in bad faith, blocking meaningful communication and causing delays. *Baltimore City Pub. Sch.,* 23 IDELR 152 (SEA Md. 1995).

It is not difficult to understand why, as discussed in Question 5 above in connection with *Bloomfield Board of Education,* 18 IDELR 1147 (SEA N.J. 1992), courts and administrative decision-makers have recognized that parents have an obligation to participate in good faith in the IEP process. But the thorny issue is how to enforce that duty, in the event of a breach, without compromising the child's right to FAPE.

The IDEA has no provision for the assessment of a monetary penalty. Certainly, exclusion of parents from the IEP process is not an option; nor is appointment of a surrogate parent. *Letter to Perryman,* EHLR 211:438 (OSEP 1987); *Dundee Cent. Sch. Dist.,* 1987-88 EHLR 509:191 (SEA N.Y. 1987).

In *Cobb County School System,* 24 IDELR 875 (SEA Ga. 1996), a hearing officer explicitly ordered the parents of an autistic preschooler who had unilaterally placed their son to "participate in good faith in planning . . . , an IEP." In theory, then, a failure to cooperate in good faith would be contempt of the hearing officer's order. But we question whether an administrative officer may—or would—in fact impose sanctions on an uncooperative parent.

In *Cobb,* whatever the parents did that suggested they would not participate in good faith—the opinion is not clear on that point— had no effect on the decision of the hearing officer to award tuition reimbursement (in the amount of $39,479) for the at-home Lovaas therapy provided during the previous year. The program was appropriate; the school district's proposed program was not, from either a procedural or substantive viewpoint.

In a more authoritative decision, a district court similarly awarded tuition reimbursement to uncooperative parents because the school district failed to diagnose the student's learning disability as a co-morbid condition and thus offer an inappropriate IEP. The parents in *Friedman v. Vance,* 24 IDELR 654 (D. Md. 1996), paid "lip service to their duty to cooperate" according to the court, but they failed to disclose that they had decided as early as May of the previous year that they planned to enroll their son in a private school for the next school year and that they were planning to be away a significant part of the summer. As a result, the school district did not have an IEP in effect at the beginning of the school year.

Assessing the conduct of both parties, the court determined that both the school district and the parents bore responsibility for the failure to have timely completed the IEP. The school district argued that it should not have to reimburse tuition for the private school because the parents contributed to the delay. The district may have made a good argument on that point, but the court refused to consider it. The IEP that was untimely, but ultimately, proposed by the school district was inadequate as a substantive matter.

Nevertheless, it does appear that, at least to some extent, courts and administrative decision-makers may take a parent's failure to participate in good faith in the IEP process into account in crafting a remedy when the substantive inappropriateness of the proposed IEP is not the issue. In addition, even when a district has failed to offer FAPE as a substantive matter, the parents' entitlement to tuition reimbursement for unilateral placement in an appropriate program may be reduced due to lack of good faith participation. That conclusion has its origin in the U.S. Supreme Court's decision in *Burlington School Committee v. Massachusetts Department of Education*, 1984-85 EHLR 556:389 (1985), in which the Court held that the parents are entitled to reimbursement for expenses incurred for a unilateral placement that is ultimately determined to have been necessary in order to provide FAPE for their child with a disability.

In so holding, however, the Court also made it clear that tuition reimbursement was an equitable—not a legal—remedy. "We do think that [the Court of Appeals] was correct in concluding that 'such relief as the court determines is appropriate' within the meaning of Section 1415(e)(2) [of the IDEA], means that equitable considerations are relevant in fashioning relief." 1984-85 EHLR at 556:396.

Among the applications of the equity principle is a consideration of the conduct of either party. *E.g., W.G. v. Board of Trustees of Target Range Sch. Dist. No. 23*, 18 IDELR 1019 (9th Cir. 1992); *Parents of Student W. v. Puyallup Sch. Dist.*, 21 IDELR 723 (9th Cir. 1994). Thus, courts may sometimes tip the balance against a party, either the school district or the parents, who they perceive to have delayed or impeded the process. *See, e.g., Hunter v. Seattle Sch. Dist. No. 1*, 1986-87 EHLR 558:302 (Wash. Ct. App. 1987) (parents not entitled to reimbursement when the school district was not given an opportunity to assess a child's needs because the student was unilaterally placed out of state and not returned home to enable evaluation).

Finally, in a case that is widely cited for its other holdings, the First Circuit Court of Appeals gave an eloquent articulation of a principle consistent with both equity and common sense. In *Roland M. v. Concord School Committee*, 16 EHLR 1129 (1st Cir. 1990), the court held that parents who, among other acts of uncooperativeness, were instrumental in the nonattendance of the student's private school teacher could not challenge the IEP on the basis of that teacher not being present at the IEP meeting. As the court opined, "The law ought not abet parties who block assembly of the required team and then, dissatisfied with the ensuing IEP, attempt to jettison it because of problems created by their own obstructionism." 16 EHLR at 1134.

The limitations on tuition reimbursement and recovery of attorneys' fees included in the 1997 Amendments seem to this author to address the concerns often expressed in administrative and judicial opinions that parents who do not act as good faith participants in the IEP process should be subject to some kind of sanction. *See* Question 2 in chapter 12, *infra,* for a brief explanation of these new limitations on remedies.

7. Do parents have a vote at IEP meetings?

As an initial matter, the IDEA does not require formal voting at IEP meetings. In fact, neither the statute nor the regulations specify how decision-making should be conducted. See Questions 9 and 11, below, in this regard. Nonetheless, it seems consistent with the IDEA's mandate that parents participate meaningfully in the IEP process that parents have a vote in those instances in which IEP meetings involve voting by participants. *But see* the discussion in Question 11 of a federal district court that ruled that a school district's IEP meeting rules under which parents were not permitted to vote passed muster under the IDEA.

8. Do parents have an equal vote at IEP meetings?

Parents have an equal vote only in the sense that their disagreement can trigger due process. As discussed in Question 7, parents may not even have a vote. But assuming parents do have a vote, equal "voting" is inconsistent with the IDEA. As discussed in more detail in Question 1, above, due process (with stay-put) is the procedure for resolving disagreements between parents and school districts. Ultimately, parents have no veto power over IEP decisions, short of disenrollment.

9. Are decisions made at IEP meetings by majority vote?

According to the Ninth Circuit Court of Appeals, a majority vote for decision-making at IEP meetings would be inconsistent with the IDEA—and could lead to nonsensical results in some cases. Rather, decision-making by consensus is the only workable approach consistent with the law. *Doe v. Maher,* 1985-86 EHLR 557:353 (9th Cir. 1986).

In *Maher,* the court rejected a parent's claim that decisions made at an IEP meeting must be made by a majority vote of the individuals present at the meeting, with each individual (and all individuals attending) having one vote. After noting that there was no express support in the IDEA for decision by majority vote—indeed, for any system—the court concluded that majority voting was inconsistent with the law.

Noting that under 34 C.F.R. § 300.344 the number of participants in an IEP meeting is indeterminate, and to some extent at the discretion of the parties, the court concluded that having a majority-vote rule could give both parents and agencies an incentive to select participants in order to gain a numerical majority. Thinking perhaps of the "court-packing" of the 1930s, the court found that creating opportunities for such gamesmanship would defeat the intent of the IDEA to make the IEP meeting a cooperative proceeding.

Moving on to consider possible alternatives to majority-vote rule, the court selected a consensus rule as most consistent with the IDEA's ideal of cooperative planning. The court acknowledged that it would not always be possible for parents and school districts to achieve a consensus and that this reality is acknowledged in the IDEA by its inclusion of due process procedures.

The district court also opined in another case that consensus-building at IEP meetings, rather than voting, is consistent with the IDEA. *Reusch v. Fountain*, 21 IDELR 1107 (D. Md. 1994). In that case, the court held that the school district's provision of extended school year services violated the IDEA—both procedurally and substantively—in almost too many ways to count. But, its majority vote concept got a lukewarm and qualified approval in a footnote.

10. What does it mean to make decisions about the IEP "by consensus"?

"Decision-making by consensus" is not a term of art in the field of education. Rather, in both judicial and administrative opinions, the term seems to be used to mean unanimous consent, although technically the term is defined as general agreement by at least most. For example, faced with a situation in which the school officials on an IEP team did not agree among themselves, the hearing officer in *DeKalb County School District*, 21 IDELR 426 (SEA Ga. 1990), opined that consensus decisions are those which are agreed to by all members of the IEP meeting. (In that case, the school district was not required to provide related services that two of the school district officials—a numerical minority—"voted against.")

But what if the public agency representatives are themselves unable to reach a consensus? That seems to be the concern motivating the school district in *Reusch v. Fountain*. Will that allow the parents, assuming they disagree with the IEP that is implemented, an independent ground to invalidate an IEP that has been ruled appropriate in due process? That appears to be the novel question asked and answered in the negative by the court in *Hawes v. Bates*, 24 IDELR 1018 (N.D. Ind. 1996).

The parents in that case had appealed the IEP proposed for their daughter two consecutive years, losing both times. The third time, the due process hearing officer refused to consider their claims, finding that the issues they raised already had been raised, reviewed and decided. The parents, acting *pro se*, appealed to the district court, and filed an unnumbered 500 page motion for summary judgment. The court noted it was difficult to review their submission. One claim the parents appeared to have raised, though, was that the IEP should be invalidated because, contrary to the *Maher* case, the IEP was not the result of a consensus among the public agency participants.

The court rejected this argument, reasoning that what is essential is the consensus of the representatives of the school district (or other agency) that is obligated to provide FAPE. "However, as made clear by *Maher,* if no consensus is reached, the local educational agency must prepare the IEP, which it has done." 24 IDELR at 1022. Ordinarily, then, the parents would have the right to request due process if they did not agree. But, in this case, that was no longer a possibility.

Regardless of whether decisions by consensus require unanimous consent or not, there appears to be more agreement about what the decision-making by consensus process entails. Consistent with the IDEA requirement for meaningful parental participation, consensus decision-making involves a sharing of views and discussion of questions, areas of disagreement and alternatives. The author is reminded, in fact, of objectives associated with jury deliberations. Voting without discussion, even if all participants would vote the same way, is suspect. As articulated by the appeals officer in *Nenana City Public Schools,* 18 IDELR 489 (SEA Alaska 1991):

> To arrive at a decision by consensus is time consuming, inefficient, and downright frustrating. But, the goal of consensus-building is group responsibility for successful implementation of a program. On the other hand the parents must accept the process. This is not a maneuver in which each member of the group sets forth his or her position—a vote is taken, the ayes have it, and the matter is settled.

18 IDELR at 491.

A good example of what decision-making by consensus is *not* is found in *Murphy v. Timberlane Regional School District,* 21 IDELR 133 (D.N.H. 1994), in which the district court ruled on the parent's motion for enforcement of the court's earlier order to provide two years of compensatory education for a 25-year-old student with spastic quadriplegia, cortical blindness and mild mental retardation. In prior rulings in that case, including the First Circuit's widely cited analysis of laches in the context of claims alleging denial of FAPE (*Murphy v. Timberlane Regional School District,* 20 IDELR 1391 (1st Cir. 1994)), the student had been awarded two years of compensatory services, with the specific program and placement to be decided by the student's IEP team. The IEP team agreed on a tentative IEP, an out-of-state residential facility that could implement the IEP was selected, and that facility agreed to accept the student. But at that point the process stopped, with the IEP team member who was the public agency representative first delaying finalizing the IEP and then refusing to sign it.

Tape recordings of the IEP meetings were made and these transcriptions, along with what appears to be extensive testimony by the IEP team members, resulted in the court's concluding that the school district intentionally prevented the IEP team from reaching a consensus regarding the student's placement. The opinion, which quotes extensively from the transcripts of the IEP meetings, illustrates well what the court viewed as obstructive conduct in violation of the IDEA mandate for collaborative decision-making.

11. Does each member of the IEP team have an equal "vote"?

"One person-one vote"—in the sense that no participant has any greater decision-making authority than another—appears to be the premise underlying the Ninth Circuit's rejection of majority voting in *Doe v. Maher*, 1985-86 EHLR 557:353 (9th Cir. 1986). While that conclusion is consistent with the IDEA mandate that parents be "equal participants" vis-à-vis school representatives (Appendix C to 34 C.F.R. Part 300, Question 26), it is a more difficult principle to apply when the differing positions of school representative attendees are involved. *See Hawes v. Bates,* 24 IDELR 1018 (N.D. Ind. 1996); *DeKalb County Sch. Dist.,* 21 IDELR 426 (SEA Ga. 1990). Part of the difficulty may be that the diffusion of authority is foreign to the more hierarchical structure of the school district—or any large enterprise. Another is that the IDEA simply does not address this issue.

According to the administrative law judge in *Mason City Community School District,* 21 IDELR 248 (SEA Iowa 1994), though, in the IEP world some animals cannot be more equal than others. In that case, the parents prevailed in their challenge to the district's proposal to graduate their daughter on the sole basis of having completed the generally applicable number of academic credits.[6] In finding that the district's decision violated the IDEA, the ALJ described the IEP meeting at which the graduation decision was made:

> [T]he process of IEP development is one of attempting to arrive at consensus about appropriate special education programs. In order to achieve that result, no one person on an IEP team can or should exercise greater power than anyone else on the team. (See 34 C.F.R. Part 300, Appendix C, No. 26). Yet that is *not* what happened here. District administrators, admittedly strangers to [the student's IEP] process, arrived on the scene at a time when the rest of the team was in the process of formulating a significant change in the IEP. The other educators on the team and [the student's] parents were headed toward a determination that [the student] should not be graduated and, instead, should be provided additional educational programming. That IEP team effort was effectively stopped when the administrators usurped the decision-making process. . . .

21 IDELR at 254.

This seems to the author to be a correct decision made for the wrong reasons. The administrators apparently were not considered part of the IEP team and thus should not have been permitted to participate in the IEP meeting in the first instance. They should have had *no* vote, exercised *no* power—equal or otherwise.

In a footnote, the court in *Reusch v. Fountain,* 21 IDELR 1107 (D. Md. 1994), approved unequal voting and surprisingly, seemed to vet allowing parents to be non-

---

[6] *See* chapter 10, *infra,* concerning graduation.

voting members of IEP teams. In effect, it seemed to approve the type of procedure struck down in *Mason City Community School District.*

> The IDEA requires no rigid voting decision in the IEP decision-making process. Consequently, [the school district] is free to adopt—as it has—a policy of consensus-building at IEP meetings in which voting is discouraged. However, voting does occur in some cases. [Parents] argue that when IEP committees do vote on critical issues, parents and teachers should be included. [The school district] denies that there is such a requirement under the IDEA.

> Under federal and state regulations, parents and teachers are statutorily named members of IEP committees. See 34 C.F.R. § 300.344. The provisions make no mention of any difference in status between them and the administration representative also required to attend such meetings. To the contrary, the regulations note that parents are to be treated as "equal participants" in the process. 34 C.F.R. § 300 Appendix C. The Court is not going to require that parents and/or teachers be given a vote in the decisional process. However, it will require that the position of the non-voting parents and teachers be considered by those voting and placed in the record of the proceedings.

21 IDELR at 1117 n.14.

Chapter 7

Behavior Management Plans and Other Special Needs

This chapter addresses the relationship between the IEP and three types of needs that students with disabilities may have: behavior management plans, assistive technology devices or services, and extended school year (ESY) programming. The first is increasingly important, as appropriate social behavior by young people becomes an ever more pressing concern in society as a whole. The latter two are what might be referred to as "big ticket" items, costly to provide when required to deliver FAPE. This introduction takes a brief look at behavior management plans, from a pedagogic perspective.

Lack of discipline in schools continues to be identified as a major concern by both the general public, and to a lesser extent, educators. Clearly there is no quick fix to the systemic discipline problems that continue to affect the school environment. While schools have attempted to react to this concern, the extent to which the measures they have taken have been successful remains a point of ongoing discussion.

One stumbling block for educators may be the perception some have that problems manifested by some students, particularly those with disabilities, are beyond school control and, further, that potential solutions are elusive and not within the means of a school. The frustration generally is one of content and pedagogy—knowing and assessing proper techniques and providing appropriate instruction to implement those techniques. Interestingly, many schools have no student discipline policies. Those that do often do not effectively communicate responsibilities to the staff members who are required to implement the policies.

One of the greatest professional challenges today is providing fair and appropriate discipline to students who disrupt the classroom, the halls, the lunchroom, the playground, the school bus and often times the community. Effective management of classroom behavior is the foremost aspect of this challenge, since adequate control of a classroom is a prerequisite to achieving instructional objectives and to safeguarding the psychological and physical well-being of children. Importantly, the management approach chosen must promote the opportunity for students to learn and must result in changed behaviors.

Despite the significant amount of attention given to this topic, serious controversy remains over which set of procedures constitutes effective discipline. Educators and mental health professionals view students' behavior problems differently and, as a result, a realistic conceptual model that suitably guides the analysis of behavioral, social, and emotional functioning and that provides the communication link among professionals has not yet been developed.

Disciplining students with disabilities adds yet another level of complexity to the challenge facing school officials. The determination of a student's level of maladjustment often is hindered by difficulty in deciding whether symptoms indicate a serious emotional problem or merely a developmental or situational difficulty. There continues to be a general lack of consensus between and among educators and mental health professionals regarding what constitutes emotional and behavioral difficulties.

Further, school officials must take into account the additional statutory rights of children with disabilities set out in federal law. Although the IDEA, Section 504 of the Rehabilitation Act, the Americans with Disabilities Act and implementing regulations for these laws are detailed, they contain no specific guidelines for the in-school discipline of students with disabilities. As a result, the possibility of litigation has further complicated the process of maintaining appropriate discipline and has frustrated school officials in their attempts to balance educational needs and the rights of students with disabilities with the school's need to discipline students.

In spite of the attention given to many discipline practices by courts and in the literature, it seems apparent that the use of productive disciplinary practices has not been effectively communicated to those expected to implement the procedures. Practical applications of learning-theory principles are more readily available today than ever; however, the adequate preparation of teachers in this regard has been impeded. There is an ever-increasing need to clarify interpretation to staff of school and classroom rules outlined in local student discipline policies and procedures. The problems that educators face, combined with the procedural requirements needed to address these problems, often result in confusion that affects the decision-making process. In many cases, this confusion has generated more frustration and concern by those attempting to provide an appropriate educational program.

Very often a discipline plan is developed as part of a student's IEP. Using the IEP process avoids misunderstanding between schools and parents and should ensure that the individual needs of the student are met. A plan created for an individual student must address and recognize to the maximum extent appropriate: (1) opportunities for interaction; (2) a continuum of placement alternatives in accordance with individual needs; and (3) appropriate placement in the least restrictive environment selected from the available options, although certainly not at all costs or to the detriment of the student or others.

Ultimately the effectiveness of a discipline plan rests on the quality of the relationship between the student and the teacher. Teachers must be given specialized training in content and pedagogy to help facilitate the implementation phase. Recognizing the central involvement and the strategic importance of the teacher's position in effective discipline planning is key to subsequent changes in student behavior.

Sometimes students with challenging behaviors perceive the school as territory in which they do not belong. Schools need to recognize that although they can act swiftly and efficiently in dealing with disciplinary issues in a manner that provides a safe and productive learning environment for all students, they must do more. Schools also must recognize the importance of assuring that students who normally would have been excluded or who feel alienated from the school environment are provided some productive means of support so they can learn from their mistakes and are given a productive and resourceful educational environment designed to habilitate them to the demands and expectations of the school and, eventually, general society.

Behavior Management Plans

1. What is a "behavior management plan"?

A behavior management plan (BMP) is intended to address prospectively how school district personnel will deal with a student's challenging, disruptive or otherwise unacceptable behaviors. While students with disabilities such as autism or mental retardation may have challenging behaviors and require behavior management plans, we also use the term here in the way it is commonly used in connection with special education law as being synonymous with a discipline plan. A BMP should outline behaviors that are prohibited, behaviors that are expected, and the positive and negative consequences for those behaviors. Such a plan will provide a clear indication of the school's response at the time of the critical behavioral event.

2. When are behavior management plans required to provide FAPE?

Generally, a school district must develop a BMP for a student whose disability-related behaviors are interfering with his or her ability to make educational progress under an otherwise appropriate program and placement.

Implementation of BMPs is an issue under Section 504 as well as the IDEA, particularly with regard to students whose classroom behavior is disruptive as a result of ADHD.

> OCR finds that when a student who is disabled within the meaning of Section 504 manifests repeated or serious misconduct such that modifying the child's negative

behavior becomes a significant component of what actually takes place in the child's educational program, the District is required to develop an individual behavioral management plan. The plan should ensure that the disabled child is able to successfully maintain the placement that is determined to most appropriately meet his or her educational needs.

Orange (CA) United Sch. Dist., 20 IDELR 770, 773 (OCR 1993).

While court litigation on the issue is scant, published administrative decisions have ruled on parental claims that a school district's failure to include a BMP in the student's IEP resulted in a denial of FAPE. For example, in *Pasadena Independent School District,* 21 IDELR 482 (SEA Cal. 1994), the hearing officer ordered the school district to develop and implement a written behavior management plan as a component of the programming for a 19-year-old student with multiple disabilities, including moderate to severe autism, mental retardation and speech/language impairments. To control aggression and encourage on-task behavior, the student's teachers restrained him by tying him to a chair by the use of a belt apparatus. Although the parents did not prevail in challenging the use of the restraining device, they did convince the hearing officer that a BMP governing, among other things, use of the belt, would benefit both school personnel and parents and thus was required.

[The student's teachers] would surely be assisted in addressing [the student's] behavioral needs with a set of specific interventions and techniques clearly stated in written form. Such a plan could, for example, unequivocally specify the circumstances, duration, and necessity for use of the belt apparatus. . . .

A written behavior management plan would provide both [the student's] teachers and his parents with a clear understanding of the acceptable parameters of use of the belt. It also gives the parties an opportunity to design a mutually agreeable set of consequences to address aggressive, uncontrollable or otherwise inappropriate behavior that is not met by either the belt or other strategies.

21 IDELR at 484.

The hearing officer in *St. Mary's County Public School,* 21 IDELR 172 (SEA Md. 1994), also found that an BMP was a necessary element of FAPE for an 11-year-old student diagnosed as having a serious emotional disturbance. The district proposed a residential placement for the child because of his history of being verbally abusive and physically aggressive. The hearing officer found from the evidence, though, that the student could succeed in a public school placement if he received a number of interventional strategies, all of which were to be set out in an individualized behavior management plan.

Finding for the school district, a hearing officer held in *Jefferson County Board of Education,* 20 IDELR 493 (SEA Ala. 1993), to the opposite effect that the absence of a BMP is not always fatal, assuming appropriate behavioral interventions are implemented nonetheless. In that dispute the parents of a student diagnosed as having attention deficit hyperactivity disorder (ADHD) and IDEA-eligible as other health impaired, claimed that the school district denied FAPE to their son because it had not developed and implemented a BMP for him. The student's documented behavior in prior school years included disruptive behavior in class, refusal to follow directions, temper outbursts, fighting, kicking, and throwing objects, although there was no evidence of such conduct in the then-current school year.

The hearing officer first determined that a BMP did not have to be included in a student's IEP. He further determined that in this case the failure to have a written BMP in the first instance did not deny FAPE to this student because his teacher had devised a modification checklist that was succeeding in controlling disruptive behavior and permitting the student to make acceptable grades in the majority of his subjects and to pass from grade to grade.

Section 614(d)(3)(B) of the 1997 Amendments appears to contain Congress' affirmation of the need for a BMP when a student's disability-related behavior impacts his or her own education or the learning environment of others. The new language, providing a level of detail not formerly found in the statute, directs IEP teams to consider "in the case of a child whose behavior impedes his or her learning, or that of others, . . . when appropriate, strategies, including positive behavioral interventions, strategies, and supports to address that behavior."

3. Is a school district required to include a behavior management plan for a student with a disability in his or her IEP?

Generally no, as a matter of meeting the requirements of the IDEA, OSEP opined in 1995. Nevertheless, an IEP should contain behavioral goals in appropriate instances. School districts should design and implement BMPs for students with disabilities in appropriate instances, notwithstanding the fact that the BMP does not have to be included in the IEP.

In response to a thoughtful inquiry, OSEP stated in *Letter to Huefner,* 23 IDELR 1072 (OSEP 1995), that the IDEA does not require inclusion of BMPs in the IEPs of students with behavioral or emotional disorders. "IEPs for disabled students who require behavioral components must include behavioral goals and objectives, but need not include behavioral methods/plans. . . . Part B does not necessarily require that IEPs for disabled students include behavior methods/plans." 23 IDELR at 1072-73.

OSEP's response explains why, as a matter of statutory interpretation, BMPs do not need to be included in an IEP:

- Educational programming for children whose disability-related behavior adversely impacts educational progress must include a behavioral component.

- When a student's educational programming includes behavioral components, the IEP must include both statements of behavioral goals and objectives, including short-term objectives (34 C.F.R. § 300.346(a)(2)), and specific special education and related services related to those identified goals and objectives (34 C.F.R. § 300.346(a)(3)).

- A student's IEP does not, however, have to include detailed educational plans or methods, i.e, instructional components. Appendix C to 34 C.F.R. Part 300, Question 41; *Letter to Hall,* 21 IDELR 58 (OSERS 1994); *Letter to Anonymous,* 17 EHLR 842 (OSEP 1991).

- A BMP is a statement of disciplinary methods. It is not a statement of goals and objectives, a specific item of special education, or a related service.

- As a result, 34 C.F.R. § 300.346 does not compel inclusion of a student's BMP in his or her IEP.

Taking the same view was the administrative law judge who ordered a school district to clarify the IEP for an eight-year-old student with Down syndrome in *Clarion-Goldfield Community School District,* 22 IDELR 267 (SEA Iowa 1994). The ALJ rejected the parents' claim that the school district was required to include the student's behavior plan in his IEP, although she did order the district to improve the statement of behavioral goals and objectives.

While there are no authoritative court decisions to the contrary, two hearing officers have taken an opposing view.

In *St. Mary's County Public School,* 21 IDELR 172 (SEA Md. 1994), the BMP was characterized as a supplementary aid and service required for a student with a disability to participate in the regular classroom (although his placement was in fact a self-contained classroom). OSEP has made its position clear that supplementary aids and services must be included in an IEP.[1] Appendix C to 34 C.F.R. Part 300, Question 48. Thus, the school district was required to include a BMP, as well as other behavioral strategies, in the student's IEP.

The hearing officer in *Etowah County Board of Education,* 20 IDELR 843 (SEA Ala. 1993), determined that an IEP which lacked a specific and complete behavior management plan denied FAPE to a student with a learning disability, a serious emotional disturbance and co-morbid ADHD. The student was repeating the seventh grade for the third time and had frequent behavioral problems which resulted in the district's filing two delinquency petitions against him.

One exception to including a BMP in the IEP would be to include in the statement of the student's current level of educational performance a description of behavior interventions that have been tried and their effectiveness. 34 C.F.R. § 300.346(a)(1).

---

[1] An arguable position, as discussed in Question 26 in chapter 2, *supra.*

For example, the IEP for a 16-year-old student with autism and behavior disorders included a description of the student's behavior, the series of behavior interventions that had been tried and their results. *North Scott Community Sch. Dist.*, 21 IDELR 226 (SEA Iowa 1994).

Whether *Letter to Huefner* will continue to be good law after July 1, 1998 is the question already being posed by some commentators in light of Section 614(d)(3)(B) of the 1997 Amendments. *See* Question 2 of this chapter. The suggestion has been made that the 1997 Amendments impliedly require the inclusion of a BMP in a student's IEP.

4. Is a school district permitted to include a behavior management plan for a student with a disability in his or her IEP?

Yes. Consistent with generally recognized IDEA principles, a school district may elect to make a student's BMP a part of his or her IEP. "[T]here is nothing in Part B that would prohibit the inclusion of behavior plans in a particular student's IEP if an IEP team determines that such plans are needed to ensure the effective implementation of the student's IEP." *Letter to Huefner*, 23 IDELR 1072 (OSEP 1995).

5. Should a school district include a behavior management plan for a student with a disability in his or her IEP?

In most cases, best practice includes developing, reviewing, implementing and documenting a BMP as part of the IEP process. Students with a propensity for misbehavior, as identified through the evaluation and assessment process, should have behavioral objectives, classroom interventions and disciplinary plans addressed and contained in their IEPs. As discussed in Question 3 above, the 1997 Amendments may, in fact, now mandate inclusion.

It is important in developing a valid BMP to utilize the IEP as a jointly agreed document. "A written behavior plan can be a mechanism to improve communication between home and school." *Pasadena Indep. Sch. Dist.*, 21 IDELR 482, 484 (SEA Cal. 1994). The BMP developed via the IEP serves as a written record of decisions jointly made by parents and school personnel outlining goals and objectives. A BMP discussed in advance with the parents is more likely to meet with success in both the home and school. In addition, a BMP that is discussed and implemented within the context of the IEP is less likely to be legally challenged by the parents.

The issue of the causal relationship between a student's disability and challenging behavior can be more readily determined by knowledgeable and informed IEP participants. Information shared from the multidisciplinary evaluation and assessment team can make the work of the IEP team more reasonable and valid. Foreshadowing the relationship of a student's disability and his or her behavior promotes positive behavioral change. At the same time it avoids possible confrontation and enhances communication between parents and school officials, because at the initial meeting issues are more likely to be discussed objectively and rationally.

Furthermore, the IEP can function as a communication vehicle used for the establishment of specific disciplinary plans, which are clearly defined and positively stated in support of specific and immediate consequences based on the student's needs. A written IEP can be used as a problem-solving document to fully explore and articulate positive disciplinary alternatives. A full and open discussion of discipline should occur in the planning meeting with the involvement of parents. For many students, there is no one quick fix for disruptive behavior. The key to finding solutions, however, is through a frank and open exploration of strategies, involvement of key personnel, and an appropriate mix of general strategies.

Recognizing the necessity that the IEP be reasonably calculated to confer an educational benefit, the IEP team can make determinate predictions of how a student's disability may or may not affect future classroom performance. If properly developed, the IEP creates an appropriate intervention plan reflective of the student's needs, as identified through the evaluation and assessment process.

If, on the other hand, a school district elects not to include a student's BMP in his or her IEP, the management of that student's behavior then falls within the broad discretion of the school. Thus, in *Oakley (KS) Unified School District #274,* 24 IDELR 393 (OCR 1995), OCR found that the school district did not discriminate against a student with a disability when it failed to discipline the student in accordance with her IEP. The IEP did not address discipline and the school district did not discipline the student because of her disability. *See also Benecic v. City of Malden,* 18 IDELR 829 (Mass. App. Ct. 1992).

6.   How are placement decisions affected by including the behavior management plan for a student with a disability in his or her IEP?

The implementation of an agreed-upon discipline plan as part of an IEP (or Section 504 accommodation plan[2]) avoids the issue of whether disciplinary action constitutes a change in placement. The importance of this issue cannot be disputed. If the IEP describes the disciplinary plan to be followed for a particular student, then change in placement procedures normally would not be invoked upon the implementation of a disciplinary action already included in the IEP.

For example, consider the learning disabled and emotionally disabled student whose circumstances were explored in the OCR Letter of Finding, *Francis Howell (MO) School District,* 18 IDELR 78 (OCR 1991):

---

[2] *See* Questions 1 and 2 in chapter 11, *infra,* concerning accommodation plans.

... [A]n annual goal in the IEP states the following: "Will improve behavior to a level required for success in regular class, special service class and the general school setting." The first objective under this goal states: "Will participate in at least one extracurricular activity throughout the school year." The second objective states: "Will follow Francis Howell High School code of conduct rules." As called for in his IEP, [the student] was participating in one extracurricular activity, interscholastic wrestling, during December 1990.

18 IDELR at 79.

The student with this IEP was unable to meet the behavioral rules for participation in interscholastic wrestling and was suspended from the extracurricular activity for two weeks. OCR found that this removal was consistent with the IEP and therefore it constituted neither discrimination or a change in placement.

[The student's] participation in an extracurricular activity and his adherence to the code of conduct are specifically related to the annual goal in his IEP of improving his behavior. These objectives are interrelated in the context of addressing his behavior in the general school setting. Therefore, the District was implementing his IEP when the District suspended him from wrestling for two weeks because of his failure to adhere to the code of conduct. The IEP goal which states that [the student] "will participate in at least one extracurricular activity throughout the school year" does not prevent the District from withholding this activity to discipline him. Moreover, District policy prohibits a student who is suspended from school or who is in [the In-School Alternative Program] from practicing or participating in extracurricular activities until the suspension is served. For these reasons, OCR finds that the District did not deny [the student] a free appropriate public education....

18 IDELR at 79.

7. May a school district call the police when the student with a disability has a behavior management plan?

Yes, according to OCR in its review of a complaint charging that the school district discriminated against a student by calling the police. The student with a disability at issue in *Chester Upland (PA) School District,* 24 IDELR 79 (OCR 1995), was involved in a physical fight with another student. Both students had bloody lips. The school district called the police, who arrested the disabled student.

The parent claimed that the district could not call in the police because the student had a behavior management plan. OCR did not agree. First, nothing in the letter of the BMP or the IEP precluded calling the police. Second, calling the police did not violate the spirit of the IEP or its behavior management component in this instance due to the dangerousness of the student's behavior. "School officials have a clear and unconditional duty to protect the health and safety of their students and employees and OCR will not disturb that responsibility absent overwhelming and significant evidence of dereliction of duty or subterfuge." 24 IDELR at 80.

The 1997 Amendments specifically address this issue in Section 615(9)(a) entitled "Referral to and action by law enforcement and judicial authorities," which states:

> Nothing in this part shall be construed to prohibit an agency from reporting a crime committed by a child with a disability to appropriate authorities or to prevent State law enforcement and judicial authorities from exercising their responsibilities with regard to the application of Federal and State law to crimes committed by a child with a disability.

8. If a behavior management plan is included in an IEP, is its choice of strategies considered an issue of educational methodology?

Apparently not, according to the district court in *Eric J. v. Huntsville City Board of Education,* 22 IDELR 858 (N.D. Ala. 1995). In that case the court reviewed in detail the BMP included in the IEP for a 14- year-old student with a learning disability, speech and language impairments, and ADHD and causally related misconduct. It closely analyzed the disruptive behaviors to be addressed and the methods by which they were to be redirected or otherwise dealt with, with no suggestion that selection of behavior management techniques was an issue of educational methodology.

Because *Eric J.* is the most detailed and authoritative published decision on this topic, the author describes in detail two contested components of the BMP, the basis for the parents' challenge to that component, and the court's resolution.

BMP component: Participation in physical education, a class the student enjoyed, rather than social skills training class, as a reward for progress in behavior management.

Parent's complaint: Inadequate as a positive reinforcer, particularly because it was the only positive reinforcer in the BMP.

Court's decision: No evidence was presented to establish that use of negative consequences, rather than positive reinforcers, is a denial of FAPE.

BMP component: Opportunity to show teacher a "red card" to show anger or frustration and leave the room to cool off, offered as an alternative to his use of profanity in class.

Parent's complaint: IEP also should have addressed other problem behaviors that were determined to be related to stress in the academic environment.

Court's decision: While no other specific situations are discussed, the techniques included in the BMP, including the red cards and time-out room, were adequate to address skills to use in other stress-related situations.

The administrative decision in *Radnor Township School District,* 21 IDELR 878 (SEA Pa. 1994), also involved a school district having to demonstrate in a contested proceeding the appropriateness of its BMP for a student, with no apparent deference being given to the school district's choice of methodology.

9. Can a student with a disability who has a behavior management plan be disciplined under the school district's disciplinary code?

Generally, disciplinary sanctions should be consistent with the intervention strategies set out in the student's behavior management plan. *See, e.g., Cabarrus County (NC) Sch. Dist.*, 22 IDELR 506 (OCR 1995) (the student's IEP identified a variety of behavioral management strategies and the disciplinary sanctions the student received were consistent with the intervention strategies contained in the IEP).

Nevertheless, students with disabilities are not immune from normal school disciplinary rules, provided the rules are administered in a nondiscriminatory manner and are not inconsistent with the student's IEP. However, in addressing critical behavioral events, the multidisciplinary team and IEP team must determine whether the offense is caused by or is a manifestation of the student's disability. *See, e.g., Stuart v. Nappi*, 1985-86 EHLR 557:101 (D. Conn. 1985).

Further, the IEP team could elect to include compliance with the school's disciplinary code in the BMP, to the extent appropriate. *See, e.g, Francis Howell (MO) Sch. Dist.*, 18 IDELR 78 (OCR 1991).

Although knowledge of the range of behavioral interventions and in-school disciplinary measures in a particular student's BMP generally are limited to the multidisciplinary and IEP teams, the school must ensure that any disciplinary action taken with respect to the student has no adverse effect on the goals and objectives of the IEP and is not applied in a discriminatory manner in violation of Section 504. *OSEP Memorandum 95-16*, 22 IDELR 531 (OSEP 1995); *Cabarrus County (NC) Sch. Dist., supra.*

These requirements extend to all school personnel, according to OCR. Thus, the school district in *West Las Vegas (NM) School District*, 20 IDELR 358 (OCR 1993), violated Section 504 with respect to the disciplining of a student with emotional, behavioral and learning disabilities who misbehaved on the bus. Although the student had an IEP which specified certain disciplinary strategies to deal with his behavior problems on the bus, the district failed to notify the bus driver of the appropriate discipline for the student. The bus driver used his own techniques to discipline the student, and these techniques were found to be inconsistent with those in the student's IEP.

While long-term suspensions trigger IDEA procedural safeguards,[3] the following measures generally are recognized as normal school disciplinary measures that have

---

[3] OSEP Memorandum 95-16, 22 IDELR 531 (OSEP 1995), in question and answer form, is a comprehensive statement of OSEP's interpretation of the IDEA with regard to the discipline of students with disabilities.

no such implications: reprimands and written warnings (*Stuart v. Nappi, supra*); time-outs (*Rodiriecus L. v. Waukegan School District No. 60*, 24 IDELR 563 (7th Cir. 1996)); use of study carrels (*Honig v. Doe*, 1987-88 EHLR 559:231 (1988)), restriction of privileges and detention (*Id.*); and in-school suspensions (*Big Beaver Falls Area School District v. Jackson*, 19 IDELR 1019 (Pa. Commw. Ct. 1993)). According to OSEP, use of such measures for students with disabilities is permissible as long as such measures are not inconsistent with a student's IEP. *OSEP Memorandum 95-16*, 22 IDELR 531 (OSEP 1995).

10. Does a school district's modification of the specific reinforcement strategies in the BMP contained in a student's IEP trigger the procedural safeguards of the IDEA?

Extrapolating from the decisions noted in Question 8 above, such changes should trigger safeguards. Nevertheless, there is a well-reasoned administrative decision that makes the case that the parents were not entitled to notice or the convening of another IEP meeting in these circumstances.

In *Pickens County Board of Education*, 22 IDELR 180 (SEA Ala. 1995), the school district included a BMP in the IEP for a six-year-old student with mental retardation and ADHD. The BMP contained time-outs and edible reinforcers. Subsequent to the creation of the IEP, the school district changed the location in which the student was placed for time-outs. Originally, he was to be given any time-outs in his classroom. But that caused too much disruption in the classroom, triggering relocation to, first, the hallway outside the classroom and, then, the auditorium. In addition, the edible reinforcer was changed to specifically identify "fruit loops." Both these actions took place without any changes being made to the IEP.

The parents charged that these changes violated their rights under the IDEA and their son's right to FAPE. The hearing officer ruled otherwise. Reciting the six required components of an IEP under state law (restating 34 C.F.R. § 300.346(a)), the hearing officer concluded that the changes did not involve significant or substantive changes to any of those elements.

> The only evidence offered in support of this issue is the fact that the physical location of the Child's "time-out" procedures was changed and that there may have been some variation in the specific positive reinforcers used in the behavior modification program. These appear to be day-to-day details which are merely the actual implementation of the broader program spelled out in the IEP. There is no evidence of any change which would require additional notice and a meeting.

22 IDELR at 185.

However, there are some changes to the BMP that do trigger procedural safeguards. Changes in the behaviors to be addressed in the BMP contained in an IEP certainly should be preceded by notice to parents and a meeting. Similarly, best practice would dictate convening a meeting if a school district proposed to modify the type of intervention or the actions to be taken in a less-than-trivial way when the intervention strategies are not effective.

Assistive Technology Devices and Services

11. Who determines if a student with a disability needs an assistive technology device (or assistive technology services)?

Ultimately, that responsibility rests with the student's IEP team. However, as is required with the determination of the educational needs of students with disabilities, generally, a multidisciplinary team first must conduct an evaluation of the student's needs for such a device or services.

Assistive technology devices and assistive technology services are terms of art under the IDEA. An assistive technology device is "any item, piece of equipment, or product system, whether acquired commercially, off the shelf, modified, or customized, that is used to increase, maintain, or improve the functional capabilities of children with disabilities." 34 C.F.R § 300.305. An assistive technology service is "any service that directly assists a child with a disability in the selection, acquisition, or use of an assistive technology device." 34 C.F.R. § 300.306.

Numerous policy letters have made it clear that school districts are required to provide assistive technology devices or services to a student with a disability if the participants on the student's IEP team determine that the student needs such a device or service in order to receive FAPE. *Letter to Anonymous,* 24 IDELR 854 (OSEP 1996); *Letter to Fisher,* 23 IDELR 565 (OSEP 1995); *Letter to Naon,* 22 IDELR 888 (OSEP 1995); *Letter to Seiler,* 20 IDELR 1216 (OSEP 1993); *Letter to Anonymous,* 18 IDELR 627 (OSEP 1991).

When the device at issue is novel or expensive (for example, an augmentative communicative device),[4] one might think that some higher-level oversight, such as when a state has state-level review of funding for residential placements, would be indicated. But, as OSEP made clear in *Letter to Anonymous,* a school board has no authority to unilaterally change any decisions made by an IEP team regarding the provision of assistive technology devices.

---

[4] An augmentative communication device is a computerized communication device with vocal output used by individuals who cannot communicate readily or at all through speech or writing, typically because of severe cognitive or physical impairments.

As one might expect, expert evaluation of a student's educational needs in connection with assistive technology is an important part of the preplacement evaluation in appropriate circumstances. OSEP emphasized this point in its *Letter to Fisher:*

> [E]ach public agency must ensure that, as part of its Part B educational evaluation when warranted by the child's suspected disability, it assesses, in accordance with the evaluation requirements of 34 C.F.R. § 300.532, the student's functional capabilities and whether they may be increased, maintained, or improved through the use of assistive technology devices or services. The evaluation should provide sufficient information to permit the IEP team to determine whether the student requires technology devices or services in order to receive FAPE.

23 IDELR at 566 (citations omitted).

To like effect, the hearing officer in *Maynard School District,* 20 IDELR 394 (SEA Ark. 1993), stated that if a student is identified as needing special education and related services, he or she is entitled to an evaluation for possible assistive technology devices to be included in the IEP.

In *Pasadena Independent School District,* 21 IDELR 482 (SEA Tex. 1994), the evaluation of a young man with multiple disabilities, including autism and mental retardation, recommended an augmentative communication device as a supplementary aid. Because the school district presented no evidence to support not providing it, a hearing officer ordered inclusion of the device in the student's IEP.

The 1997 Amendments codify the OSEP policy letters cited above, providing in Section 614(d)(3)(v) that IEP Teams consider "whether the child requires assistive technology devices and services."

12. Should the assistive technology devices or services the IEP team determines are required for FAPE be included in the IEP?

Yes. All the OSEP policy letters cited in Question 11, as well as other similar letters, make it clear that any such services must be included in the student's IEP. For example, in *Letter to Anonymous,* 18 IDELR 627 (OSEP 1991), OSEP states: "[T]he child's IEP must include a specific statement of such [assistive technology devices or] services. 34 C.F.R. § 300.346." To the extent appropriate, that statement must include the amount of services. Appendix C to 34 C.F.R. Part 300, Question 51.

Further, as with all other items of special education, related services or supplementary aids and services, all assistive technology devices included in a student's IEP must be provided. *See, e.g., Boone County (WV) Sch. Dist.,* 24 IDELR 475 (OCR 1995) (the school district provided all the assistive technology devices and services included in the student's IEP, including a touch screen, a computer and an augmentative communication device).

What is not clear is where in the IEP assistive technology or services should be addressed. As discussed in Question 13 below, an assistive technology device or service may be considered as special education, a related service, or a supplementary aid or service. 34 C.F.R. § 300.308. Should the item to be provided be included in the appropriate section of the IEP or should there be a new section? That was the question posed to OSEP in *Letter to Anonymous,* 24 IDELR 854 (OSEP 1996). OSEP's response: It is a matter of state or local law or policy. "Structure and organization of the IEP document is left to the discretion of the State and local education agency." 24 IDELR at 854.

Interestingly, in light of the new language contained in Section 614(d)(3)(v) of the 1997 Amendments (set out in Question 11), a statement of necessary assistive technology aids and services is not specifically included as a required component of an IEP document. As discussed in Question 13 below, it is not clear whether such an item is considered special education or a related service, making identification required on that basis. Further, it is not clear whether such an item should be considered as included within the scope of the newly defined term "supplementary aids and services" (Section 602(29)), compelling identification in the IEP document on that basis. Section 614(d)(3)(v).

13. Is a necessary assistive technology device considered special education or a related service?

According to IDEA regulations, an assistive technology device (or service) can be either special education or a related service. It can even be a supplementary aid or service.

34 C.F.R. § 300.308 provides:

Each public agency shall ensure that assistive technology devices or services, or both, as those terms are defined in §§ 300.5-.6, are made available to a child with a disability if required as part of the child's—

(a) Special education under § 300.17;

(b) Related services under § 300.16; or

(c) Supplementary aids and services under § 300.550(b)(2).

As explained by OSEP in its *Letter to Seiler,* 20 IDELR 1216 (OSEP 1993), the effect of this regulation is to limit the provision of assistive technology and services to those which are required for a child to receive FAPE. Not every device or service that helps a child to improve, maintain or increase functional capabilities will, for that reason alone, be required for FAPE.

The impact of classifying the device or service as one or the other of the three possible categories is not particularly clear. In theory, different standards apply to determinations about whether a student needs individualized instruction (special education), a related service, or a supplementary aid or service. Few published opinions explore how the categorization makes a difference in deciding whether or not to provide, once the IEP team determines that the device or item of service is needed for educational purposes.[5]

One administrative opinion that approaches this issue well is *Board of Education of Smithtown Central School District,* 22 IDELR 818 (SEA N.Y. 1995). In that case, the parents of an eight-year-old with multiple disabilities claimed that a frequency modulated auditory trainer (FM trainer) would amplify the voice of the child's teacher and enable him to be less distracted by the background noise in his classroom.

The parents' expert, seemingly adopting a maximization standard, testified that it would be " 'more of a struggle' for the child to benefit from instruction without the service." The review officer, though, made it clear that the *Rowley* standard applies when considering whether an assistive technology device should be provided. Because the child was making academic progress and social gains without the device, he did not need it to receive FAPE.

More pertinently for our question, the parents also argued that the FM trainer was necessary as a supplementary aid or service to ensure that the student remains in his least restrictive environment. Again the review officer rejected their position. Supplementary aids and services under 34 C.F.R. § 300.308(c) relate to assistive technology or services required to assist in regular education classroom placement. In this instance, the student's LRE was a special education class and would remain so, even with an FM trainer.

What is clear, though, is that to the extent a student needs an assistive technology device for FAPE, the school district is financially responsible for its acquisition, as well as its maintenance. *See, e.g., Letter to Cohen,* 19 IDELR 278 (OSEP 1992); *Letter to Anonymous,* 18 IDELR 627 (OSEP 1991). In that respect, assistive technology devices are unlike technological devices that medically fragile students may need to attend school.

14. How does an IEP team make decisions about whether to provide an assistive technology device or service to a student with a disability?

The IEP team must determine whether a child, in light of his or her particular educational needs, requires an assistive technology device or service in order to receive FAPE in accordance with applicable IEP requirements (34 C.F.R. §§ 300.340-300.350). *See, e.g., Letter to Anonymous,* 18 IDELR 627 (OSEP 1991).

---

[5] *See* Question 14 in this chapter, *infra.*

Consistent with the requirement for individualization of review, the Department of Education does not maintain a predetermined listing of assistive technology devices or services. That was the question asked and answered by OSEP in *Letter to Naon,* 22 IDELR 888 (OSEP 1995), and the implications are clear. School districts should not base their own decisions about which devices or services to provide to a student with a disability on a categorical basis. *See also* the discussion of *Board of Educ. of Smithtown Cent. Sch. Dist.,* 22 IDELR 818 (SEA N.Y. 1995) in Question 13, *supra.*

15. If the student needs an assistive technology device both inside and outside school, must the school district provide it?

OSEP has traditionally taken the position that, as a general matter, a school district is not required to purchase devices the student would require regardless of whether or not he or she was attending school. However, this exclusion does not apply if the IEP team determines, as it is permitted to do, that the student needs the device or service to receive FAPE and accordingly includes it in his or her IEP. *See, e.g, Letter to Anonymous,* 24 IDELR 388 (OSEP 1995); *Letter to Bachus,* 22 IDELR 629 (OSEP 1994); *Letter to Galloway,* 22 IDELR 373 (OSEP 1994). In *Letter to Anonymous,* for example, OSEP stated that a public agency's obligation to maintain or purchase a pulmonary nebulizer device would depend on how that device was characterized and addressed in the student's IEP.

Left unstated in all these policy letters are any criteria for determining when a student who needs an assistive technology device inside and outside school would "need" or "not need" the device to provide FAPE. In fact, in its response in *Letter to Bachus,* OSEP declined to address directly that portion of the inquiry that asked if the parent's inability to afford the device for the student (in that instance, eyeglasses) made the school district's provision necessary.

16. Is a school district responsible for providing eyeglasses, a hearing aid or other personally prescribed device for a student as an assistive technology device?

Generally no, but it is possible that a school district would consider such a personal device an assistive technology device, thus requiring the IEP team to include a personal device in the IEP of a student with a disability in those instances when provision is necessary for FAPE.

While personal use devices such as eyeglasses or hearing aids are not "high tech," they may nonetheless be considered assistive technology devices for purposes of the IDEA. *Letter to Seiler,* 20 IDELR 1216 (OSEP 1993). The 1990 amendments to the IDEA added the provision of assistive technology devices and services to the schools' mandates under the IDEA, but failed to make clear whether items such as eyeglasses or hearing aids were covered devices. The definitions of the devices and services added to the IDEA were taken directly from the Technology Related Assistance for Individuals Act of 1988. Because the preamble to this act and the discussion of the IDEA amendments refer to new technology and advancements, eyeglasses and hearing aids would not seem to qualify as covered new devices. But both pieces of legislation were deliberately written quite broadly. As a result, the question of school districts' responsibility for provision of such items remains essentially unanswered.

The 1997 Amendments do nothing to resolve this uncertainty, perpetuating the IDEA's definitions of assistive technology devices in Section 602(1).

17. Are school districts required to provide personal computers for home use by students with disabilities?

They may be in some instances, but that decision, like all others concerning the educational programming for students with disabilities, must be made on an individual basis.

Computers are clearly high-technology devices that may provide particular support for students with motor or learning disabilities, among other things. They also may be assistive technology devices, as defined in 34 C.F.R. § 300.5, that can be used for educational purposes. Nevertheless, not every student with a disability who would benefit from provision of a computer to use at home is entitled to receive one as a district-funded assistive technology device.

The decision as to whether a child needs to use an assistive technology device or service in settings other than school (such as the child's home) must be made on an individual basis. School districts are required to provide computers for use at home by students with disabilities only if such home use is necessary for the provision of FAPE and is so specified in the student's IEP. *Letter to Anonymous,* 18 IDELR 627 (OSEP 1991).

With the growing awareness of the educational benefits possible with home computer use, there likely will be more decisions like *Garcia v. California State Department of Education Hearing Office,* 24 IDELR 547 (E.D. Cal. 1996). In that case, the parents claimed provision of a multimedia computer for home use was necessary to provide FAPE for a sixth grader with hearing deficiencies and a learning disability. The district court affirmed the hearing officer's finding from the testimony of teachers that the student would not need a computer to do homework and had access to a computer at school for other purposes consistent with his IEP.

18. Is the choice of the particular assistive technology device within the sole discretion of the school district?

Generally, the choice of a particular assistive technology device is left to the school district, provided the device it selects provides an appropriate level of educational benefit or support. But, in a few published administrative decisions the parents have successfully challenged the school district's selection.

The parents in *Greenwood County School District #52*, 19 IDELR 355 (SEA Cal. 1992), convinced a hearing officer that the school district should purchase an augmentative communication device called "The Liberator" for their 13-year-old daughter with multiple disabilities and limited communication skills. The district had proposed purchasing the less expensive device called "The Intro Talker," but the parents presented expert testimony that the student had the potential to acquire the higher-level language skills for which only their preferred device provided options.

The school district argued that cost consideration was an allowable factor in its choice of device. While the hearing officer generally agreed, it found that cost cannot be the end of the story. "While cost is a consideration, it cannot be the determining factor under [the IDEA]. The law requires that [the student's] IEP offer an educational program which gives her an opportunity to progress." 19 IDELR at 356.

The parents of a four-year-old student with developmental disabilities also prevailed in a due process challenge to the school district's selection of an assistive device to load their child on and off the school bus. In *Davis School District*, 18 IDELR 696 (SEA Utah 1992), the school district argued that the choice of a stroller-type device for loading and unloading the student was not an educational issue, but a transportation methodology issue within its sole discretion. The parents argued that, to the contrary, the device was an assistive technology device (properly considered a related service) and thus subject to the IEP process. The hearing officer agreed, allowing the parents to present evidence that the device they favored was necessary to provide FAPE.

School districts have had some success in published administrative decisions concerning selection of computers as assistive technology devices. For example, the review officer in *Board of East Hampton Bays Union Free School District*, 21 IDELR 881 (SEA N.Y. 1994), held that, when the student's IEP team recommended that he be provided a lap-top computer without further recommending either a model or software, the school principal acted within his discretion in replacing the computer with another model. (The difference: the replacement did not have software for games.)

The student in *Granite School District*, 22 IDELR 405 (SEA Utah 1995), couldn't even get a lap-top. In that case the hearing officer held that the school district has the discretion to supply the assistive technology needs identified in the IEP by allowing the student access to a computer in the classroom. Similarly, the hearing officer considering the parent's claims in *In re Child with a Disability*, 21 IDELR 749 (SEA Conn. 1994), ruled that the school district was not required to replace a computer that had been provided for the student's home use with one of the same make or model. Instead, replacement with a letterboard met IDEA requirements because the letterboard also provided FAPE.

19. Is a school district responsible for damages and repair to a computer provided for home use?

Generally yes. When a district provides a personal computer for home use as an assistive technology device in accordance with a student's IEP, the computer remains the property of the district, with the student's use being allowed on a restricted loan basis. It is consistent with the IDEA to make the school district responsible for at least reasonable repairs.

The definition of assistive technology services in 34 C.F.R. § 300.6(b)-(c) includes not only "purchasing, leasing, or otherwise providing for the assistive technology devices," but also "supplying . . . repairing or replacing . . . them." Thus, OSEP has stated that when a school district purchases a computer for use by a student at school or at home, it is responsible for maintaining the computer. *Letter to Anonymous,* 21 IDELR 1057 (OSEP 1994).

It is possible for a school district to make parents responsible for repairs resulting from damage caused by unauthorized or unwarranted use. Arguably, restrictions on unauthorized use and responsibility for unwarranted damages to a computer provided for use at home are defensible, provided they take into consideration the nature and severity of the child's disability. Any mutual agreement made regarding how to address these issues should be formalized in the IEP.

20. If a student's IEP includes use of an at-home computer purchased by the parents, is the school district responsible for repairs or replacement?

While the IDEA does not require school districts to assume such responsibility, OSEP believes it would be reasonable and consistent with the statute if they did so.

In *Letter to Anonymous,* 21 IDELR 1057 (OSEP 1994), OSEP responded to an inquiry concerning a school district's responsibility for repairs to a computer purchased by parents by stating:

> Federal law . . . does not specify the responsibility of a public agency . . . where parents elect to purchase a needed device from their own funds, and the public agency, with parental permission, uses the family owned device in connection with the implementation of the student's IEP either at school or at home, as specified in the IEP. In many cases, it may be reasonable for public agencies to assume liability for family-owned devices used to implement a child's IEP either at school or at home, since the public agency is responsible for providing assistive technology devices and services that are necessary parts of the child's special education, related services, or supplementary aids and services, as specified in the child's IEP. Further, without the use of the family-owned device specified in the IEP, the public agency would be required both to provide and maintain a needed device. On the other hand, there may be situations in which assuming liability for a family-owned device would

create a greater responsibility for the public agency than the responsibility that exists under Federal law.

21 IDELR at 1059.

Extended School Year Programming

21. Is the school district's decision of whether to provide extended school year (ESY) programming unilateral or subject to the IEP process?

There is no doubt that school districts must involve parents in the determination of whether to provide ESY programming to students with disabilities. Accordingly, the school district must convene an IEP meeting to discuss the issue. The decision whether or not to provide, or what to provide and where to provide it, is reviewable in due process.

The traditional school year continues for approximately nine months or 180 school days. Addressing the issue of whether this time limitation can be raised to relieve school districts of providing summer services to all children with disabilities, most, if not all, courts have answered no. *See, e.g, Battle v. Pennsylvania,* 1979-80 EHLR 551:647 (3d Cir. 1980); *Georgia Ass'n of Retarded Citizens v. McDaniel,* 1984-85 EHLR 556:187 (11th Cir. 1983); *Crawford v. Pittman,* 1983-84 EHLR 555:107 (5th Cir. 1983). All told, there is no serious doubt that written or unwritten policies restricting all children to a fixed school year violates the IDEA. *See also Gebhardt v. Ambach,* 1982-83 EHLR 554:130 (W.D.N.Y. 1982) (State school for blind could not simply decline to provide ESY services because its facility would be closed for renovations during the summer; it had to take affirmative actions to make other arrangements for students whose IEPs called for ESY).

Having established the entitlement, courts were then called on to resolve a second wave of litigation, in these instances attempting to establish standards to determine which children should receive ESY services. Two leading cases propose different standards: the Fifth Circuit's *Alamo Heights Independent School District v. State Board of Education,* 1985-86 EHLR 557:315 (5th Cir. 1986) and the Tenth Circuit's *Johnson v. Independent School District No. 4,* 17 EHLR 170 (10th Cir. 1990).

Alamo Heights established the need for the IEP team to conduct a regression-recoupment analysis to determine if ESY services were a necessary part of an appropriate education. All children experience regression, loss of learned skills during extended school breaks resulting in the need to relearn at the start of the new school year. When a child with a disability has a sufficiently severe regression-recoupment problem, ESY services are a component of his or her appropriate educational program. Regression-recoupment problems triggering the need for ESY services occur when: (1) a child suffers an inordinate or disproportionate degree of regression during that portion of the year in which the customary 180-day school year is not in session, and (2) it takes an inordinate or unacceptable length of time for the child to recoup those lost skills (academic, emotional or behavioral) upon returning to school.

Johnson took a multifactorial approach under which regression-recoupment was just one of many items the IEP team needed to consider. In a footnote, the court identified a range of factors that may need to be considered, making it clear, however, that those factors were neither exhaustive nor necessarily all pertinent in any particular case.

- Degree of regression suffered in the past

- Exact time of the regression

- Ability of the parents to provide educational structure at home

- Student's rate of progress

- Student's behavioral and physical problems

- Availability of alternative resources

- Ability of the student to interact with nondisabled children

- Areas of the student's curriculum that need continuous attention

- Student's vocational needs

- Whether the requested services are "extraordinary" for the student's disabling condition, as opposed to an integral part of a program for populations of students with the same disabilities

17 EHLR at 176 n.9.

Whatever the particular substantive standards, there is universal agreement about the procedure for assessing those standards. As OSEP has confirmed in numerous policy letters: The determination as to whether or not a child with a disability needs ESY services to receive FAPE must be made by the child's IEP team, based on a consideration of the child's unique needs and consistent with the procedures for IEP meetings set out in 34 C.F.R. §§ 300.340-300.350. *See, e.g., Letter to Harkin,* EHLR 213:263 (OSEP 1989); *Letter to Myers,* EHLR 213:255 (OSEP 1989); *Letter to Baugh,* EHLR 211:481 (OSEP 1987).

Although many new published decisions concern an individual child's entitlement to ESY services, few recent disputes involve the school district's procedural compliance as a general matter. School districts appear to consistently convene IEP meetings to evaluate the child's individual needs.

The school district involved in the decision in *Reusch v. Fountain,* 21 IDELR 1107 (D. Md. 1994), was a notable exception. In that case the District Court for the District of Maryland found a startling number of procedural and substantive violations and concluded that the school district's attitude toward ESY, taken as a whole, was "hostile." The author discusses here those sections of the opinion that addressed procedural violations of the IEP process.

The district had a two-step review procedure for ESY services eligibility: (1) review by a school-level committee (similar to the traditional IEP meeting), (2) followed by review by a district-level committee. At the first step, ESY eligibility could be either denied or referred to consideration by the second level of review. That second level had final authority for eligibility determinations, as well as sole authority to determine the duration, location and content of the services. The school-level meeting could not determine eligibility. Its denials were not reviewed at the district level as a matter of course; the parents had to affirmatively request review by the district level. The plaintiff parents claimed that the unique system of review (no other services in the district were subject to this process) was designed to—and did—enable the district to evade its responsibilities to provide FAPE to all eligible students with disabilities by, among other things, diminishing the decision-making authority of the IEP team and marginalizing parental and teacher participation in ESY programming.

While the court did acknowledge that school districts could have legitimate administrative concerns about how to most efficiently provide ESY, it agreed with the parents that the school district's two-step process was not "the benign engine of efficiency" the school district claimed it was. Rather, it deprived students with disabilities of their right to receive ESY when appropriate.

In a footnote, the court pointed out that the school district attempted to bolster their legal position with personal attacks on the plaintiffs and their counsel. The court took no such approach. Rather than dwelling on the school district's motivation, it presented a precise legal analysis of the manner in which the review process violated the IEP procedural requirements set out at 34 C.F.R. §§ 300.344-300.345.

> It is readily apparent that the [school district's] two-level structure undermines the viability of the [IEP] committees. An IEP committee not authorized to factor ESY into a student's overall educational program cannot be deemed a properly constituted IEP committee. . . .
>
> . . .
>
> The Court further finds the two-step process to create problems regarding parent and teacher participation and timely and individualized decision-making guaranteed under the IDEA. . . . In the [school district scheme] the extra [district level] meeting creates scheduling conflicts and additional burdens and inconveniences that interfere with those rights. In particular, the centralized [ ] meetings effectively prevent a large number of school-based teachers from being present at the ESY discussions of their students.

21 IDELR at 1112.

Apparently, the court decision in *Reusch v. Fountain,* did not make the requirements for deciding if ESY services should be provided clear in all parts of the state. In *Howard*

County Public Schools, 24 IDELR 719 (SEA Md. 1996), the parents of a nine-year-old student with autism were awarded reimbursement for the cost of a summer program in which they unilaterally enrolled their son because the school district failed to develop a proper IEP for ESY services. The IEP team failed to properly consider all the critical life skills objectives from the student's current IEP. Rather, the IEP team appeared to do a cursory review of the IEP, failing to consider the student's distinct needs and behaviors.

Chapter 8

Incarceration, Expulsion and Transfers

FAPE for imprisoned students with disabilities? Yes. It is a settled issue that a youth with a disability does not lose his or her entitlement to FAPE because of criminal conduct and consequential punishment. If that individual has a disability and was duly enrolled in school without yet having graduated at the time of imprisonment, his or her right to FAPE continues, just as it would for a hospitalization or other change in placement not occasioned by educational needs.

Such a right exists in theory, but how often could it be an issue in practice? The reader may be surprised at the increasing number of youths with disabilities who are both IDEA-eligible and convicted felons serving their time in adult prisons.

Some states are surprised, apparently, because they have been caught short not providing mandated services to those eligible members of their prison populations. Since 1992, the United States Department of Education has issued findings to 26 states which either were not providing services to the inmates properly or not providing them at all.

Corrective actions were adopted by each of those states to satisfy federal requirements. That put the state of California in a weak position. In October 1996 OSEP formally warned the state that it could become ineligible for $280 million in federal grants if state education officials did not provide special education to disabled youths in its adult prisons, a population that numbered between 6,500 and 8,500 in 1995. California has agreed to provide FAPE by accepting a compliance offer to phase in special education over three years. A hearing with OSEP, scheduled to take place after publication of this book, will determine whether the state needs the full three years for implementation.

Even with the best intentions, states face enormous challenges in providing special education to disabled youths in the prison environment. In most states, special education programs in prisons are administered by the state's corrections department. In other states, either the department of education or a separate local educational agency (LEA) handles the programs. Regardless of who administers the programs, provision of services in prisons implicates concerns totally distinct from educating children in public school settings. The IEP for an incarcerated student must be designed to reflect prison placements. It cannot address the inmate's educational needs without carefully considering the legitimate security and operational concerns of the prison and classification of the student-inmate.

Clarifications and changes made in the 1997 Amendments, as discussed in relevant part in this chapter, may relieve some of the confusion and make provision of FAPE by educational agencies less burdensome, but ultimately leaves the larger problems of an ever-increasing population of criminal youth unresolved.

Incarcerated Students

1. Is a school district required to provide FAPE for a student with a disability who becomes incarcerated?

Some public entity within the state is required to provide FAPE for incarcerated students, but whether the responsible public agency is the school district the student attended before being taken into custody is a matter of state law.

While the obligation to continue to provide special education services to criminals may stick in the craw of some state legislatures, federal law is unambiguous on this point: States are obligated to provide special education services to otherwise eligible prison inmates or pretrial detainees. The fact that they have been charged with or convicted of a crime does not diminish the substantive rights, procedural safeguards and remedies provided under the IDEA to students with disabilities and their parents. *State of Connecticut—Unified Sch. Dist. #1 v. Department of Educ.*, 24 IDELR 685 (Conn. Super. Ct. 1996); *Nashua Sch. Dist. v. State of New Hampshire*, 23 IDELR 427 (N.H. 1995); *Alexander S. v. Boyd*, 22 IDELR 139 (D.S.C. 1995); *Donnell C. v. Illinois State Bd. of Educ.*, 20 IDELR 514 (N.D. Ill. 1993).

The issue of educational services for incarcerated students with disabilities affects more of the youthful prison population than one might think. OCR noted in 1986 that "most correctional authorities agree that there is an extremely high incidence of learning disabilities among youthful offenders." *California Dep't of Youth Authority*, EHLR 352:307 (OCR 1986). Presenting testimony in *Alexander S. v. Boyd*, the South Carolina Department of Juvenile Justice admitted that perhaps as many as 50 percent of the state's juvenile prison population need special education.

Despite the clear mandate that special education services be provided to eligible inmates,[1] the IDEA takes its typical "hands-off" approach concerning which public

---

[1] IDEA regulations at 34 C.F.R. § 300.2(b)(4) extend the requirements of the law to all state correctional facilities involved in the education of children with disabilities.

agency within a state is responsible for providing and funding such services. 34 C.F.R. §§ 300.152, 300.600.

Some states have created special school districts given responsibility for some or all of the state's prison population, much like an intermediate unit. *State of Connecticut—Unified School District #1 v. Department of Education,* explains how this kind of statutory scheme plays out. Neighboring state New Hampshire takes the opposite approach. In *Nashua School District v. State of New Hampshire* school districts unsuccessfully challenged the state law requiring local school districts to enter state prisons, perform evaluations, hold IEP meetings and develop IEPs for incarcerated special education students.

The 1997 Amendments provide that incarcerated students with disabilities retain their entitlement to FAPE (with two exceptions discussed in Question 3 of this chapter and Question 1 of chapter 10). The state, however, has discretion to assign to any (state) public agency the responsibility for compliance for those young people with disabilities who have been convicted as adults and are incarcerated in adult prisons. Section 612(a)(11)(C).

2. Is the responsible public agency required to provide, or arrange for the provision of, all of the services listed in a newly incarcerated student's most recently approved IEP?

No. Generally the special circumstances of imprisonment—confinement, conformity to established prison routines, and generally applicable rules, court dates, and the like—make continuation of an IEP designed for implementation in a school environment impossible, or nearly so. Thus, the responsible public agency has no duty to implement the student's most recently approved IEP in all cases. *State of Connecticut—Unified Sch. Dist. #1 v. Department of Educ.,* 24 IDELR 685 (Conn. Super. Ct. 1996).

The same holds true when the nature of the student's confinement changes, according to the district court for the District of New Hampshire in its well-reasoned opinion in *New Hampshire Department of Education and New Hampshire Department of Corrections v. City of Manchester,* 23 IDELR 1057 (D.N.H. 1996). The responsible agency need not continue a previously approved IEP agreed to in contemplation of different circumstances.

The student in that case was a 20-year-old man with emotional and learning disabilities serving 15 to 30 years for manslaughter. After due process, the responsible school district was ordered to develop an IEP to be implemented in prison.[2] That IEP provided for a minimum of 5.25 hours of daily instruction and counseling, to be provided in the education building at the state prison. At the time the IEP was designed, the student's security risk classification permitted him to attend classes in that building. However, several times the student's problem behavior resulted in a change in his security classification to one

---

[2] *See* Question 4, *infra,* concerning IEP meeting requirements for incarcerated students.

involving housing in a separate building and limited contact with the general prison population. Following the general guidelines, the student could not attend his classes or counseling as envisioned in the IEP and did not receive the specified 5.25 hours of daily instruction. He was provided some services, but they were limited to once-a-week meetings with an instructor to receive and review in-cell work assignments.

The school district (recall that in New Hampshire local school districts are responsible for providing FAPE to imprisoned students) argued that it had implied authority to implement the agreed IEP only to the extent permitted by emerging prison security interests. The student claimed otherwise: the IEP was a contract that, once agreed to, must be implemented regardless of the student's situation vis-à-vis prison security interests or disciplinary concerns.

The court, in ruling on the student's claims, took a middle ground, as discussed in Question 3 below, allowing modifications and requiring compliance with IDEA procedural safeguards. On the way to its holding, the court discussed why the IDEA does not require provision of all the services listed in an incarcerated student's most recently approved IEP in all cases.

> At the outset it should be recognized that the tail of [the student's] IEP cannot wag the dog of his prison sentence, nor can it serve to exempt him from legitimate administrative and disciplinary systems in place within the prison. Stated somewhat differently, [the student] is not entitled to an IEP which effectively insulates him from prison discipline and control if a different IEP could be developed which might serve both his educational needs and the prison's valid security interests, or at least one that did not undermine legitimate penological interests.

23 IDELR at 1061.

3. When the educational needs of an incarcerated student with a disability, as identified in his or her IEP, conflict with the need of a prison to maintain security and control, which takes precedence?

While more cases debating this important issue may be forthcoming, currently the only opinion is that of the district court in *New Hampshire Department of Education and New Hampshire Department of Corrections v. City of Manchester*, 23 IDELR 1057 (D.N.H. 1996). That court declined to take a firm position, although there is a suggestion that, if push comes to shove, a prison's legitimate interest in security and discipline take precedence over a disabled prisoner's educational needs.

As discussed in more detail in Question 2 above, the school district could not implement the student-prisoner's IEP because he had been reclassified for security purposes such that he was not permitted to leave his cell to attend classes and counseling sessions. Instead of 5.25 hours of daily classroom instruction and services, he received only one hour of one-on-one instruction weekly.

A hearing officer held that the school district had violated the IDEA and ordered implementation of the IEP as written, with the prison being given the option of implementing the IEP by appropriately modifying the student-prisoner's separate housing unit (SHU) or by allowing him to participate in the program for the general population, despite his security classification. The necessary minimum modifications, according to the hearing officer, included

> the creation of a separate area within the SHU to be used as a classroom for [the student] and other educationally handicapped students, the designation of a separate study area within SHU . . . , and the provision of "interactive" audio and/or video equipment so that [the student] might have "access" to other students when receiving daily instruction in courses where more than one student is normally present.

23 IDELR at 1063 n.4.

This was too much for the district court. It refused to affirm the hearing officer's order for relief, instead ordering the parties to convene an IEP meeting to, in essence, negotiate in good faith and with flexibility, what type of program could provide both an educational benefit for the student and protect the prison's interest in preserving order and discipline.

The court proceeded on the premise that individuals of good will can accommodate both the student and the prison. But what if they can't? What if these interests are irreconcilable? The court need not—and did not—squarely confront this issue. What it did say in this regard is revealing, however, of where it might stand.

> Dangerous prisoners cannot use an IEP as a "free pass" to avoid legitimate penological restrictions and roam the general population. Nor can a prisoner's IEP operate, without regard for penological concerns, to require the prison to (a) assign personal guards to escort such a prisoner to, during, and from his educational classes, (b) restructure its disciplinary programs, or (c) substantially reconfigure its physical plant simply to accommodate that inmates's current IEP, at least not when the IEP can be appropriately modified to satisfactorily address all competing interests. This is particularly true when the inmate's own deliberate and volitional misconduct results in his removal from the general population, thereby frustrating the prison's efforts to deliver the educational program described in the IEP.

23 IDELR at 1061.

The balance between prison security and disabled students' rights to receive services while incarcerated caught the attention of Congress, which addressed the issue in the 1997 Amendments. Congress weighed in on the side of security in Section 612(d)(6)(B), which states as follows:

> If a child with a disability is convicted as an adult under State law and incarcerated in an adult prison, the child's IEP Team may modify the child's IEP or placement notwithstanding the requirements of sections 612(a)(5)(A)

and 614(d)(1)(A) [the least restrictive environment or IEP document provisions of the law] if the State has demonstrated a bona fide security or compelling penological interest that cannot otherwise be accommodated.

Neither "bona fide" nor "compelling" is further defined, raising the possibility of continuing disputes on this issue.

4. Must a responsible public agency convene an IEP meeting to develop an IEP for a newly incarcerated student with a disability?

Generally, yes, although limited case law relieves an agency in the case of short-term stays.

A responsible public agency generally must convene an IEP meeting to develop an IEP at the beginning of the period of detention. *See, e.g., State of Connecticut—Unified Sch. Dist. #1 v. Department of Educ.*, 24 IDELR 685 (Conn. Super. Ct. 1996); *Alexander S. v. Boyd*, 22 IDELR 139 (D.S.C. 1995). As a general matter, a school district can change a student's placement without conducting an IEP meeting if the same programming is to be provided in the new setting. But the likelihood that an IEP designed for another setting can be implemented *in toto* in prison is so small that a meeting for review and revision should almost always be held.

As discussed by the court in *Alexander S. v. Boyd*, though, the administrative burdens imposed on state agencies in complying with this aspect of federal special education law can outweigh the benefits to the disabled students involved when the student will be residing in the detention facility only for a short-time.

In that case, state law interpreted federal requirements to mandate development of two IEPs: one for the juvenile's stay at the Reception and Evaluation Center ("Center"), where officials considered long-term confinement of the student, and another upon any confinement to a long-term institution. By law, the juvenile offender could not remain at the Center for more than 45 days; evidence at trial established that the average stay was 21 days.

The class action plaintiffs challenged, among other things, the failure of the state to ensure that IEPs were developed upon placement at the Center. The state conceded that this was the case, but the court found that ordering that such IEPs be developed would be a "drain on the resources and staff" of the state's Department of Juvenile Justice, resources and staff more urgently needed to adequately serve those disabled students who are committed to long-term institutions. Looking for a more beneficial resolution, the court requested and then relied on an interpretive memorandum prepared by the United States Department of Justice, Civil Rights Division[3] that opined:

---

[3] Not cited sufficiently for identification.

In the case of short-term temporary confinement, the State may meet its obligation under IDEA and Section 504 . . . by implementing the IEP from the previous school district or placement instead of developing a new one. The IEP must be implemented to the extent possible in the temporary setting. To the extent the implementation of the old IEP is impossible, services that approximate, as close as possible, the old IEP must be provided.

22 IDELR at 153.

The court thus held that the Center was not required to develop new IEPs, but rather was required to implement the most recently approved IEP to the extent possible while the students remained in that placement. Interestingly, while OCR was not cited in the opinion, it took the same position with regard to short-term transitional placements of juveniles in 1986 in *California Department of Youth Authority,* EHLR 352:307 (OCR 1986). Similarly, in *Del Norte County (CA) Office of Education,* 20 IDELR 1070 (OCR 1993), OCR found that the county office of education fulfilled its obligations under Section 504 when the juvenile hall in which juveniles were placed for short-term incarceration informally contacted the county and continued to provide the services received in the home school, to the extent possible.

Expelled Students

5. Must the school district convene an IEP meeting to develop an IEP for use during a student's long-term suspension or expulsion?

The threshold issue is whether a school district is obligated to continue to provide educational services to a properly expelled (or long-term suspended) student with a disability. Assuming that question is answered in the affirmative, it seems clear that an IEP meeting will need to be convened.

The school district's duty to provide services to properly expelled students with disabilities is a subject beyond the scope of this publication. Briefly, until the enactment of the 1997 Amendments neither the IDEA statute nor its regulations explicitly addressed whether school districts could expel students with disabilities. This is a sensitive issue involving the intersection of federal and state law.

Courts had spoken, though, about expelling students with disabilities for misconduct related to their disabilities. As explained by OSEP in its *Letter to Lieberman,* 20 IDELR 1463 (OSEP 1993):

Generally, student discipline is a state and local matter. However, when students with specified disabilities are involved, the requirements of IDEA become relevant. In brief, in the case of *Honig v. Doe* [1987-88 EHLR 559:231] (1988), the U.S.

> Supreme Court interpreted the IDEA as precluding school authorities from unilaterally removing [without parental consent] a student with a disability from school for more than 10 school days for misconduct growing out of the student's disability.

20 IDELR at 1464.

Parental consent is not the entire issue, either. Under pre-*Honig* court interpretations of the IDEA, school districts cannot impose a long-term suspension or expulsion on account of misconduct that is related to a student's disability. *See, e.g., S-1 v. Turlington,* 1980-81 EHLR 552:267 (5th Cir. 1981).

More controversy surrounded the question of whether a school district had to continue to provide educational services to a "properly expelled" student (one expelled for misconduct determined to be unrelated to his or her disability). OSEP consistently took the position that the IDEA requires school districts to continue to provide educational services to properly expelled or long-term suspended students. Its most recent pronouncement to that effect was the comprehensive *OSEP Memorandum 95-16,* 22 IDELR 531 (OSEP 1995). OSEP's position was supported by the Seventh Circuit Court of Appeals in *Metropolitan School District v. Davila,* 18 IDELR 1226 (7th Cir. 1992), but rejected by the Fourth Circuit in *Virginia Department of Education v. Riley,* 25 IDELR 309 (4th Cir. 1997). Congress supported the view of OSEP, stating in Section 612(a)(1)(A) of the 1997 Amendments that properly suspended or expelled students (those disciplined for conduct not related to their disabilities) are entitled to FAPE.

OSEP Memorandum 95-16 does not explicitly address the precise contours of the programming required for properly expelled or suspended students with disabilities. In fact, it declines to do so. The memorandum does make clear that the IDEA mandate of individualized programming continues in these situations. "During the period of disciplinary exclusion from school, each disabled student must continue to be offered a program of appropriate educational services that is individually designed to meet his or her unique learning needs." 22 IDELR at 536.

It is equally clear that the student's IEP will need to be changed to reflect his or her new out-of-school circumstances. Thus, an IEP meeting should be convened. That was the holding of the hearing officer in *Beaumont Independent School District,* 21 IDELR 261 (SEA Tex. 1994). In that case, the school district should have developed an IEP setting forth the services and placement it proposed to offer a properly expelled student, and its failure to do so denied the student FAPE. (The violation was found insignificant, however, because the parents could have maintained appropriate educational services for the student pending the hearing by invoking the stay-put provision and returning the student to his pre-expulsion placement).

6. Must a school district convene an IEP meeting before it takes action to suspend a student with a disability for 10 days or less?

No. Under the IDEA, school districts *may* elect to do so, and in some circumstances convening an IEP meeting is advisable. As explained by OSEP in *OSEP Memorandum 95-16*, 22 IDELR 531 (OSEP 1995):

> There are no specific actions under Federal law that school districts are required to take during this time period. If the school district believes that further action to address the misconduct and prevent future misconduct is warranted, it is advisable to use the period of suspension for preparatory steps. For example, school officials may convene a meeting to initiate review of the student's current IEP to determine whether implementation of a behavior management plan would be appropriate. If long-term disciplinary measures are being considered, this time also could be used to convene an appropriate group to determine whether the misconduct was a manifestation of the student's disability.

22 IDELR at 535.

The 1997 Amendments made significant changes to the rules governing the discipline of students with disabilities. See Section 615(k). Among them is the requirement set out in Section 615(k)(1) concerning, inter alia, short-term suspensions and similar disciplinary actions. Under subsection 615(k)(1)(B) the school district must take the following action either before or not later than 10 days after suspending a student with a disability:

(i) [I]f the local educational agency did not conduct a functional behavioral assessment and implement a behavioral intervention plan for such a behavior before the behavior that resulted in the suspension . . ., the agency shall convene an IEP meeting to develop an assessment plan to address that behavior; or

(ii) if the child already has a behavioral intervention plan, the IEP team shall review the plan and modify it, as necessary, to address the behavior.

7. Must a school district convene an IEP meeting to make a manifestation determination?

Under the IDEA the answer is no, although the individuals empowered to make a manifestation determination may, at the school district's option, be those who are required participants on the IEP team under 34 C.F.R. § 300.344(a)(1)—(5). Under the 1997 Amendments the answer is yes, as Section 615(k)(4) vests authority solely in the IEP Team.

As a threshold matter, a manifestation determination is not a decision about appropriate educational programming, although such a decision may flow from the determination. Rather, a manifestation determination is a determination about the relationship between misconduct and disability—whether the misconduct is: (1) a manifestation of the student's disability;[4] (2) a result of an inappropriate placement or program; or (3) unrelated to either the student's disability or failure to be provided a FAPE.

Under the IDEA, when a school district proposes to sanction the misconduct of student with a disability by expulsion, suspension for an indefinite period, or suspension for more than 10 consecutive school days, it first must make a manifestation determination. (A similar determination is required under Section 504. *OSEP Memorandum 95-16,* 22 IDELR 531 (OSEP 1995).)

Neither the IDEA nor its regulations specify who should make the manifestation determination. OSEP's position, as expressed consistently in policy letters and memoranda, is that the manifestation determination must be made by a group of persons knowledgeable about the student and the meaning of the evaluation data. That group may be either those persons who constitute the student's IEP team under 34 C.F.R. § 300.344(a)(1)-(5) or his or her multidisciplinary team under 34 C.F.R. § 300.533(a)(3). *OSEP Memorandum 95-16,* 22 IDELR 531 (OSEP 1995); *Letter to Case,* 22 IDELR 370 (OSEP 1994).

In some instances, school-level administrators who serve as disciplinarians make it clear to the school's special educators that an upcoming manifestation determination had better not impede the disciplinarian's ability to suspend or expel a student. To reduce pressure of this nature, some school districts have proposed the use of an "impartial team" from another school to make the manifestation determination. Despite this laudable objective, such an alternative does not comply with the requirement that the determination be made by persons knowledgeable about the student. *Letter to Case, supra.*

If a manifestation determination team is composed of the same individuals who make up the MDT for evaluations and placements, parents are not entitled to participate. Nonetheless, OCR has indicated that a manifestation determination team should include a parent. *Mobile County (AL) Sch. Dist.,* EHLR 353:378 (OCR 1989); *McKeesport (PA) Area Sch. Dist.,* EHLR 353:266 (OCR 1989).

---

[4] Courts have established different standards of required relatedness. In the Fourth Circuit Court of Appeals, for example, the standard is whether the misconduct is causally related to the disabling condition. School Board of the County of Prince William (VA) v. Malone, 1984-85 EHLR 556:406 (4th Cir. 1985). In the Fifth Circuit, the subtly less stringent standard requires that the misconduct bear a relationship to the disabling condition. S-1 v. Turlington, 1980-81 EHLR 552:267 (5th Cir. 1981).

Section 615(k)(4)(C) of the 1997 Amendments addresses manifestation determinations in detail. Subsection 615(k)(4)(C)(ii) sets the standard to be used by the IEP TEAM in deciding if a student's behavior was a manifestation of his or her disability.

Interstate/Intrastate Transfers

8. Must a school district implement the IEP of a student with a disability who transfers from a school district in another state?

No, each state has ultimate responsibility for establishing the standards under which special education and related services are provided for children with disabilities within that state. 34 C.F.R. § 300.600. Nothing in the IDEA compels a state to accept an IEP designed and found appropriate in another state.

This is the case even in those instances in which the parents of a student transferring from another state and the receiving school district are unable to agree on the student's new educational program, or even the interim placement pending resolution of their dispute. Further, the school district is not required to "approximate the services" contained in the previous IEP. Instead, as explained in *OSEP Memorandum 96-5*, 24 IDELR 320 (OSEP 1995), the school district into which the student has transferred should place the student in the regular educational program in accordance with 34 C.F.R. § 300.513(b).[5]

9. Must a school district convene an IEP meeting when a student with a disability transfers from another state?

The receiving district need not convene an IEP meeting in all instances, according to the guidance provided in *OSEP Memorandum 96-5*, 24 IDELR 320 (OSEP 1995).

After years of declining to respond to inquiries about how to handle interstate transfers, OSEP set out guidance to "assist States and school districts in safeguarding the rights of disabled students and their parents in interstate transfer situations." 24 IDELR at 321.

When a student with a disability transfers from a school district in one state (District A) to a district in another state (District B), the first step for District B is to determine whether or not to adopt the most recent evaluation and IEP performed by District A. District B could elect to implement the most recent IEP developed by District A, provided that District B determines that: (1) the student has a disability; (2) the most recent evaluation conducted by District A meets state and federal requirements; and (3) the most recent IEP developed by District A meets state education standards and federal IDEA requirements.

If these three conditions are met, District B is not required to conduct another IEP meeting provided that:

---

[5] 34 C.F.R. § 300.513(b) is the section of the IDEA stay-put provision that provides that, in the case of an initial admission to public school, "the child, with the consent of the parents, must be placed in the public school program until the completion of all the proceedings."

- a copy of the current IEP is available;

- the parents agree to use of the current IEP;

- District B believes the IEP is appropriate for the student; and

- District B can implement the IEP.

Of course, if District B does not agree with either the evaluation or the IEP of District A, then it must comply with the IDEA regulations concerning evaluations and/or IEP meetings, including all pertinent timelines.

While likely an unusual circumstance, a 1991 OCR Letter of Finding concluded that in the particular circumstances at issue, the school district was required by Section 504 to convene an IEP meeting for a student transferring from a school district in another state. The student in *Carpinteria (CA) Unified School District,* 17 EHLR 1035 (SEA Calif. 1991), an 18-year-old with a learning disability, re-enrolled in the school district after attending public school out-of-state for less than one full school year. The district placed him in regular education, contending that it did not offer to provide him special education services at his request. The student had an unsuccessful school year, marked by another transfer, re-enrollment and home study and capped by a complaint alleging a failure to provide FAPE. OCR found that the school district had a duty to convene an IEP meeting upon the student's re-enrollment because it was aware of his "previous special education background" prior to his transfer out-of-state. According to OCR "[t]he District failed to provide [the student] with an appropriate education when it failed to convene an IEP meeting on a timely basis, develop an appropriate program for him after his return from [the out-of-state district] and by failing to implement his prior IEP." 17 EHLR at 1037.

10. If a school district rejects the most recent evaluation conducted by an out-of-state transferring district, must the school district implement the transferring state's IEP pending completion of its own evaluation?

No. According to *OSEP Memorandum 96-5,* 24 IDELR 320 (OSEP 1995), the student should be placed according to an agreed-upon interim IEP or, in the absence an agreement between the parents and the district, in a regular education placement. Naturally, once the evaluation is completed, an IEP meeting must be convened in accordance with the regulatory requirements of 34 C.F.R. § 300.343(c).

11. Must a school district implement the IEP of a student with a disability who transfers from a school district within the same state?

Generally yes. Unlike OSEP interpretation of the requirements imposed on school districts in connection with interstate transfers,[6] OSEP's intrastate transfer policy requires the receiving school district to implement the IEP and placement developed by the sending district until such time as a revised IEP is developed. *Letter to Reynolds,* EHLR 213:238 (OSERS 1989). If the parents and the receiving district are unable to agree on an interim placement, the district must implement the old IEP to the extent possible until a new IEP is developed and implemented. *Letter to Nerney,* EHLR 213:267 (OSEP 1989).

12. What should a receiving school district do when it cannot implement the IEP designed by the sending district in an intrastate transfer?

According to OSEP, the receiving school district must provide services that approximate, as closely as possible, those called for in the IEP of the sending school district. *Letter to Campbell,* EHLR 213:265 (OSEP 1989).

13. Under what circumstances must the receiving district convene an IEP meeting in the case of an intrastate transfer?

In the case of an intrastate transfer, both local school districts, the transferring and the receiving districts, and the SEA itself have an ongoing obligation under Part B to ensure timely transmission of records so the student continues to receive FAPE. 34 C.F.R. § 300.600. Nevertheless, if for some reason the student's IEP is unavailable, or if either the receiving school district or the parents believe it is not appropriate, then an IEP meeting must be convened. *Letter to Anonymous,* 25 IDELR 525 (OSEP 1996).

14. What actions must a receiving school district take pending development of the IEP for a student with a disability transferring from another school district within the state?

It is inconsistent with the receiving district's responsibility to provide FAPE for an incoming student with a disability already identified as IDEA-eligible to be placed,

---

[6] *See* Question 9, *supra.*

even temporarily, without appropriate special education services. *See, e.g, Letter to Campbell,* EHLR 213:265 (OSEP 1989) (30-day interruption of services was a denial of FAPE).

Thus the receiving school district must take two actions:

1. Convene the IEP meeting within a short time after the student's enrollment. OSEP opines that the meeting should be held within one week, in the normal course of events. *Letter to Anonymous,* 25 IDELR 525 (OSEP 1996).

2. Place the student in an interim program, receiving at least some appropriate services, pending finalization of the IEP.

Chapter 9

Private School Students

This chapter discusses the IDEA requirements for the development and review of IEPs for children with disabilities who attend private schools or facilities in three different scenarios—public placement; parents' unilateral placement triggered by dissatisfaction with the public program offered by the school district; and unilateral placement by parents who seek only special education or related services for their children. Frequently, this third category involves parental placement in a sectarian school.

It is not surprising that, after 20 years, the remaining unsettled legal issues under the IDEA are marginal issues, in the sense that they concern only a discrete minority of all eligible children with disabilities. Continued services for properly suspended students with disabilities is one such issue; programming for incarcerated students another. In the author's view, though, the "hottest" issue is the one we touch on here: the extent to which school districts are obliged to provide services to parentally placed students.

The 105th Congress also found the responsibility of public school districts to unilaterally placed students with disabilities a "hot" issue. As discussed in this chapter, the 1997 Amendments include provisions intended to resolve the ambiguities in the law that have spawned recent litigation in this area.

But do they? Not according to commentators. The language itself, requiring that funds "expended for the provision of [such] services by a local educational agency . . . equal a proportionate amount of Federal funds made available under this part," is vague. The explanatory language contained in the Senate's Committee Report—"the amount consistent with the number and location of private school children with disabilities in the State"—is no more enlightening. At first reading, and even after several readings, the author has difficulty distinguishing this new directive from the prior EDGAR-derived regulations, universally acknowledged as confusing. Thus the impact of the new provisions contained in the 1997 Amendments on this area of the law won't be known until the topic is subjected to judicial scrutiny and, ultimately, Supreme Court review.

Which leaves us right where we were before the enactment of the 1997 Amendments. Thus an exploration of recent circuit court rulings, issued in rapid fire order starting in 1996, remains a helpful introduction to this chapter. The analysis provided here is likely to be only part of the story by the time this publication reaches your hands. Nevertheless, even though we are dealing with a moving target, we believe an analysis of the "current" state of the law will help the reader understand the IEP process with regard to private school students.

In 1995 four new decisions upset what, for a long while, had been the conventional wisdom on serving parentally placed private school students with disabilities. These district court level decisions essentially placed the rights of private and public school students on an equal plane, rejecting the long-standing policy of the Department of Education. In practice, OSEP's vague "equitable opportunities" standard left a considerable amount of discretion in the hands of schools to decide which private school students to serve, and to what extent and in what manner.

Almost as if by chain-reaction, one by one, each of those cases supporting IDEA entitlements for parentally placed private school students was appealed by the school districts to the various appellate level courts governing the locales in which they were situated. And, one by one, three of these circuit courts issued their decisions throughout 1996 and in early 1997, with one case still pending as the author pens this analysis. With their release, the law on services for private school students has once again been largely rewritten.

On the spectrum of services for private school students, each of these circuit court decisions took a unique position as to the intensity of services which are required, leaving confusion in their wake.

First came the Seventh Circuit in *K.R. v. Anderson Community School Corp.,* 23 IDELR 1137 (7th Cir. 1996), the appeal of the renegade district court pronouncement which led the movement toward full benefits for private school students. This time around, the Seventh Circuit did an about-face, reversing the district court's decision and endorsing OSEP's "equitable opportunities" standard. Applying that standard, the court held that the school district was not obligated to provide an instructional assistant to a seven-year-old student with multiple disabilities on the premises of the private school.

The Second Circuit's decision in *Russman v. Sobol,* 24 IDELR 274 (2d Cir. 1996), followed on the heels of *Anderson,* but remained true to the view that services for parentally placed private school students are an obligation of the school district, not a discretionary provision of assistance. Affirming the district court's earlier holding, the ruling entitled an 11-year-old student with mental retardation to receive the services of a consultant teacher and a teaching aide on the premises of her parochial school.

The Fifth Circuit complicated matters further with the issuance of *Cefalu v. East Baton Rouge Parish School Board,* 25 IDELR 142 (5th Cir. 1997), which, on its face, appears to be a compromise approach somewhere in between the two extremes of *Anderson* and *Russman*. First, the Fifth Circuit devised its own three-part test to govern the provision of on-site services for private school students. It then proceeded to send the case back to the district court to apply the test and decide whether the 14-year-old student with a hearing impairment was entitled to a speech interpreter on private school premises.

In searching for the true meaning behind these cases, one is naturally tempted to reduce them to the simplest possible level: *Anderson* is the "discretionary" view of private school services; *Russman* is the mandatory entitlement approach; and *Cefalu* is the moderate—fact-sensitive—compromise.

However, as one looks beyond the specific disposition in each case, it becomes clear that the courts themselves did not think there is a simple rule delineating the duties of school districts to serve private school students. For example, in the *Anderson* decision, which is the one adhering to the most limited view of the obligation to provide services for private school students, the court noted that the district already was providing the student with a full range of related services—including speech, occupational and physical therapy, and transportation to the public school site where those services were provided—when it refused to provide an instructional assistant on private premises. Regarding schools' obligation to serve private school students, the Seventh Circuit observed that "a complete failure to provide any services, especially those that can be provided at a neutral or public school at flexible times, would be strong evidence that the public school has abused its discretion." Thus, even under the most minimalistic notion of the rights of private school students, *Anderson* does not advocate complete discretion in serving this group.

Just as *Anderson* stops short of seeing the duties of public schools as completely discretionary, *Russman*—the circuit court decision taking the most expansive outlook on private school services—does not stand for the proposition that private school students have an unconditional right to receive services at the location of their choice. Instead, closer scrutiny of *Russman* reveals that the Second Circuit's apparent directive for mandatory benefits is somewhat less. Consider the court's reasoning: "Where the provision of services at a distant private school would entail significant additional costs, e.g., transportation to be borne by the state, public school authorities may fulfill their IDEA obligations by offering the services at a local public school." In its next breath, though, the court observed that, "[w]here the cost of special services does not vary with where they are provided, the IDEA and regulations regarding voluntary private school students make little sense if such services may be made available only in the public schools." Thus the Second Circuit gives a strong indication that the costs of the services involved carry some weight in the overall analysis of serving private school students and may possibly curtail provision of services.

Cefalu, the last of the circuit court decisions, added an unusual twist with its three-part test to determine a school district's obligations for a particular student with a disability attending a private school. Step one requires the student to make a show of "genuine need"—as opposed to "mere convenience"—for the on-site services. In step two, if the student has such a need the burden shifts to the district to either provide the services or demonstrate a "justifiable reason," either economic or non-economic, for refusing to do so. In step three, if the district does meet the burden for refusal the student is given one last chance to demonstrate that the district has taken a position that is irrational, arbitrary or simply contrary to the IDEA. According to the court, if the three-part test were properly applied, private school students with disabilities would receive comparable services on-site when they could be provided in that location at the same approximate cost as if delivered at another site. Like the *Russman* court, the court in *Cefalu* implied the financial costs of the services could serve as a limitation on those rights.

Beyond their ambiguity, these three cases have in common their concern with students with severe disabilities whose parents seek the provision of intensive services directly on the premises of their private schools. The fringe of a marginal issue, one might say. Thus we are left guessing about how, indeed whether, the rules of law set forth in these cases would be applied in other situations, such as more moderately disabled students or less intensive services.

Public Placements in Private Schools or Facilities

1. Under what circumstances may school districts place students with disabilities in private schools or facilities?

IDEA regulations at 34 C.F.R. § 300.400 explicitly recognize that some students with disabilities may be "placed in or referred to a private school or facility as a means of providing special education and related services." While the IDEA does not establish by regulation or policy standards for deciding if a student with a disability should be placed in a private school or facility, the least restrictive environment (LRE) mandate of the IDEA makes it clear that such a placement should be made only when a student's disability is of such nature and severity that he or she cannot be educated in any public school setting.

2. Are IEPs required for students with disabilities who have been publicly placed in private schools or facilities?

Yes, students who have been publicly placed retain all their rights under the IDEA. Regulations at 34 C.F.R. § 401(a)(1) make state educational agencies ultimately responsible for ensuring, among other things, that such students are provided with special education and related services "in conformance with an IEP that meets the requirements of Sections 300.340-300.350." Of those, sections 300.340-300.347 and 300.350 apply to students attending both public and private schools; section 300.348 concerns students publicly placed in private schools (*see* Questions 3 through 10 in this chapter, below), and section 300.349 concerns parentally placed private school children with disabilities receiving services from a public agency (*see* Questions 3 through 10 in this chapter).

3. Is the IEP process the same when the school district has placed the student in a private school or facility as when the student is unilaterally placed?

Not entirely. The IDEA imposes additional procedural requirements in connection with the development of IEPs for students who are publicly placed in private schools or facilities. It also establishes different requirements for review and revision of IEPs for such students, once placed.

When a school district (or other responsible public agency) proposes private placement at public expense, IDEA regulations at 34 C.F.R. § 300.348(a) make it clear that an IEP meeting, attended by a representative of the school or facility in which the student is to be placed, must be held beforehand to develop the IEP which will be implemented in that placement. That meeting must comply with the requirements of 34 C.F.R. § 300.343, which in turn implicates the requirements of 34 C.F.R. § 300.344 concerning meeting participants; 34 C.F.R. § 300.345 concerning parental rights and participation; and 34 C.F.R. § 300.346 concerning the required contents of the IEP document.

As is the case with students with disabilities enrolled in and attending public schools, the decision of the IEP team is final. As OSEP opined, the decision of the IEP team to publicly place a student in a private school or facility is determinative and cannot be overridden by the Board of Education of the school district (*Letter to Anonymous,* 18 IDELR 627 (OSEP 1991)) or the state educational agency (*Letter to Tucker,* 18 IDELR 965 (OSEP 1992)). This is the case even when state law and regulation establish parameters for state approval of a private school for purposes of state funding.

Once the student is placed, the IEP review and revision procedure deviates somewhat from that set out in 34 C.F.R. § 300.343(d) by recognizing that distance considerations may make the attendance of all required parties at one site for a follow-on IEP meetings not feasible. 34 C.F.R. § 300.348(b)(1) states that: "[a]fter a child with a disability enters a private school or facility, any meetings to review and revise the child's IEP may be initiated and conducted by the private school or facility at the discretion of the public agency." In essence, once the student has been placed, the regulation vests the placing agency with discretion to either conduct the meetings itself or have the private school do so. *Andersen v. District of Columbia,* 1988-89 EHLR 441:508 (D.C. Cir. 1981).

4. Is the IEP document the same when the school district has placed the student in a private school or facility as when the student is publicly placed?

Generally yes, the content requirements of 34 C.F.R. § 300.346 apply in both cases, although the services themselves will of course vary to take into account the particular aspects of the private placement.

In *Letter to Favorito*, 24 IDELR 295 (OSEP 1995), OSEP responded to an interesting query that highlighted a content requirement applicable to public placements in private schools or facilities. In such placements the IEP team is charged with considering if structural changes—lighting, carpeting, cooling, and the like—are required to enable that school or facility to implement the student's IEP. According to OSEP, the school district may consider such required structural changes as elements of an appropriate educational program, with the characterization of such items treated as either assistive technology or related services, at the discretion of the IEP team. The implication of this letter is that, either way, the IEP team must identify any such changes as an element of the IEP under 34 C.F.R. § 300.346.

5. May a school district hold the required IEP meeting that precedes placement without the attendance in person of a representative of the private school or facility?

Yes, provided an attempt to ensure the attendance of a representative is made and alternative means of participation are used. However, even when the parents and the public agency have agreed in principle that a public placement in a private school or facility is required, another IEP meeting must be held after the specific school or facility has been identified and the student has been accepted for placement.

While regulations at 34 C.F.R. § 300.348 state that the placing agency shall ensure that a representative of the private school or facility attend the meeting, they also recognize that attendance may not always be possible and the meeting should be held regardless. Accordingly, as is the case in 34 C.F.R. § 300.345 in connection with parental participation, the regulations at 34 C.F.R. § 300.348(a)(2) compel school districts to secure some type of involvement even when personal attendance is not possible. "If the representative cannot attend, the agency shall use other methods to ensure participation by the private school or facility, including individual or conference telephone calls."

In many cases, the student's need for private school or facility placement and the program that he or she should receive in such a placement already has been agreed to by the parents and the necessary state and local personnel before the private school is contacted. In those instances, the meetings already held do not satisfy the requirement that an IEP meeting with a representative of the private school or facility be held. A subsequent meeting must be held and the attendance of a school representative solicited.

Patterson C. v. Board of Education, 1986-87 EHLR 558:384 (4th Cir. 1987); Notice of Interpretation on IEP Requirements, Appendix C to 34 C.F.R. Part 300, Question 59).

6. What are the school district's responsibilities if the private school or facility conducts IEP meetings?

Both 34 C.F.R. §§ 300.348(c) and 300.401 make it clear that both the placing agency and the state educational agency remain ultimately responsible for the provision of FAPE to a publicly placed child, even in those instances when the placing agency has, in its discretion, authorized the private school to initiate and conduct meetings to review and revise the publicly placed student's IEP.

As a general matter, 34 C.F.R. § 300.401 sets out the SEA's responsibilities:

Each SEA shall ensure that a child with a disability who is placed in or referred to a private school or facility by a public agency:

(a) Is provided special education and related services—

(1) In conformance with an IEP that meets the requirements of §§ 300.340-300.350;

(2) At no cost to the parents; and

(3) At a school or facility that meets the standards that apply to the SEA and the LEAs (including the requirements of this part); and

(b) Has all of the rights of a child with a disability who is served by a public agency.

According to OSEP, the SEA may either ensure compliance directly or delegate some responsibility for ensuring compliance to the placing school district. *Letter to Black,* EHLR 211:434 (OSEP 1987).

With regard to involvement in IEP review, 34 C.F.R. § 300.348(b) is intended to ensure that a school district (or other placing agency) not abdicate its responsibility for the student's education because it has placed the student in a private school and authorized that school to review and revise IEPs. *Letter to Anonymous,* 21 IDELR 673 (OSEP 1994). Thus, the regulations impose two requirements on the school district when the private school or facility is conducting the IEPs: (1) to ensure continuing involvement by parents and an agency representative in any decisions about the child's IEP; and (2) to agree to any proposed changes before implementation. 34 C.F.R. § 300.348(b)(2).

7. Must a school district representative attend IEP meetings conducted by a private school or facility?

Generally, yes, attendance of a school district representative is required, even when the district has elected to have the private school or facility initiate and conduct the

IEP meetings. While 34 C.F.R. § 300.348(b) states that school districts must remain "involved" in decisions about changes in the student's IEP, there is otherwise little guidance about the nature of the required monitoring of IEP proceedings for compliance with the IDEA called for in 34 C.F.R. § 401. However, the general rule of 34 C.F.R. § 300.344(a)(1) still applies, making attendance by a representative mandatory.

In *Letter to Sutler,* 18 IDELR 307 (OSEP 1991), OSEP stated that 34 C.F.R. § 300.348 is not intended to create an exception to the mandatory attendance requirements of 34 C.F.R. § 300.344. Thus, in the ordinary course, both parents and a representative of the school district should attend IEP meetings initiated and conducted by the private school.

Adopting that interpretation of the interaction of 34 C.F.R. § 300.344 and 300.348, the court in *Smith v. Henson,* 18 IDELR 897 (D.D.C. 1992), held that the school district committed a substantial procedural error when it failed to participate in developing the IEPs for students with learning disabilities who had been publicly placed at the Lab School. When the district subsequently proposed to change the placement of the students, so that the IEPs developed at the Lab School would be implemented at a public school, the parents filed for due process. Upholding the hearing officer's rulings in favor of the students, the court ruled that the failure to ensure that a representative of the district attend the IEP meetings at the Lab School "rendered the IEPs invalid to serve as the basis for changing the students' placement." 18 IDELR at 898.

Attendance in person may not always be necessary, however. In *Letter to Sutler,* OSEP opined that if all the required participants of an IEP meeting (as determined under 34 C.F.R. § 300.344) agree to an alternative method for participation other than attendance, then the absence of a public agency representative may be permissible on a case-by-case basis.

8. May a school district which elects to initiate and conduct IEP meetings for review and revision of the IEP for a student publicly placed in a private school secure the participation of the student's teacher by telephone?

While neither the IDEA statute nor its regulations provide a clear answer, OSEP opines in a policy letter that participation of the student's teacher by telephone may be permissible in appropriate instances. *Letter to Sarzynski,* 23 IDELR 993 (OSEP 1996).

The inquirer in *Letter to Sarzynski* raised an issue of significant practical application that is not clearly addressed in what should be the pertinent section of the IDEA regulations, 34 C.F.R. § 300.348(b). The problem, the inquirer said, results when a student is publicly placed in a private facility located at some distance from where the public agency will be conducting the IEP meeting. While the student's teacher at the facility is clearly required to attend (34 C.F.R. § 300.344), the expense and logistical problems involved in securing such personal attendance can be great. Participation by telephone conference calling seems like it should be a workable and compliant alternative, but the regulation seems to permit such alternative arrangements only for securing the participation of a private school representative for the IEP meeting held prior to initial placement (34 C.F.R. § 300.348(a)).

In responding, OSEP agreed that pertinent sections of the regulations, 34 C.F.R. § 300.348(b) and 34 C.F.R. § 300.344, are silent on the use of alternative methods to secure the participation of required participants, other than parents and representatives of public agencies, at IEP meetings to review the IEPs of publicly placed students.

Using the same approach it did in *Letter to Sutler,* 18 IDELR 307 (OSEP 1991) (concerning telephonic participation of public agency representatives at IEP meetings conducted by private schools), OSEP concluded that alternative methods, including conference calling, used to secure the participation of the student's private school teacher at a meeting to review the IEP is permissible, on a case-by-case basis.

9. Must a school district convene an IEP meeting prior to changing the placement of publicly placed students from one private school to another?

It depends on whether the change in schools is accompanied by a change in programming, according to OSEP. In *Letter to Green,* 22 IDELR 639 (OSEP 1995), the inquirer posed the situation of a private school at which students with disabilities had been publicly placed becoming decertified, necessitating enrollment in another private school or facility, this one approved. The relevant question, OSEP opined, in determining whether an IEP meeting should take place prior to implementing a change is whether the change in location (from one private school to another) would substantially or materially alter the student's current educational program, and thus constitute a change in placement. If the change is only a change in location and the student's most recent IEP was developed within the last 12 months, then the school district is not required to hold an IEP meeting prior to the implementation of the change. However, if the school district believes that an IEP meeting is necessary to ensure effective implementation of the existing IEP, it may choose to hold one before the change takes place.

The hearing officer in *City of Chicago School District No. 299, Cook County,* 21 IDELR 889 (SEA Ill. 1994), took the same approach, holding that the school district was not required to convene an IEP meeting to consider the transfer of a 15-year-old student with severe mental retardation from one private school to another. The former facility had lost its status as a state-approved facility and the transfer involved the implementation an existing, valid IEP in the new facility.

10. Must the IEP of a residentially placed student include exit criteria?

Exit criteria are not required but they may be included, according to OSEP.

Exit criteria are the minimum amount of educational/behavioral progress that when achieved, trigger the review of the educational placement of a student placed at a residential facility to determine whether he or she can be moved to a less restrictive placement. In two 1995 policy letters—*Letter to Allen,* 23 IDELR 996 (OSEP 1995) and *Letter to Lund,* 23 IDELR 994 (OSEP 1995)—OSEP stated that a state's use of exit criteria as an additional component of an IEP furthers, rather than inhibits, compliance with the IDEA. Inclusion of such criteria helps to ensure that students do not remain in residential placements any longer than is educationally appropriate. They further help guard against premature transfer from that setting.

OSEP further found the inquirers' use of exit criteria consistent with the IDEA because of two assurances made about the role of those criteria in placement determinations:

- Each placement determination was based on the entire IEP.

- Such criteria were not the sole determinant for a change in placement. They served only as an indicator that change may be appropriate and a review should be undertaken.

Unilateral Placements after Disputes about FAPE

11. When parents who dispute the appropriateness of the program offered by the school district unilaterally place their child in a private school or facility, must the school district invite a representative or teacher from that school to attend the IEP meeting?

Two federal circuit courts have ruled on this issue—reaching different conclusions.

In *W.G. v. Board of Trustees of Target Range School District No. 23,* 18 IDELR 1019 (9th Cir. 1992), the Ninth Circuit awarded tuition reimbursement for the parents due to a raft of procedural errors committed by the school district, including the failure to invite a private school representative or teacher to the IEP meeting for an elementary school student with a significant learning disability. A close reading of the case, though, reveals that the court's reliance on 34 C.F.R. § 300.349 (then 300.348) was something of a stretch.

The following circumstances led to the ill-fated IEP meeting. Dissatisfied with their son's educational progress and other difficulties, the parents of a fourth-grade student requested an IEE in 1985, the result of which was a diagnosis of learning disability. A multidisciplinary team meeting, convened to review the IEE, refused to identify the student as IDEA-eligible. Thereupon the parents enrolled him in a private school for the school year starting in September 1985. In 1987 that school conducted an evaluation, also finding that the student was learning disabled. The private school contacted the school district, Target Range, and a public agency representative attended a meeting at the private school to discuss the diagnosis. This time Target Range agreed that the student was eligible for services under the IDEA and scheduled a meeting of representatives of both schools to develop an IEP. The parents advised Target Range that they would arrange for representatives of the private school to attend. The private school representatives were unable to attend, however, and the meeting was conducted without them.

The proposed IEP called for implementation of a particular program, the Scott Foresman Focus Program, at the public school. The parents objected to the program and placement, and they filed for due process. The court found, however, that it did not even have to address the adequacy of the proposed program, as a substantive matter. The procedural errors committed by Target Range were severe enough in themselves to constitute a denial of FAPE.[1]

Of those errors, the one pertinent to this question was the school's failure to make efforts to include either the student's private school teacher or another representative of the private school in the IEP process. The court first held that the absence of the student's private school teacher violated the mandatory attendance requirement of 34 C.F.R. § 300.344.

Further, it held that the failure to secure the attendance of a private school representative violated 34 C.F.R. § 300.349 [then 300.348]. But does it? The author thinks an argument to the opposite effect can be made. Section 300.344 says nothing about requiring that the private school teacher be selected as the child's teacher. In fact, the later Ninth Circuit's decision in *Clyde K. v. Puyallup School District,* 21 IDELR 664 (9th Cir. 1994), confirmed that the IEP meeting attendee designated as the child's teacher does not have to be a teacher who has previously taught the student.

Section 300.349, on the other hand, does require that a "representative" of the private school attend IEP meetings when the student is enrolled in a private school. But that section applies to the provision of specialized instruction or related services when the parents' unilateral placement was not motivated by the alleged failure of the school district to offer an appropriate educational program in the public school.[2] But that was *not* the case in *Target Range.* The parents claimed the student was denied FAPE and Target Range's proposed IEP contemplated the student's return to the public school.

It is possible that the First Circuit Court of Appeals would agree with the position of the Ninth Circuit in *Target Range.* In *Roland M. v. Concord School Committee,* 16

---

[1] *See* Question 10 in chapter 12, *infra.*

[2] *See* Questions 13 through 15 in this chapter, *infra.*

EHLR 1129 (1st Cir. 1990), the court suggested that failure to include the unilaterally placed student's private school teacher as a required IEP team member was a denial of FAPE. However, the court found the parents were foreclosed in their ability to raise procedural objections to the composition of the IEP meeting by their own conduct.

The Third Circuit Court of Appeals adopted what the author believes is the better reasoned view—that a private school representative is not a mandatory attendee at an IEP meeting held for a unilaterally placed student for whom the school district is offering to provide FAPE at the public school—in *Fuhrmann v. East Hanover Board of Education,* 19 IDELR 1065 (3d Cir. 1993). In that case the parents of a developmentally disabled student enrolled their son in a private school because they did not believe the school district offered an appropriate program. When the district convened an IEP meeting to propose a public program for the next school year, it did not invite representatives of the private school to attend. The parents claimed that omission violated the requirements of 34 C.F.R. § 300.248(a)(2) (then 300.347(a)(2)).

The court rejected the parents' argument, holding that reliance on that section of the regulation was "inapplicable." In a footnote, the court explained how it interpreted the IEP meeting requirements for students attending private schools.

> To the extent that petitioner [parent] argues that the procedures set forth in 34 C.F.R. Sections 300.348(a)(2) and 300.349 [then 300.347(a)(2) and 300.348] were violated with respect to the 1990-91 school year [the year after the student was enrolled in the private school], that argument must be rejected. [The parent] suggests that the hearing officer's finding that G.F. [the student] was in a private school as a result of a unilateral decision of the Fuhrmanns was incorrect and that, therefore, his dismissal of the procedural challenges under these two code sections was erroneous. Petitioner's arguments fail, quite simply, because neither of these two code sections apply to this case.
>
> Both of these regulations are aimed at ensuring that a public agency that would otherwise be responsible for the education of a handicapped child does not abdicate that responsibility merely because the a child is or will be enrolled at a private institution. Section 300.348(a)(2) [then 300.347(a)(2)] dictates that before a public agency places a child in a private facility, the agency must initiate a meeting to develop an IEP and must include in that meeting a representative of the private facility. Because East Hanover did not seek to place G.F. at a private facility for 1990-91, it had no duty to include any private school representative in the IEP development process. Section 300.349 [then 300.348] sets forth guidelines for a public agency to follow when a handicapped child is enrolled in a private school and receives special education or related services from the public agency. Here, however, there is no indication that, while enrolled at [the private school], G.F. received any services from a public agency. Rather he was enrolled at [the private school] in lieu of the services offered by the public agency. Clearly, neither section applies to this case.

19 IDELR at 1069 n.5 (citations omitted).

Most recently, the federal district court for the District of Vermont has adopted the view of the *Target Range* court, although it did not cite to that case—or any other—in support of its decision. In *Briere v. Fair Haven Grade School District,* 25 IDELR 55 (D. Vt. 1996), the court held that the school district violated the requirements of 34 C.F.R. § 300.344 because it did not have any of the teachers who instructed the unilaterally placed student at the IEP meeting.

12. Must unilaterally placed students receive services under IEPs for their parents to be entitled to tuition reimbursement?

No. The topic of tuition reimbursement as a remedy for denial of FAPE is beyond the scope of this publication. But, the author notes that the U.S. Supreme Court's decision in *Florence County School District Four v. Carter,* 20 IDELR 532 (1993), stated clearly that IEP requirements do not apply if a child with a disability is unilaterally placed by his or her parents. In that case, the Court held that parents should be reimbursed for costs incurred in placing their child with learning disabilities in a private school because the private school provided an appropriate educational program for the child, in the sense of providing a program under which the child received educational benefit. The IDEA's requirements that FAPE must be provided under public supervision (34 C.F.R. § 300.8(a)), meet the standards of the state educational agency (34 C.F.R. § 300.8(b)) and be provided in accordance with an IEP (34 C.F.R. § 300.8(d)) was binding on public agencies, but "did not make sense in the context of a parental placement."

Services for Unilaterally Placed Students

13. Must a school district convene an IEP meeting to determine whether it will serve a child with a disability unilaterally enrolled in a private or parochial school?

The issue of a private school student's entitlement to services, in those instances in which the parents are not seeking FAPE from a public school placement, is unsettled. At this time, there is little in the 1997 Amendments concerning unilaterally placed students to clarify the rights, if any, such students have under the IDEA. *See* the introduction to this chapter for a brief discussion.

OSEP's view is that an IEP meeting need not be held to determine if an individual student must be served. Rather, the consultation requirements set out in EDGAR regulations at 34 C.F.R. §§ 76.651- 76.662[3] govern that determination. One district court takes an opposing view. *Natchez-Adams School District,* 23 IDELR 982 (S.D. Miss. 1996).

The threshold issue of the extent to which school districts must provide services to unilaterally placed students who have been offered FAPE in the public school setting is one of the most unsettled in special education law, a detailed exploration of which is beyond the scope of these Questions. (Although we do discuss the latest case law concerning this issue in the beginning paragraphs of this chapter.) In brief, OSEP has its own view: a school district has only "limited obligations" and need not provide services at all.

OSEP's interpretation is not binding on the judiciary. Three federal circuit courts of appeal have ruled on a school district's obligation to privately placed students in the context of a student needing services that can be provided only on-site. The Seventh Circuit signed on to that interpretation in *K.R. v. Anderson Community School Corp.,* 23 IDELR 1137 (7th Cir. 1996). The Second Circuit, on the other hand, came close to finding that private school students have an entitlement to services. *Russman v. Sobel,* 24 IDELR 274 (2d Cir. 1996). The Fifth Circuit declined to adopt the views of either, instead crafting its own unique test for determining whether services must be provided on-site in *Cefalu v. East Baton Rouge Parish School Board,* 25 IDELR 142 (5th Cir. 1996).

Whatever the differences in interpretation among the circuit courts and OSEP, none of the circuit court opinions cited above dispute that the IDEA extends benefits of some sort to private school students with disabilities. IDEA regulations at 34 C.F.R. § 403(a) confirm that school districts are obligated to make services available to private school students with disabilities in accordance with 34 C.F.R. §§ 300.451-300.452. Those sections in turn incorporate the requirements set out in EDGAR regulations at 34 C.F.R. §§ 76.651-76.662.

However, neither the above-referenced IDEA regulations nor the incorporated EDGAR regulations explicitly impose a requirement to convene an IEP meeting to determine if a school district will serve a privately placed student. Instead, the EDGAR regulations at 34 C.F.R. § 76.652 set out the consultation requirement generally applicable when considering which private school students will receive services under any federally supported program and how those services will be provided:

---

[3] Education Department General Administrative Regulations (EDGAR) promulgated by the U.S. Department of Education, concern various aspects of the federal government's role in state and local educational systems and include the following parts, codified at 34 CFR Part:

    75   Direct Grant Programs

    76   State-Administered Programs

    77   Definitions that Apply to Department Regulations

    79   Intergovernmental Review of Department of Education Programs and Activities

    80   Uniform Administrative Requirements for Grants and Cooperative Agreements to State and Local Governments

    81   General Education Provisions Act-Enforcement

    86   Drug-Free Schools and Campuses.

(a) An applicant for a subgrant [e.g., a school district] shall consult with appropriate representatives of students enrolled in private schools during all phases of the development and design of the project covered by the application, including consideration of:

(1) Which children will receive benefits under the project; . . .

(3) What benefits will be provided;

(4) How the benefits will be provided. . . .

As OSEP makes clear in, among other pronouncements, its *Letter to Cernosia,* 22 IDELR 365 (OSEP 1994), the required consultation is in no significant way a substitute for the procedurally rigorous IEP meeting. For example, the EDGAR regulation at 34 C.F.R. § 76.652 does not specify which individuals are "appropriate representatives of students enrolled in private schools."

Neither does Part B impose any IEP process or documentation requirements when the consultation is in connection with IDEA services. Rather, that determination is left to the discretion of state and local authorities. Similarly, in its *Letter to Champagne,* 21 IDELR 1136 (OSEP 1995), in the course of its explanation of why refusals to provide services are not subject to due process challenges, OSEP implies that such refusals need not be made in the course of IEP meetings. As stated by the Seventh Circuit in *K.R. v. Anderson,* "[t]he consultation mandated under Section 76.652 is entirely separate from the consultation required to formulate the IEP."

The court in *Natchez-Adams School District* also agreed that school districts must follow the consultation process set out in the EDGAR regulations in deciding which private school students will be served and what services will be provided to those children who are served. In that case, the court held that the school district failed to comply with the EDGAR regulations because it simply refused to provide services to any private school students. But, the court continued to opine, with no citation to authority, that the school district violated the IDEA because it failed to develop and implement a complete IEP for the student. Its interpretation of the IDEA, which we question, is that the "the IDEA, through its implementing regulations ensures access to educational services by requiring the responsible public agency to design and implement an IEP for each child with a disability." 23 IDELR at 987.

14. Must a school district prepare an IEP if it decides to provide services to a unilaterally placed private school student?

Yes, a public agency must prepare an IEP for those private school students whom, through the consultation process set out in 34 C.F.R. §§ 300.451(b) and 76.652, it has determined to serve. *Letter to Williams,* 18 IDELR 742 (OSEP 1992).

IDEA regulations at 34 C.F.R. § 300.349(a) state:

If a child with a disability is enrolled in a parochial or other private school and receives special education or related services, from a public agency, the public agency shall—

(a) Initiate and conduct meetings to develop, review and revise an IEP for the child in accordance with § 300.343.

Metropolitan Nashville v. Guest, 23 IDELR 232 (M.D. Tenn. 1995), is a fluky case that emphasizes the need to always be clear about whether the school district is offering a private placement at public expense or just services for a unilaterally placed student or preschooler. The child in that case was a three-year-old diagnosed with autism who was enrolled in a private day care facility (Belle Meade), when he was 18 months old, before his diagnosis was made in the course of an evaluation undertaken at parental expense. After delays and misidentifications, not pertinent here, the public agency proposed an IEP in August 1993 that offered various services three days a week at the Early Childhood Education Center at the Martha Vaugh School, with the child remaining at Belle Meade the other two days at his parent's expense.

The parent became dissatisfied with the IEP in short order, resulting in the public agency's convening another IEP meeting in October 1993. Believing her son required a full-time placement in a setting with nondisabled students, unlike the Martha Vaugh School, she advocated full-time placement at Belle Meade.

That's where things got hairy. The agency either agreed to change the location at which the IEP services were provided from Martha Vaugh to Belle Meade *or* it agreed to finance the child's full program at Belle Meade. Reviewing the IEP document itself and transcripts of the October 1993 meeting and considering the testimony of agency representatives at the due process hearing, the hearing officer found for the parent. The district court agreed. Its exploration of "who-said-what-when" is so rich, that we reproduce it below.

Q: [Attorney]: So you are saying then that this paragraph that you wrote and recorded here [on the IEP] is not true?

A: [Special Education Consultant] Let me read it again. At today's meeting, it was recommended that he remain in the least restrictive environment of Belle Meade Children's Center. We are not saying that we placed him there, and all, and, again, I wrote the L.R.E. there, not for educational use, but you are interpreting it differently.

Q: You mean in this I.E.P. when you use the word least restrictive environment, you did not mean that in the sense of education?

A: Not in terms of his educational placement; no.

Q: Okay. So you are saying that this document says that his educational placement is somewhere other than Belle Meade; is that correct?

A: Yes.

Q: And where does this document say his educational placement is, if it is not in Belle Meade?

A: It does not say that he is in any other educational placement at all.

Q: Joel has speech/language goals; correct?

A: Yes, he does.

Q: He has occupational therapy goals; is that correct?

A: Yes, he does.

Q: Does he have any other goals and objectives?

A: No. Only service-related goals.

Q: Why not?

A: Because we are not providing the educational programming for him at Belle Meade. The educational goals were written into the one that was developed August 26, for the early childhood educational programming.

Q: Well, if you look at the I.E.P. of October 12, and directing your attention to page 112.

A: Okay. It says continue current I.E.P. goals. Yes.

Q: And isn't that referring to the I.E.P. of 8/26/93?

A: Yes, it is.

Q: So what you just said a few minutes ago was completely untrue, isn't that correct?

A: I'm looking at this. To be very honest; yes.

23 IDELR at 236.

15. Must a representative of the private school attend an IEP meeting convened for a unilaterally placed student receiving special education or related services from the school district?

Yes, although, as is the case when the initial IEP for a public placement is at issue, the school district may use alternative means, such as telephone conferencing, to ensure participation. 34 C.F.R. § 300.349(b).

Chapter 10

Transition Planning and Graduation

In 1990, Congress amended the IDEA to add new obligations for school systems, including the duty to provide transition services. As a result, the IDEA now requires that IEPs for older students include a plan for a coordinated set of services designed to move special education students successfully from school to post-school settings, such as college, vocational training, independent living and employment. This mandate was created due to Congressional concern that high-school age students in special education remained at risk of dropping out of school or otherwise leaving the school setting unprepared for adult life and responsibility. Although one might envision other ways to address these concerns, Congress imposed on IEP teams the duty to carefully consider where each student is heading after school and to determine what services are needed to assist the student in reaching his or her post-school goals.

Transition undoubtedly imposes new and expansive duties on public school districts. The questions-and-answers in this chapter review the statutory and regulatory provisions and decisional law (by courts and hearing officers) regarding how school districts must proceed to comply with the procedural mandates. The following paragraphs look beyond the procedural aspects of the law to discuss the substantive scope of transition services and the role of other agencies in transition services.

In sum, the IDEA defines transition services as encompassing a broad range of services and outcomes. In terms of the scope of services, the law requires "a coordinated set of activities," defined in terms of a laundry list that includes "instruction, community experiences . . . employment and other post-school adult objectives, and when appropriate, acquisition of daily living skills." It is apparent that such activities potentially can involve a broad range of services—including vocational training, individualized curriculum beyond the standard offerings of public high schools, and community based instruction—and that Congress' sweeping language indicates a legislative intent for an expansive and flexible range of services. Indeed, the Official Comment in the regulations states that the list of activities is not intended to be exhaustive.

As with special education in general, the touchstone will be individualization and appropriateness: services must be tailored to the particular needs of the individual student. Schools should be wary of falling into a "one size fits all" approach, even, for example, when the school's career preparation program is outstanding.

In terms of the scope of outcomes, the definition of transition services contemplates that the coordinated set of activities can be designed to lead to a variety of goals, depending, again, on the particular needs of the individual student. The post-school options toward which transition services can be directed include postsecondary education, vocational training, integrated employment, continuing and adult education, independent living and community participation. Again, while the list of outcomes may be long, it is also flexible.

The IDEA emphasizes interagency linkages as a necessary component of the provision of substantively appropriate services. As a matter of procedural requirements, the IDEA establishes a duty to include in the IEP a statement of the interagency responsibilities or linkages involved in preparing the student to leave the school setting, when appropriate.

As a starting point for considering interagency responsibility, the IDEA makes clear that the duty of schools to provide transition services does not relieve any other agencies, including vocational rehabilitation service agencies, of their preexisting and overlapping duty to provide specific services to eligible clients. Recognition of this overlapping responsibility is critical, as many of the specific services grouped under the umbrella of transition are within the scope of services available from state vocational rehabilitation agencies. Further, most students eligible for special education under the detailed federal and state special education regulations also will be eligible clients of the vocational rehabilitation agency under its more general standard of eligibility.

The first problem, of course, is getting vocational rehabilitation and other potentially responsible agencies to the table. In this regard, the regulations require that the school "shall invite . . . a representative of any public agency that is likely to be responsible" for transition, such as vocational rehabilitation. If the representative does not come, the school "shall take other steps to obtain the participation of the other agency in the planning of any transition services." 34 C.F.R. § 300.344.

Once the participation of vocational rehabilitation and/or other agencies is secured, the next problem may be a refusal on the part of the agency to commit resources or provide the services it has agreed to provide. In this event, the IDEA places default responsibility squarely on the school system.

As suggested previously, the substantive and procedural obligations of schools and vocational rehabilitation agencies are very similar and include multiple areas of overlap. For whatever reasons, however, contested cases usually center on the responsibility of schools. Very few cases have been brought against vocational rehabilitation agencies.

Unfortunately, all too often involved agencies are engaged in turf wars or are nowhere to be seen. Despite these circumstances, effective advocacy for students with disabilities must take into account the responsibility of other agencies, such as vocational rehabilitation. The more agencies brought to the table, the more resources can be marshalled to benefit the student. A limited, but growing, number of judicial decisions have adjudicated parents' claims that the student was denied FAPE because he or she did not receive adequate transition services. A majority of those decisions have been resolved in favor of the parents or the student. School districts can take several practical approaches to bring all possible resource agencies to the table, which in turn will help minimize legal risk:

- Consider the interrelationship between graduation criteria and transition planning in the IEP process.

- Bring in vocational rehabilitation agency representatives on a timely basis—well in advance of termination of special education—rather than simply following the traditional route of sequential services.

- Make sure to use parent and student partnerships and involvement, as required by the IDEA.

- When developing planning documents designed to implement transition, special educators should assure that all of the specific activities required, such as community experiences, adult living skills and instruction, are accounted for in the IEP, even if they are not needed or appropriate for that student.

- Make sure all identified areas of need are addressed far in advance of graduation. Otherwise they can be the basis for an award of compensatory education for an adult student.

- Work closely with the vocational education program in the school to develop expertise in the roles and services of other agencies. Try to meet with the other agencies—vocational rehabilitation, community mental health, community colleges and private rehabilitation agencies—in advance of disputes which may arise regarding a specific student.

Transition Planning

1. Who is entitled to transition planning?

All IDEA-eligible students are entitled to transition planning. Beginning no later than age 16, and "when deemed appropriate" at age 14 or younger, the IEP for all students with disabilities must include a statement of needed transition services. 20 U.S.C. § 1401(a)(20)(D).

Several years after passage of the IDEA (then the Education for All Handicapped Children Act) in 1975, some commentators began to question the degree to which special education students were being successfully transitioned from school to post-school activities. Although the IDEA made public education available to all children and youth with disabilities, concerns were expressed about the post-school outcomes for these students.

Studies showed that special education students had high dropout rates and many who did graduate went on to be unemployed or underemployed shortly thereafter. Although special educators were certainly providing activities designed to prepare students with disabilities to be as successful and independent as possible, the law itself did not contain specific guidelines about what services were properly considered part of public education, as opposed to post-school training or support. *See, e.g., Gorski v. Lynchburg Sch. Bd.,* 1988-89 EHLR 441:415 (4th Cir. 1989) (the parents and school district disputed whether the vocational training requested by the parents was required as part of FAPE or was a post-school activity). Further, there was no direction about how the transition process itself should be implemented or documented or what goal it was intended to achieve.

Thus, in 1990 Congress passed amendments to the Act requiring that specifically identified transition services (34 C.F.R. § 300.18) be provided to all eligible students and that planning to provide them become an integral part of the special education process (34 C.F.R. §§ 300.340- 300.350).[1]

Thus the IDEA provides at 20 U.S.C. § 1401(a)(20)(D) that an IEP shall include: "a statement of the needed transition services for students beginning no later than age 16 and annually thereafter (and when appropriate for the individual, beginning at age 14 or younger), including, when appropriate, a statement of the interagency responsibilities or linkages (or both) before the student leaves the school setting."

In its 1995 Reauthorization proposal, the Department of Education advocated that transition planning for all students with disabilities begin at age 14. The 1997 Amendments essentially retain the IDEA's age 16 rule. The age 14 floor was removed, with the Amendments stating instead that the IEP should contain a statement of needed transition services at a "younger age [than age 16], if determined appropriate by the IEP Team." Section 614(d)(1)(A)(viii)(II). The Amendments do, however, add a requirement that a statement of "transition service needs" be included in the IEPs of students with disabilities beginning at age 14. That requirement, Section 614(d)(1)(A)(vii)(I), is set out in Question 12 of this chapter.

Rather than expanding the entitlement to transition services, the 1997 Amendments restrict the rights of some students. Adult prisoners incarcerated in adult prisons who "age-out" prior to their scheduled release are not entitled to transition planning or transition services. Section 614(d)(6)(A)(ii).

---

[1] *See* Questions 5 and 6 in this chapter, *infra,* concerning aspects of these procedural requirements uniquely concerned with the transition planning process.

2.   Who determines when transition planning is appropriate for a student younger than 16?

That decision is left up to a student's IEP team. Note 3 to 34 C.F.R. § 300.346. *Letter to Hamilton*, 23 IDELR 721 (OSEP 1995), makes that clear. In *Hamilton*, OSEP also describes generally the criteria the IEP team should take into consideration when deciding when to begin transition planning.

It should be noted that the IDEA transition planning requirements are a floor. Some states may require that transitional planning occur before age 16 for all students. In addition, state and local grantees under the federal Carl. D. Perkins Vocational and Applied Technology Act must provide information about vocational opportunities to students with disabilities and their parents "at least one year before the students enter or are of an appropriate age for the grade level in which vocational education programs are first offered in the state, but in no event later than the beginning of the 9th grade." 20 U.S.C. § 2328(b)(1).

3.   In what circumstances is transition planning appropriate before the student reaches age 16?

The student's IEP team decides when transition planning prior to age 16 is appropriate based on an individual consideration of the student's circumstances and needs. 34 C.F.R. § 300.346(b); *Letter to Bereuter*, 20 IDELR 536 (OSEP 1993).

Although the language of the regulation provides no guidance about when transition services for students under the age of 16 would be deemed appropriate, Congress, in its legislative history, gave some indication of when it expects consideration should be given to the need for transition planning for younger students:

> The Committee encourages [that consideration be given to the need for transition services for students age 14 or younger] because of their concern that age 16 may be too late for many students, particularly those at risk of dropping out of school and those with the most severe disabilities.
>
> Even for those students who stay in school until age 18, many will need more than two years of transitional services. Students with disabilities are now dropping out of school before age 16, feeling that the education system has little to offer them.
>
> Initiating services at a younger age will be critical.[2]

In *Oregon City School District #462*, 23 IDELR 689 (SEA Or. 1996), the parents of a 16-year-old student with severe attention deficit hyperactivity disorder and attendant severe behavioral difficulties claimed the school district failed to provide FAPE because,

---

[2] H.R. REP. No. 101-544, at 19 (1990).

among other things, it failed to consider the student's need for transitional planning before his 16th birthday, specifically that it failed to consider transition planning at the IEP meeting held when the student was 15. The hearing officer agreed, although his reasoning was rather conclusory: the severity of the student's condition warranted earlier consideration.

But the school district's "omission" was a wrong without a remedy. The student had otherwise received FAPE, the hearing officer found. And, in any event, for reasons related to the specific circumstances, the link between the school district's failure to take action and any resulting denial of FAPE was speculative.

4. Must transition services be provided to all students with disabilities starting at age 16?

No. It is vital to keep in mind the distinction made in the IDEA between transition planning, which is a process, and the transition services themselves. The law, as discussed in Question 1 above, requires that a student's IEP team, meeting to develop, review or revise his or her IEP, consider the need for the provision of transition services no later than when the student turns 16 and at least annually thereafter. That's transition planning.

That planning, however, may not identify a need for providing transition services at age 16, or at any age. Like all other aspects of special education programming, transition services must be provided to meet the individual needs of each eligible student. As explained by OSEP in *Letter to Hamilton,* 23 IDELR 721 (OSEP 1995): "[E]ach disabled student's need for transition services, including the nature and extent of services, and the date for initiation of those services must be determined on an individual basis in light of the student's unique needs and the IEP process must be used as the vehicle for making those determinations." 23 IDELR at 722.

5. Who must attend IEP meetings at which transition services are being considered?

In addition to the mandatory attendees specified in IDEA regulations at 34 C.F.R. § 300.344(a), when a purpose of the IEP meeting is transition planning, 34 C.F.R. § 300.344(c) sets out additional requirements:

(1) If a purpose of the meeting is the consideration of transition services for a student, the public agency shall invite—

(i) The student; and

(ii) A representative of any other agency that is likely to be responsible for providing or paying for transition services.

Note 2 to the regulation makes it clear that transition services planning should be considered one of the purposes of the annual IEP meeting held for a student who is at least 16 years old.

Note the difference between the generally applicable requirement concerning attendance of the child set out in 34 C.F.R. § 300.344(a)(4) and 34 C.F.R. § 300.344(c)(1)(i). The former generally allows the parents to decide whether the child should attend; the latter compels the district to invite him or her.

6. Can an IEP team consider transition services at a meeting not attended by the student?

Yes, provided the student is invited and the school district takes "other steps to ensure that the student's preferences and interests are considered." 34 C.F.R. § 300.344(c)(2). The IEP meeting generally will be considered validly constituted even if the student does not attend.

In *Novato Unified School District,* 22 IDELR 1056 (SEA Cal. 1995), the school district did not invite the student, an 18-year-old with a serious emotional disturbance, but that deviation from this seemingly critical procedural requirement of the IDEA, surprisingly, did not result in a denial of FAPE. The hearing officer gave two reasons. First, one of the other attendees, a psychologist who was well-acquainted with the student, communicated the student's preferences about where he wanted to live after he finished his schooling. Second, the parents and the school district, and their advisors, mutually agreed that it was not in the student's best interests to participate in the meeting. The hearing officer does warn, though, that his waiving the requirement in this case should not be taken too far. "While [the student's non-participation] was considered a clinically sound practice, federal law requires that the student be invited." 21 IDELR at 1064.

7. Which agencies are likely to be responsible for providing transition services?

Both federal and state laws establish obligations independent of the IDEA to provide or pay for transition services for students with disabilities who meet the eligibility criteria for that program. As discussed in Question 19 below concerning graduation, upon leaving school the student and his or her family will be responsible for identifying where to obtain needed adult services and establishing eligibility. Transition IEP meetings provide an early opportunity for the student to meet representatives of relevant adult service agencies.

The legislative history of the transition amendments makes clear that responsibility for transition does not fall solely on the local educational agency. Any agency, other than the school district, that is financially and legally responsible for providing transition services to students is termed a "participating agency." 34 C.F.R. § 300.340.

The transition process thus can potentially involve many players beyond school personnel. Examples of agencies that administer such programs include the state department of vocational rehabilitation (DVR), state department of social services (DSS), Social Security Administration (SSA), and state department of mental health. These agencies provide a variety of services, including vocational training, job coaching, assistance in finding employment, funding for job-related equipment, counseling, and assistance in independent living.

A detailed explanation of participating agencies and the services they provide to students with disabilities is beyond the scope of this publication, although the author briefly discusses three agencies likely to be involved with students who have moderate to severe disabilities.[3]

For many students with disabilities, the primary adult service agency will be the state department of vocational rehabilitation. The Rehabilitation Act of 1973, 29 U.S.C. §§ 701-797, requires that each state establish such an agency. A student is eligible for vocational rehabilitation services if: (1) he or she has a physical or mental impairment which for such individual constitutes or results in a substantial impediment to employment; and (2) he or she can benefit in terms of an employment outcome from vocational rehabilitation services. 29 U.S.C. § 706(8)(A).

Other students with disabilities may be eligible for services, including case management, assistance with community living, and supported employment, provided by a state agency established pursuant to the Developmental Disabilities Assistance and Bill of Rights Act of 1975, 42 U.S.C. §§ 6000-6083. When originally passed the Act used a diagnostic definition for eligibility, however, 1978 amendments adopted a more functional approach to determining eligibility. As defined at 42 U.S.C. § 6001(8), an individual five years of age or older is eligible if he or she has a severe, chronic disability that is:

(A) attributable to a mental or physical impairment or combination of mental and physical impairment;

(B) manifested before age 22;

(C) likely to continue indefinitely;

(D) results in substantial functional limitations in 3 or more of the following areas of major life activity:

    1. self-care;

    2. receptive and expressive language;

    3. learning;

    4. mobility;

    5. self-direction;

---

[3] For a more detailed explanation of the role of participating agencies in providing post-school services *see* L. GARFINKEL, LEGAL ISSUES IN TRANSITIONING STUDENTS 1995.

6. capacity for independent living;

7. economic self-sufficiency; and

(E) reflects the person's need for a combination and sequence of special, interdisciplinary or generic services, supports or other assistance that is of lifelong or extended duration and is individually planned and coordinated.

The U.S. Social Security Administration (SSA) administers a cash assistance program known as Supplemental Security Income (SSI) to individuals with disabilities and financial need. An individual is disabled for SSI purposes if he or she is unable to engage in "substantial gainful activity," 42 U.S.C. § 1382c(a)(3)(A), because of a medically determinable physical or mental impairment which is expected to last for a continuous period of at least 12 months (or end in death). To determine if an adult (individual over the age of 18) is disabled for SSI purposes, the disability is compared to the impairments listed in the Code of Federal Regulations.[4] This listing contains impairments considered severe enough to prevent a person from working for one year or more. If the impairment is on the list or is equal to one on the list, the person is considered disabled without further analysis. If the impairment is not listed or is not equal to one on the list, then SSA assesses the person's ability to do any kind of work for which he or she would be otherwise suited, based on age, education and work experience.

8. What must the school district do if a representative of an agency likely to be responsible for providing or paying for transition services does not attend the IEP meeting?

IDEA regulations require the school district to take other steps to obtain the agency's participation in the planning of any required transition services. 34 C.F.R. § 300.344(c)(3). To the author's knowledge, neither IDEA regulations nor OSEP policy letters address what other steps should be taken; no reported decisions on either a judicial or administrative level provide guidance about how to—or how not to—seek to assure participation in the IEP process. Nevertheless, one approach, at least with regard to other state agencies, could be to initiate an action to compel compliance with the state's interagency agreement, assuming responsibilities for transition services are covered in that document.[5]

---

[4] 20 C.F.R. § 404, Subpart P, Appendix 1.

[5] As a related matter, *see* Question 17 in this chapter, *infra,* concerning how a school district must proceed if a participating agency refuses to provide the agreed-upon transition services.

9. Are there special requirements for parental notification about IEP meetings at which transition services will be discussed?

Yes. Aside from the generally applicable requirements concerning the content of parental notice set out in 34 C.F.R. § 300.345(b)(1),[6] special requirements for meetings convened to discuss, among other things, transition planning are set out in 34 C.F.R. § 300.345(b)(2). This section requires the school district to inform the parents of three things: (1) that one purpose of the meeting is consideration of transition; (2) that the student is invited to the meeting; and (3) the identity of any other agency that will be invited to send a representative.

10. Is there a required format for documenting transition planning?

Clearly, the school district should document the fact that there has been transition planning, as well as document the agreed-upon transition services, but there is no standard format for so documenting required by federal law.[7] In other words, while a statement of needed transition services is a required content element for IEPs under 34 C.F.R. § 300.346(b), there are no format requirements in 34 C.F.R. § 300.346(b) or elsewhere in the IDEA statute or regulations. Thus, a school district can choose to simply incorporate transition planning into the student's IEP. While not required by the IDEA, many school districts have developed a separate addendum to the IEP known as the Individualized Transition Plan (ITP).

Two administrative decisions emphasize that the format chosen by the school district to document its transition planning efforts needs to reflect the accomplishment of a meaningful effort. According to the administrative decision-maker in *Mason City Community School District,* 21 IDELR 248 (SEA Iowa 1994), the school district's use of a "mere checklist" was indicative of the superficiality of its efforts on behalf of a 19-year-old student with a disability who it proposed graduating, despite her not having substantially met IEP goals and objectives.[8]

Yet another hearing officer decision signals the dangers of using a "checklist" approach. In *Pasadena Independent School District,* 21 IDELR 482 (SEA Tex. 1994), a case involving a young woman with multiple cognitive, behavioral and communication deficits, the hearing officer summarized the duties of the school to initiate transition planning and determine appropriate post-school outcomes as part of the IEP process

---

[6] *See* Question 27 in chapter 5, *supra.*

[7] There are, however, requirements about content. *See* Questions 11 and 12 in this chapter, *infra.*

[8] *See* Question 19 in this chapter, *infra.*

and then compared these legal duties with the school's documentation of efforts. "The transition plan included in [the student's IEP] is woefully inadequate. A review of the pertinent exhibit shows that the plan is little more than a blank piece of paper with minimal attention to the regulatory requirements." 21 IDELR at 484.

11. Must the transition plan set out in the IEP contain goals and objectives?

No. Although annual goals and short-term objectives are required with respect to other educational services in the IEP, 34 C.F.R. § 300.346(a)(2), the IDEA does not specifically require that transition plans be stated in terms of annual goals and short-term objectives. Nevertheless, their use may be an appropriate method of documenting transition planning in some cases and is not prohibited.

12. What information about transition must be included in the IEP of a student with a disability?

In sum, the IDEA defines transition services as encompassing a broad range of services. The IEP must list all those services that the school district is required to provide for a particular student, based on the IEP team's consideration of his or her particular needs. In addition, if the IEP team has decided not to provide a particular transition service, it must articulate why the student does not require it. Finally, the IEP must identify the other agencies, both participating agencies (as defined in 34 § 300.340(b)) and other public agencies, to be involved in the student's transition from the school environment.

34 C.F.R. § 300.346(b) specifies the required content of IEPs covering transition services. That regulation identifies three distinct requirements.

- A statement of needed transition services, as defined in 34 C.F.R. § 300.18 (34 C.F.R. § 300.346(b)(1))

- When appropriate, "a statement of each public agency's and each participating agency's responsibilities or linkages, or both, before the student leaves the school setting" (34 C.F.R. § 300.346(b)(1))

- When the IEP team determines that certain transition services (those identified in 34 C.F.R. § 300.18(b)(2)(i)-(iii) are not required, a statement "to that effect and the basis upon which that determination was made" (34 C.F.R. § 300.346(b)(2))

Section 614(d)(1)(A)(vii) of the 1997 Amendments codify the prior requirements for statements of needed transition services and interagency responsibilities and add two additional related required statements.

- "[B]eginning at age 14, and updated annually, a statement of the transition service needs of the child under the applicable components of the child's IEP that focuses on the child's courses of study (such as participation in advanced-placement courses or a vocational education program)." Section 614(d)(1)(A)(vii)(I). According to the Committee Report to accompany the Senate's Reauthorization bill, "[t]he purpose of this requirement is to focus attention on how the child's educational program can be planned to help the child make a successful transition to his or her goals for life after secondary school. This provision is designed to augment, and not replace, the separate transition services requirement. . . ." S. Rep. No. 105-17, at 22 (1997).

- "[B]eginning at age 16 (or younger, if determined appropriate by the IEP Team), a statement of needed transition services for the child, including, when appropriate, a statement of the interagency responsibilities or any needed linkages." Section 614(d)(A)(vii)(II).

- "[B]eginning at least one year before the child reaches the age of majority under State law, a statement that the child has been informed of his or her rights under this title, if any, that will transfer to the child on reaching the age of majority under Section 615(m)." Section 614(d)(A)(vii)(III). *See also* Question 36 of chapter 5, *supra.*

Transition services are themselves defined in 34 C.F.R. § 300.18 as: "a coordinated set of activities for a student, designed within an outcome-oriented process, that promotes movement from school to post-school activities, including postsecondary education, vocational training, integrated employment (including supported employment), continuing and adult education, adult services, independent living, or community participation."

This definition is indeed quite a mouthful, for it identifies the services themselves (coordinated set of activities), the process the school district is obliged to follow (outcome-oriented), and the scope of the possible outcomes for the student that the IEP team should consider.

Because the definition of transition services contemplates that the coordinated set of activities[9] in the IEP statement of transition services be designed to lead to a variety of goals, we describe in more detail the post-school activities listed above.

Postsecondary Education. Numerous options for postsecondary education are available to transitioning students with disabilities, including technical trade schools, vocational centers, public community colleges and four-year colleges and universities. The outcome for one student with muscular dystrophy, for example, was a job that utilized his academic and computer skills and involved instruction in computer programming at the postsecondary level. As a result, provision of community college courses

---

[9] *See* Question 13 in this chapter, *infra.*

in computer training during high school was a transition service. *Chuhran v. Walled Lake Consolidated Schs.*, 22 IDELR 450 (6th Cir. 1995).

Vocational Training. Special education students may be mainstreamed into regular education vocational classes, such as metalshop, woodshop, welding and auto repair, with or without modification to the regular curriculum, as well as specially designed vocational instruction.

Integrated Employment (including supported employment). The IDEA does not define the terms "integrated employment" or "supported employment," but one proceeds on the premise that the definitions found in the Rehabilitation Act of 1973 and its implementing regulations apply. Thus, in integrated work settings individuals with disabilities interact on a regular basis with nondisabled workers or the public in the performance of job duties. Supported employment is work performed in an integrated work setting with ongoing support services for wages that meet minimum rates of the Fair Labor Standards Act (34 C.F.R. § 361.1(c)(2)). Transition activities that promote integrated or supported employment include career exploration, job searching, vocational education, job shadowing, preparing a resume and interviewing for a job.

Continuing and Adult Education. Adult education programs provide instruction to students age 16 or older who are not being served by the public high school and are not attending college. Adult education may include vocational programs, such as carpentry, health care and industrial arts. Continuing education is distinguished from adult education in that it typically provides personal enrichment rather than voca-tional training.

Adult Services. After a student graduates or "ages out" of high school, he or she must contact appropriate adult service providers and demonstrate eligibility for these services. Because the application process for some adult agencies can take several months, transitional planning can include assistance in processing an application prior to graduation and visiting agencies.

Independent Living. Transitional planning may include an exploration of where the student will live after graduation. Options vary, depending on, among other things, the student's self-care ability, and include the family home, rental housing, foster homes, group homes or personal care facilities.

Community Participation. Finally, transitional planning also may include devel-oping the student's participation in recreation and leisure in the community. Such planning may focus on development of personal and social skills necessary to participate in the community, such as taking turns and maintaining eye contact.

13. What are the transition activities that must be considered by the IEP team and included in the IEP?

A student's IEP team must consider what transition services constitute the "coordi-nated set of activities, designed within an outcome-oriented process, which promotes movement from school to post-school activities" (20 U.S.C. § 1410(a)(20)) for that particular student, taking into account his or her preferences and interests (20 U.S.C. § 1410(a)(19)).

The coordinated set of activities that should always be considered for inclusion in the IEP are:

- instruction (34 C.F.R. § 300.18(b)(2)(i));

- community experiences (34 C.F.R. § 300.18(b)(2)(ii)); and

- development of employment and other post-school adult living objectives (34 C.F.R. § 300.18(b)(2)(iii)).

As discussed in Question 12 above, if the IEP team agrees that any of such services are not required for a particular student, then his or her IEP must specifically so state and must articulate the basis for the decision. 34 C.F.R. § 300.346(b)(2); *Letter to Cernosia*, 19 IDELR 933 (OSEP 1993). Thus, even if the IEP team determines that no transition activities are required for a particular student, the IEP process of consideration must be documented.

In addition, to the extent appropriate, the coordinated set of activities includes those related to the "acquisition of daily living skills and functional vocational evaluation." 34 C.F.R. § 300.18.

Determination of a student's specific transition services is more a matter of FAPE as a substantive matter than a matter of compliance with the IEP procedural requirements, which is the subject of this publication. Two recent decisions involve parents who disputed the substantive adequacy of the proffered transition services: *Yankton School District v. Schramm*, 23 IDELR 42 (D.S.D. 1995) and *Montgomery County Public Schools*, 22 IDELR 754 (SEA Md. 1995). These cases may be just the tip of the iceberg.

14. What information must be included in the IEP about the responsibilities of other agencies in connection with transition planning?

The statement of needed transition services should include a commitment by any participating agency (for example, a state department of vocational rehabilitation) to meet any financial responsibilities it may have in the provision of transition services.

IDEA regulations at 34 C.F.R. § 300.346(b)(1) state that, when it is appropriate for a particular student, the IEP "must include a statement of each public agency's and each participating agency's responsibilities or linkages, or both, before the student leaves the school setting." While there is no definition of linkages, that term generally is understood to involve the district taking a leadership position in contacting agencies expected to provide services to the student once he or she exits the school system and acting as a liaison between the parents and the other agencies while the student is enrolled in school. This is as opposed to the responsibilities other agencies may have for funding or providing the transition services themselves. *See also Letter to Bereuter,* 20 IDELR 536 (OSEP 1993).

The importance of this requirement—the objective it is intended to further—is aptly illustrated by the deficiencies in the school district's transition planning in *Yankton School District v. Schramm,* 23 IDELR 42 (D.S.D. 1995), *aff'd,* 24 IDELR 704 (8th Cir. 1996). That case concerned a student with cerebral palsy who used a walker and a wheelchair. Although she had no cognitive disabilities, the court affirmed the hearing officer's finding that the student required transition services in the areas of instruction, community experience and self-help skills, and also would probably need services provided or funded by other agencies once she graduated high school.

With regard to these linkages, the IEP process was woefully short, with that shortfall reflected in the IEP.

> The District contends that it fulfills its responsibility to develop and implement interagency participation in transition services if it communicates to the disabled student and her parents the kinds of agencies in the community that may be able to help the student in the future and provides the student and her family with "linkages" to those agencies. . . . The transition plan drafted at that meeting states that vocational rehabilitation services, Supplemental Security Income and "other programs available" were explained and that Tracy will need "Public and Private Transportation with assistive devices when appropriate." The District wrote that, "If Tracy is eligible for SSI she will also be eligible for Medicaid," and that "Prairie Freedom Center will be contacted by [the student's mother.]" . . . Tracy and her parents were assigned follow-up responsibility in every area, with the exception that [one individual] (whose position is not identified) was named as additionally responsible for "Post-Secondary Education and Vocational" and [another individual] was named as additionally responsible regarding finances and medical services.

> The Court finds that such a minimal approach to school district responsibility for transition services planning and implementation fails to comport with the expectation of Congress. . . . The Court will require the District to convene a transition planning meeting for Tracy at which and after which the District will provide leadership in planning and implementing necessary transition services. . . .

23 IDELR at 47.

15. Must the transition plan in the IEP of a student who will be attending college state the particular test-taking strategies that should be used with the student?

No, according to the state review panel in the only case to the author's knowledge that addresses this particular issue. Such disputes probably will become more prevalent, though, as the entire issue of accommodations for students with learning disabilities attending postsecondary schools has been heating up in the past few years.

In *Lower Moreland Township School District,* 25 IDELR 351 (SEA Pa. 1996), the student whose IEP was at issue was a senior with a mild learning disability who had been accepted by the University of Pittsburgh prior to his parents' filing for due process. The parents had approved an IEP at the start of their son's senior year which called for "non-traditional test-taking methods" including additional time, and adapted length and format of tests. Upon acceptance of the student, the University of Pittsburgh requested information about the student's special needs as a learning disabled student, including an IEP.

The parents apparently did not authorize or request forwarding of the IEP. Rather, in May of the year set for graduation, the parents filed for due process, seeking, among other things, revision of the IEP to include "a very detailed optimal statement of how testing would be done." 25 IDELR at 352.

While the review panel understood the parents' desire to make their best case for the specific accommodations they believed vital to their son's college success, it refused to order the school district to provide this assistance. For purposes of the student's actual senior year experience, the statement of accommodations in the IEP was appropriate. The student made educational progress and had been, in fact, accepted by a "fine university." Turning to the parents' alternative claim, that a more specific statement of testing accommodations was a required part of the student's transition plan, the panel found no basis in the law to support the parents' position.

16. Can a school district assign responsibilities to parents in a transition plan?

No, school districts cannot unilaterally delegate their responsibilities to parents. This was made clear in *Yankton School District v. Schramm,* 23 IDELR 42 (D.S.D. 1995), discussed in Question 14 above.

The hearing officer in *In re Child with Disabilities,* 21 IDELR 624 (SEA Conn. 1994), also reached the same conclusion. The school district in that case violated the IDEA when it assigned the parents the responsibility to investigate work study options. Instead, it should have included in the IEP the process it was going to follow to secure the work site and training for the students and then followed through on that process to identify a work site.

17. What obligations does a school district have if an agency who has a commitment to provide transition services included in the IEP fails or refuses to provide them?

If a participating agency fails to provide agreed-upon services, the IDEA requires that the IEP team meet to identify other ways to meet the student's transition objectives. 20 U.S.C. § 1401(a)(20)(F); *Letter to Anonymous,* 21 IDELR 673 (OSEP 1994).

Agencies have an obligation independent of the IDEA to provide or pay for transition services to students with disabilities who meet the eligibility criteria of that agency. The IDEA does not relieve them of any responsibility they would otherwise have. 34 C.F.R. § 300.347(b). Nevertheless, the school district is the party ultimately responsible to the student for ensuring that transition services called for in the student's IEP are implemented. *See generally* 20 U.S.C. § 1412(b).

Thus, 34 C.F.R. § 300.347(a) states:

> If a participating agency fails to provide agreed-upon transition services contained in the IEP of a student with a disability, the public agency responsible for the student's education shall, as soon as possible, initiate a meeting for the purpose of identifying alternative strategies to meet the transition objectives and, if necessary, revising the student's IEP.

The school district's obligation in this regard is illustrated in a case decided under Section 504. In *Martinsville (VA) City Public Schools,* 16 EHLR 1088 (OCR 1990), the student's IEP called for full-time attendance in a community workshop, but the particular workshop refused to allow full-time attendance. OCR found that the district should have reconvened the IEP team to pursue other options to fulfill the transition goal of vocational placement. Had the case been brought under the IDEA, the result would certainly have been the same.

While the school district must ensure that transition planning and services continue even when a participating agency defaults, the district can simultaneously take action to attempt to force the defaulting agency to fulfill its obligations to the student. Each state plan for special education sets forth policies and procedures for developing and implementing interagency agreements between school districts and other agencies that must provide or pay for services for students with disabilities. 20 U.S.C. § 1413(a)(13). Such agreements also establish procedures for resolving interagency disputes, although how those procedures play out when the dispute concerns transition services is unclear, and is likely to remain so until a dispute percolates through a state's judicial system.

Section 612(a)(12)(B)(ii) of the 1997 Amendments specifically applies the general rule of the IDEA (at 20 U.S.C. Section 1412(6)) to transition services, among other things. This section makes the school district or other responsible educational agency responsible for paying for or providing such services if the public agency that is otherwise responsible refuses to do so and creates a federal right to claim reimbursement from the defaulting agency (under procedures established by the state).

18. Does a school district's failure to comply with the procedural requirements for transition planning result in a denial of FAPE?

Compliance with the IDEA's procedural requirements for IEP design and implementation is a factor in determining whether a student with a disability has received

FAPE, although noncompliance is not always fatal. Courts often have held that procedural violations do not deny FAPE unless they result in a substantial deprivation of a student's or parent's rights.[10] That general principle has been applied by courts in connection with noncompliance with the procedural requirements for transition planning.

In *Chuhran v. Walled Lake Consolidated Schools,* 22 IDELR 450 (6th Cir. 1995), the court affirmed the lower court's decision (20 IDELR 1035) that the school district's failure to prepare a written transition plan was an "insubstantial" technical defect because the student had been provided adequate transition services, agreed to at properly convened and conducted IEP meetings.

To like effect, the Tenth Circuit Court of Appeals in *Urban v. Jefferson County School District R-1,* 24 IDELR 465, 496 (10th Cir. 1996), stated that "it is important to distinguish between the statement of transition services in the IEP and the provision of transition services." While the student's IEP did not contain an explicit statement of transition services, the court found from the evidence that appropriate services had been provided nonetheless; the student did not challenge the quality of the services. Furthermore, the IEP contained language that addressed his needs for community awareness and daily living skills. Without a corresponding substantive violation, the procedural defect did not deprive the student of an appropriate education.

Graduation

19. May a school district graduate a student with a disability who has not met all of the goals and objectives set out in his or her IEP?

Generally, no is the answer provided by both long-standing and more recent authoritative case law. Assuming the goals and objectives in the child's IEP are realistically achievable, as they must be to comply with the IDEA, then the child who has not met them in the course of his or her schooling has not received the educational benefit to which he or she is entitled. While no specific statutory or regulatory provision dictates this result, both OSEP and courts interpreting the IDEA consider this conclusion a necessary consequence of the law.

Whether a student with a disability can be properly graduated is a vital, and frequently disputed, issue. And one can see why. "The award of a diploma to a student with a disability has significant consequences. Whereas prior to graduation the student is entitled to receive a multitude of services from one central source (the school district), after graduation the student is responsible for identifying and establishing eligibility

---

[10] *See* Question 10 in chapter 12, *infra,* for a more detailed discussion.

for appropriate services from a potentially vast array of adult agencies." *Novato Unified Sch. Dist.*, 22 IDELR 1056 (SEA Cal. 1995).

Generally, a student's eligibility terminates on the earlier of the date: (1) he or she reaches the maximum age for entitlement to services or (2) he or she is properly graduated. 20 U.S.C. § 1401(a)(10). *See, e.g., Letter to Richards*, 17 EHLR 288 (OSEP 1990); *Gorski v. Lynchburg Sch. Bd.*, 1988-89 EHLR 441:415 (4th Cir. 1989). The IDEA does not require any state to provide a postsecondary education to a student with a disability. *Gorski v. Lynchburg Sch. Bd., supra; Cronin v. Board of East Ramapo Sch. Dist.*, 1988-89 EHLR 441:124 (D.N.J. 1988). Because the maximum age for eligibility is through age 21 in most states (34 C.F.R. § 300.300(a)), some students with disabilities may be able to receive more educational services if they are not graduated. While some students will be entitled to receive supportive services from other agencies or programs after graduation, the uncertainty and disruption resulting from the termination of school district responsibility should not go unappreciated.

Just as some parents may wish to prolong the termination of eligibility as long as possible, some school districts are just as eager to hasten the departure of some students with disabilities. *Honig v. Doe*, 1987-88 EHLR 559:231 (1988). This was the circumstance ruled on by the U.S. Supreme Court in *Helms v. Independent School District No. 3*, 750 F.2d 820 (10th Cir. 1984), where the Court held that the graduation of students with disabilities was a sham designed to terminate responsibility at the earliest possible moment under circumstances where students without disabilities were provided with additional schooling. In that case, students with disabilities were passed through from year to year with little consideration of whether they had satisfied the goals included in their IEPs, while nondisabled students were retained if they did not satisfy the academic requirements established for promotion from grade to grade.

The inevitable conflict thus results as parents, fearful about their child's future, question whether the school district has failed to consider the interests of their child in proposing graduation. The situation is well described by the administrative law judge in *Millburn Township Board of Education*, 20 IDELR 463 (SEA N.J. 1993):

> [T]he parents' objection to the school district's determination to graduate their son ... stemmed from their belief that he had not attained the recommended target established in the particular IEP, and therefore graduation would leave him not only without any program, but without any success with respect to going on in life. And they argued that therefore this graduation, while it wasn't a complete sham in the classic sense, nevertheless would violate the meaning and spirit of the special education laws. . . .

With this background, the following discussion deals with administrative decisions and OSEP policy letters concerning the relationship between IEP goals and objectives and the decision to graduate a student with a disability.[11]

---

[11] Disputes concerning graduation almost inevitably involve disputes about the provision of what we now term "transition services." Prior to the inclusion of the transition services requirement to the IDEA

Generally, a school district establishing that a student with a disability has successfully met the goals and objectives contained in his or her IEP (assuming that IEP provides an appropriate program) and should therefore be graduated will prevail in a dispute with parents seeking an extension of services. That was the ruling of the Third Circuit in *Wexler v. Westfield Board of Education,* 1985-86 EHLR 557:282 (3d Cir. 1986) and the Fourth Circuit in *Gorski v. Lynchburg School District, supra.* OSEP endorsed this position in, among other policy letters, *Letter to Richards,* 17 EHLR 288 (OSEP 1990).

On the other hand, as illustrated by the administrative decision in *Mason City Community School District,* 21 IDELR 248 (SEA Iowa 1994), if a parent establishes that the decision to graduate was not made on the basis of achievement of IEP goals and objectives, then the school district may remain obligated to provide further services. The parents in *Mason City* successfully challenged the school district's proposal to graduate their 19-year-old multidisabled daughter. At the last IEP meeting held before the proposed graduation date, members of the IEP team identified need for further growth for the student to achieve her social, emotional and job skill goals and objectives. Nevertheless, the school district supported graduation solely on the basis of the student having accumulated 40 credits (with each credit indicating successful completion of an academic course in regular education, special education, or regular education with accommodations). The administrative law judge found that the use of credits for purposes of determining graduation was essentially meaningless in this instance. Because the student had not substantially completed her IEP goals and objectives and additional educational opportunity would likely allow her to do so, the district could not graduate her, as proposed.

This is not to say that a student who has failed to substantially complete his or her IEP goals cannot be properly graduated. School districts, after all, cannot be responsible for failures due to lack of effort on the student's part. Further, IDEA regulations make it clear that the IEP is not an educational contract guaranteeing success. 34 C.F.R. § 300.350.

One interesting administrative decision has, in fact, supported the school district's decision to graduate a 20-year-old student with a disability notwithstanding his failure to meet the social-emotional, vocational and daily living skills goals and objectives of his IEP. In *Hamilton County School District,* 23 IDELR 772 (SEA Tenn. 1996), the school district had placed the student in an out-of-state (Connecticut) residential school. Upon completion of the academic and credit requirements of his IEP, the student graduated, receiving a high school diploma in accordance with general Connecticut

---

(20 U.S.C. § 1410(a)(19)), the child's entitlement to services to help prepare him or her for post-school life was more uncertain, but the core concerns motivating parents in graduation disputes was even so grounded in a claim that the school district, in failing to adequately equip the student for the future, failed to provide FAPE. We discuss transition services, in relation to the IEP process, in Questions 1 through 18 in this chapter, *supra.*

criteria. The parent filed for due process, challenging the district's decision to graduate him. The administrative law judge found that the student had not achieved the nonacademic goals in his IEP, but affirmed the graduation nonetheless, refusing to order the school district to provide additional services.

The reasoning is persuasive on a superficial basis. Some students will have lifelong difficulties; there has to be an end at some point to a school's obligations. But on a more critical level, the author believes the administrative law judge's reasoning flawed. The IDEA establishes maximum ages for eligibility. By neglecting to take into account that students may "age out" of eligibility, the ALJ discounted the legitimacy of the severely disabled student's nonacademic goals—agreed to by the school district in the first instance—and the significance of his failure to achieve them. Such goals, if properly designed, should not have been intended to do anything more than allow the student to receive an educational benefit under the IDEA's FAPE standard. They should have been realistic and attainable. Thus, the author finds the ALJ's philosophizing about burdening school districts with responsibility for students not achieving unreachable goals a nice piece of rhetoric, but off the point. But, judge for yourself. Here is an extended excerpt from the opinion.

> Congress intended that local school systems provide educational benefits to disabled children, but a school system is not responsible for the continued care and treatment of the student simply because he may not be able to function in an unrestricted environment or can not return to his home for reasons unrelated to his educational placement. The Supreme Court made this point clear in its seminal decision in *Board of Education of Hendrick Hudson Central School District v. Rowley,* 1981-82 EHLR 553:656 (1982), wherein the Court stated in footnote 23 as follows:
>
>> Because many mildly handicapped children will achieve self-sufficiency without state assistance while personal independence for the severely handicapped may be an unreachable goal, "self-sufficiency" as a substantive standard is at once inadequate protection and an over demanding requirement. We thus view these referenced in the legislative history as evidence of Congress' intention that the services provided handicapped children be educationally beneficial, whatever the nature or severity of their handicap.
>
> A school system is not required to guarantee that the Student will be self-sufficient once he completes his course of study with the school system. In this case, the Student has completed his educational requirements and has graduated with a Connecticut diploma. Pursuant to the [IDEA], the Student is not eligible for post-graduate services. The undisputed facts are that the student has met all academic requirements for graduation and has graduated.

23 IDELR at 774.

20. Should an IEP contain graduation criteria?

Yes and no. IDEA regulations at 34 C.F.R. § 346 do not include a requirement that an IEP contain specifically identified graduation criteria or a graduation plan.

Nonetheless, the IEP must contain goals and objectives (34 C.F.R. § 300.346(a)(2)) and a transition plan (34 C.F.R. § 300.346(b)). Generally speaking, graduation criteria can be described in terms of accomplishment of those goals and objectives, plus receipt of the specified transition services.[12] Further, because graduation is considered a significant change in placement for purposes of students eligible for services under Section 504 and the ADA only, an IEP or accommodation plan promulgated under these laws should reflect the criteria necessary for graduation. *Letter to Runkel,* 25 IDELR 387 (OCR 1996).

Because in this area the IDEA acts as a floor, states could establish a specific requirement to include graduation criteria in an IEP. That was the case in *Mason City Community School District,* 21 IDELR 241 (SEA Iowa 1994). Iowa state law mandated inclusion in the IEP of the criteria to be used in judging whether graduation should occur.

Despite the lack of a federal requirement for inclusion of specific graduation criteria in a student's IEP, the school district's decision to graduate a student still must be made by an IEP team, as discussed in Question 21 below. Further, long-standing authoritative case law has held that graduation is a change in placement, thus triggering the IDEA's procedural safeguards. *Gorski v. Lynchburg Sch. Bd.,* 1988-89 EHLR 441:415 (4th Cir. 1989); *Wexler v. Westfield Bd. of Educ.,* 1985-86 EHLR 557:282 (3d Cir. 1986).

21. Must the school district convene an IEP meeting prior to graduating a student with a disability?

Yes, it should, and failure to do so generally will nullify the decision to graduate the student. According to OSEP, under the IDEA each school district should initiate and conduct a review of the child's IEP at an appropriate time to assure that graduation requirements will be met and the goals and objectives of the IEP will be completed. *Letter to Richards,* 17 EHLR 288 (OSEP 1990).

One of the relatively few authoritative state court decisions concerning the IDEA, *Stock v. Massachusetts Hospital School,* 1983-84 EHLR 555:550 (Mass. 1984), invalidated a public agency's unilateral decision to graduate an 18-year-old student with multiple cognitive and physical disabilities. In that case, the student's teachers proposed that the student graduate and prepared an IEP to that effect without convening an IEP meeting or providing any notice to the student or his parents. The agency obtained the student's signature on the IEP document and claimed that was an effective consent to the graduation. The court found the unilateral decision violated the IDEA. In fact, in view of the student's severe disabilities and limited comprehension, the court found the agency's actions highly improper.

---

[12] *See* Question 19 in this chapter, *supra,* concerning accomplishment of goals and objectives in connection with graduation and this chapter generally concerning transition services.

While ordinarily an IEP developed without any parental participation would be invalidated on that basis alone, one surprising administrative decision, *Montgomery County Public Schools,* 22 IDELR 754 (SEA Md. 1995), upheld a graduation decision that was made without first conducting an IEP meeting or otherwise notifying or securing the input of the parents. The school district proposed to graduate a 17-year-old student with a serious emotional disturbance and autism who had received special education and related services through his entire schooling, from grades one through 12. Despite his disabilities the student did well with his academic progress and met all the state's generally applicable criteria for graduation from a public high school. The parents, believing the student's behavior problems needed to be addressed further, requested an IEP meeting in February of his senior year to review the graduation decision. The school district graduated the student without honoring the request for a meeting.

When the parents sought due process, both the local hearing officer and the review officer upheld the school district's decision. Both agreed that the district violated both state and federal procedural requirements, that the violation was a serious breach of the student's rights, and that the parents were correct in claiming that the student has not achieved "100%" of his potential. Despite these findings, no relief was ordered. "It is quite clear from the evidence that [the student] has gone as far as one can go within the system; and while in the system, reasonable effort was made to advance him." 22 IDELR at 756.

In one of the differences between the IDEA and Section 504, OCR stated in *Letter to Runkel,* 25 IDELR 387 (OCR 1996), that neither Section 504 nor the ADA (Title II) require an IEP meeting before a student covered under those laws graduates from high school. Nevertheless, while there is no express requirement for a "formal" determination about whether a student should be graduated, such procedures are advisable.

Other Terminations of Services

22. Must a school district convene an IEP meeting prior to terminating special education services?

Generally, yes. As explained by OSEP in *Letter to Hagen-Gilden,* 24 IDELR 294 (1996):

> [W]hen a decision to terminate the special education and related services to a child with a disability is based on the child's educational progress and accomplishments of the child's IEP's goals and objectives, that decision must be made by the IEP team during a properly convened IEP meeting that meets the participant requirements of 34 C.F.R. § 300.344.

24 IDELR at 295; *accord Letter to Steinke,* 21 IDELR 379 (OSEP 1994).

Letter to Hagen-Gilden does identify one exception to the requirement for convening an IEP meeting. If the multidisciplinary team determines (as a result of a reevaluation[13]) that the student is no longer IDEA-eligible, then an IEP meeting need not be held prior to the termination of services.

In an interesting case, a school district claimed unsuccessfully in *Beede v. Town of Washington School District,* 18 IDELR 1295 (D. Vt. 1992), that it did not have to convene an IEP meeting to terminate a student's special education services because the IEP contained a "sunset provision" under which the IEP and the student's eligibility expired one year from its date of origin. Specifically, the IEP contained a statement "buried within the document" that "it is believed that Amy would benefit from one year of language remediating." The court found that, in proceeding in this way, the district violated both the letter and the spirit of the IDEA.

The 1997 Amendments appear to overturn OSEP's *Letter to Hagen-Gilden* in connection with a determination that a student is no longer IDEA-eligible. Although it is not expressed clearly, Section 614(c)(4) appears to require that such determinations be made by "the IEP Team and other qualified professionals."

---

[13] Conducted in accordance with 34 C.F.R. § 300.534.

Chapter 11

Section 504, Part H (New Part C) and Public Agencies

This chapter, in the main, addresses Section 504 of the Rehabilitation Act of 1973 and Part H of the IDEA (providing early intervention services to eligible infants and toddlers). While generally there is no intersection between Part B (providing special education to preschool and school age children with disabilities) and Part H (although a state may choose to serve children from birth through age 2 under Part B), Section 504 can be thought of as a "wider but less deep" alternative to Part B.

This introduction addresses Section 504. In a nutshell—and subject to all the reservations that result from broad generalizations—all IDEA-eligible children of school age also are eligible under Section 504, but the opposite is not the case. While Section 504 appears to provide the same services and programming to students with disabilities as the IDEA, in practice students with the most intense needs receive support in accordance with the IDEA.

Unlike the IDEA, which is a funding statute, Section 504 is an antidiscrimination law. It provides, in pertinent part:

> No otherwise qualified individual with a disability in the United States, as defined in [29 U.S.C. § 706(8)], shall, solely by reason of her or his disability, be excluded from participation in, be denied the benefits of, or be subjected to discrimination under any program or activity receiving Federal financial assistance or under any program or activity conducted by any Executive agency or by the United States Postal Service.

29 U.S.C. § 794.

Virtually every school district receives federal financial assistance, and thus Section 504 applies to each. Nonetheless, despite Section 504's wide applicability and the long time it has been on the books, implementation has been difficult for many schools, in large part due to confusion regarding the districts' role(s). Although Section 504 consists of nondiscrimination language, its regulations for secondary and elementary education parallel the approach under the IDEA.

In fact, in many ways Section 504, in its application to secondary and elementary education in the public schools, is similar to the requirements under the IDEA. In many other ways, however, the responsibilities and requirements under Section 504 differ from those under the IDEA.

For one thing, the IDEA sets forth very detailed and comprehensive rules for states to follow to ensure that children with disabilities receive a free appropriate public education (FAPE). Unlike the IDEA, Section 504 does not set out comprehensive rules for school districts to follow when educating children with disabilities, although the regulations promulgated pursuant to Section 504 by the United States Department of Education (DOE) do set out some specific criteria for school districts to follow when providing special education services to children with disabilities. The DOE regulations provide, however, that with respect to the provision of FAPE, a school district's procedural compliance with the IDEA is one means of complying with the procedural requirements of Section 504.

A significant difference between the laws, in relation to school age students with disabilities, is the eligibility criteria. The IDEA protects only students who, by virtue of their disabilities, require special educational services. Section 504, however, prohibits discrimination against all school age children, regardless of whether or not they require special education services.

There are numerous instances in which Section 504, but not the IDEA, might apply to school age children. One such instance involves a child who suffers from an illness that has not progressed to the point that the child requires special education, but whose illness does affect the child to such a degree that accommodations are required to allow the child to continue in the regular classroom. For example, a child with a moderate case of cystic fibrosis could attend regular classes if accommodated by the provision of respiratory therapy services during the day.

Other situations in which school children might be covered by Section 504, but not the IDEA, include temporarily injured children; children or youths who are alcoholics or drug addicts; students with diabetes, asthmatic bronchitis, allergies, severe asthma or juvenile arthritis; morbidly obese children; children with AIDS; and children with Attention Deficit Disorder (ADD). With respect to ADD, the DOE's Office for Civil Rights developed a policy statement to provide guidance to school districts on their responsibilities toward children with ADD.

Section 504

1. Is an IEP required for students with disabilities eligible only under Section 504?

No, although Section 504 likewise requires that schools design an individualized program to meet a student's needs, 34 C.F.R. § 104.33(b)(1), sometimes called an individual accommodation plan, and that requirement can be met by developing an IEP. 34 C.F.R. § 104.33(b)(2). *Accord Letter to Pollo,* 21 IDELR 1132 (OSEP 1994) (IEPs are not required for students covered solely under Section 504; however a school district may opt to use an IEP). In fact, while not recommended, Section 504 permits informal or even verbal accommodation plans, assuming the other procedural safeguards of Section 504 can be met using this approach. *See M.H. v. Montana High Sch. Ass'n,* 25 IDELR 42 (Mont. 1996).

Does that mean you should follow the IDEA's IEP procedures for all students with disabilities, even those protected only by Section 504? Some education experts do not recommend it. For students protected by Section 504, but ineligible for IDEA services, it is preferable to avoid the complex IDEA procedures in drafting individual accommodation plans. For one thing, using the same approach to meet two different requirements may create some confusion among school personnel as to who is a Section 504-eligible student and who is an IDEA-eligible student. That confusion could lead to misuse of federal funds, since IDEA funds cannot be used for ineligible students. Another reason for not using the IDEA IEP procedure is simplicity. The numerous content requirements of an IEP[1] are in many cases unnecessary to develop an appropriate accommodation plan for a Section 504 student.

2. What information should be included in a Section 504 accommodation plan?

An accommodation plan must address the following five concerns:

1. *Nature of the student's disability and the major life activity it limits.* Keep in mind that students are eligible for Section 504 protection if they have a physical or mental impairment that substantially limits one or more major life activities or if they have a record of or are regarded as having such an impairment. 34 C.F.R. § 104.3(j). In the school context, the major life activity affected most frequently is learning; however, it is not limited to that. A student with asthma, for example, may be eligible for accommodations if the condition substantially limits the major life activity of breathing. It's the job of the multidisciplinary team that evaluates the student to determine

---

[1] *See* chapter 2, *supra.*

if the disability substantially limits a major life activity. *See Letter to McKethan,* 23 IDELR 504 (OCR 1994).

2. *The basis for determining the disability.* Section 504, like the IDEA, requires schools to meet certain evaluation procedures, which must be documented in the accommodation plan. 34 C.F.R. § 104.35(b).

3. *The educational impact of the disability.* The multidisciplinary team must describe how the disability affects the child's educational performance so proper accommodations can be prescribed.

4. *Necessary accommodations.* Keep in mind that Section 504's FAPE standard requires schools to provide services that "are designed to meet the individual needs of handicapped persons as adequately as the needs of non-handicapped persons are met." 34 C.F.R. § 104.33(b)(1)(i). Because this standard differs from the IDEA's standard, it is possible in some cases for the required services to also differ from those mandated under the IDEA.

5. *Placement in the least restrictive environment.* Section 504 has an LRE requirement, codified at 34 C.F.R. § 104.34, that is similar to the LRE mandate of the IDEA.

3. May a parent of an IDEA-eligible student demand that the school district provide services under a Section 504 accommodation plan rather than an IEP?

No, according to OCR in its *Letter to McKethan,* 25 IDELR 295 (OCR 1996). Once a school district finds a student to have a disability within the meaning of the IDEA and develops an IEP in accordance with the IDEA, parents cannot refuse to accept the IDEA services as specified therein and instead require the school district to develop an accommodation plan under Section 504. OCR explained that for students who qualify for services under the IDEA (and as a result, Section 504), the use of an IDEA IEP is the way in which the Section 504 requirements regarding documentation of programming (34 C.F.R. § 104.33) are met. According to OCR, a rejection of the services offered under an IEP that complies with IDEA requirements amounts to a rejection of services under Section 504, as well.

Americans with Disabilities Act

4. Is an IEP required for students with disabilities eligible under the Americans with Disabilities Act?

No, the same standards governing permissive use of IEPs under Section 504 apply.[2]

The Americans with Disabilities Act of 1990 (ADA) is a broad mandate to eliminate discrimination against persons with disabilities in virtually all aspects of public life in

---

[2] *See* Question 1 in this chapter, *supra.*

our society, from seeking employment to buying a lottery ticket. Title II of the ADA prohibits "public entities" (a defined term that includes public schools, as well as courthouses, town halls, libraries and municipal government entities) from discriminating on the basis of disability.

Implementing regulations at 28 C.F.R. Part 35 clarify the nature of a public entity's duties under Title II by identifying general requirements concerning, among other things, employment, program accessibility and communications. The breadth of the nondiscrimination mandate of Title II can hardly be overstated; in essence, every action taken by a public school must be evaluated for consistency with the Title's requirements.

Because they are written for a wide array of public entities, the regulations, like the ADA statute itself, contain no explicit reference obligating school districts to provide FAPE to children with disabilities. However, OCR has interpreted the ADA as incorporating all Section 504 protections that may afford students with disabilities more extensive rights. *See e.g., Newburyport (MA) Pub. Sch.,* 21 IDELR 813 (OCR 1994). The FAPE requirement found in Section 504 provides greater protection for students with disabilities than the reasonable modification requirement of the ADA. *Urban v. Jefferson County Sch. Dist. R-1,* 24 IDELR 465 (10th Cir. 1997). *Accord Prins v. Independent Sch. Dist. No. 761,* 23 IDELR 544 (D. Minn. 1995).

As a result, OCR interprets the ADA Title II regulations to require school districts to provide FAPE to the same extent as is required under Section 504. *Madera (CA) Unified Sch. Dist.,* 22 IDELR 510 (OCR 1995). Thus, OCR imposes the same procedural requirements on school districts with respect to FAPE as govern educational decisions under Section 504. As stated in *Madera:*

> When read in conjunction, . . . Section 504 and Title II regulations require the District to: 1) provide adequate notice of evaluation and placement meetings to parents/guardians of disabled students in order to allow meaningful input and participation, and 2) consider relevant information provided by parents/guardians in reaching evaluation or placement decisions.

22 IDELR at 511.

Transition from Part H

5. *What is an "individualized family service plan"?*

Just as an IEP is the main document for mapping the services to be given a child with disabilities under Part B of the IDEA, the principal document for identifying services for an infant or toddler under Part H is the individualized family service plan or IFSP. The IFSP is defined in Part H regulations at 34 C.F.R. § 303.340(b) as "a written plan for providing early intervention services to a child eligible under this part and the child's family."

The IFSP process is similar to the IEP process, mandating meetings attended by a designated group of individuals and stressing the importance of parental participation. Services provided under the IFSP, termed early intervention services, bear some resemblance to the components of special education and related services under Part B, although naturally there are age and developmental level differences in the particulars of the services provided. In addition, there are three types of services unique to Part H: (1) family support services, (2) nutrition services and (3) case management.

6. Must an IFSP contain the same information as an IEP?

No, although there is a great deal of similarity as a result of the common process for assessing the individual child's unique needs and the ways in which services will be provided for that child.

Part H regulations at 34 C.F.R. § 303.344 establish content requirements for IFSPs. According to the regulation, the IFSP must contain:

- information about the child's status, including the child's present levels of physical development, cognitive development, language and speech development, psychosocial development and self-help skills (34 C.F.R. § 303.344(a));

- with the family's permission, a statement of the family's strengths and needs relating to enhancing the development of the child (34 C.F.R. § 303.344(b));

- an outcome statement, with criteria, procedures and time lines (34 C.F.R. § 303.344(c));

- a listing of the specific early intervention services necessary to meet the unique needs of the child and the family to achieve the outcomes and give the frequency, intensity, location and method of services and the payment arrangements, if any (34 C.F.R. § 303.344(d));

- to the extent appropriate, a listing of medical and other services that the child needs but that are not required under the Part H program and the steps that will be undertaken to get the services (34 C.F.R. § 303.344(e)); and

- the projected dates for the initiation of the services and the anticipated duration of the services (34 C.F.R. § 303.344(f)).

The IFSP content requirements set out in Part C of the 1997 Amendments at Section 636(d) continue to differ from those for Part B IEPs; now they also differ from those in Part H. For our purposes, the most pertinent change is the requirement that the document specifically address the students' transition from coverage under Part C to Part B.

Section 636(d) provides that the IFSP shall contain a statement of:

- the infant's or toddler's present levels of physical development, cognitive development, communication development, social or emotional development, and adaptive development (Section 636(d)(1));

- the family's resources, priorities and concerns relating to enhancing the development of the infant or toddler (Section 636(d)(2));

- the major outcomes expected to be achieved for the infant or toddler and his or her family, criteria for determining progress made toward such outcomes (any revisions of either outcomes or services to achieve them are required.) (Section 636(d)(3));

- the specific early intervention services necessary to meet the unique needs of the infant or toddler and the family, including the frequency, intensity and method of delivery (Section 636(d)(4));

- the natural environments in which the early intervention services will be provided, including a justification of the extent, if any, to which the services will not be provided (Section 636(d)(5));

- the date the services will begin and their anticipated duration (Section 636(d)(6));

- the identification of the service coordinator from the profession most immediately relevant to the infant's or toddler's or family's needs who will be responsible for the implementation of the plan and coordination with other agencies and persons (Section 636(d)(7)); and

- the steps to be taken to support the transition of the toddler with a disability to preschool or other appropriate services (Section 636(d)(8)).

7. May a responsible public agency use an IFSP rather than an IEP to provide FAPE to preschool age children?

Yes. According to OSEP the IDEA permits states to elect to allow its school districts and intermediate educational units to use an IFSP instead of an IEP to provide FAPE to children with disabilities transitioning from Part H up until the sixth birthday, assuming the parents consent. *OSEP Memorandum 14*, 19 IDELR 1130 (OSEP 1993). The 1997 Amendments also so provide. Section 614(d)(2)(B).

8. Does the mandated process for the development of an initial IEP for a child with a disability differ when the child has been receiving early intervention services under Part H?

Yes, 1991 amendments to the IDEA included changes to Part B and Part H (the Early Intervention Program for Infants and Toddlers with Disabilities) to allow states greater flexibility in implementing a system for transitioning children with disabilities from early intervention services under Part H (20 U.S.C. §§ 1471-1485) to preschool special education programs under Part B (20 U.S.C. §§ 1411-1420). Under the law, the lead agency charged with administration of Part H need not be the state educational agency. For that reason, coordination is vital when a child is transferring from one program to another to ensure there is no interruption in services. Part H at 20 U.S.C. § 1478(a)(8) requires the lead agency to initiate the transition process no later than 90 days prior to the child's third birthday.

Part B regulations at 34 C.F.R. § 300.154 describe this requirement, approached from the other end, as follows:

> Each State plan must set forth policies and procedures relating to the smooth transition for those individuals participating in the early intervention program under Part H of the Act who will participate in preschool programs assisted under this part, including a method of ensuring that when a child turns age 3 an IEP or, if consistent with sections 614(a)(5) and 677(d) of the Act [the requirement that either an IEP or an IFSP be developed for the provision of services] an individualized family service plan, has been developed and implemented by the child's third birthday.

Thus, both Part B and Part H require that responsible agencies develop a transition process to ensure that when a child becomes eligible for Part B services at age three, an educational program is in place. That program can be either an IEP, or at the option of the state, an IFSP. 20 U.S.C. § 1413(a)(15).

It is important to note that not all children with disabilities who receive services under Part H will be eligible for services under Part B. In brief, Part H has eligibility categories that may not be the basis for Part B qualification. Thus, one of the results of the required transition planning could be a determination that the child is no longer eligible for any IDEA educational services. In such an instance, parents are accorded the procedural safeguards set out in Part B, much as applies for other determinations of non-eligibility. *OSEP Memorandum 14*, 19 IDELR 1130 (OSEP 1993).

9. If a state's procedures for transitioning children with disabilities from Part H to Part B include a transition conference, can an eligible child's initial IEP or IFSP be developed at this meeting?

Yes. According to OSEP, "[t]he decision of whether to provide FAPE according to an IEP or IFSP may be made at this [transition] conference and the document may be developed at this meeting, if appropriate requirements are met." *OSEP Memorandum 14*, 19 IDELR 1130, 1132 (OSEP 1993). The Memorandum goes on to state that these appropriate requirements include all the substantive rights and procedural protections (other than the Part B IEP content requirements in the case of use of an IFSP) apply.

10.   Is a school district required to provide under Part B the same services identified in a child's Part H IFSP?

No. While Part B requires coordination to assure continuity of services,[3] it does not compel provision of all the same services. School districts are free to conduct an initial evaluation of the child and convene an IEP meeting to design the IEP from scratch, provided the generally applicable time frames for evaluation, holding IEP meetings and implementing IEPs are adhered to. *OSEP Memorandum 14,* 19 IDELR 1130 (OSEP 1993).

Two Pennsylvania administrative decisions confirm this. In *Boyertown Area School District,* 2 ECLPR ¶ 47 (SEA Pa. 1994), a child with cerebral palsy was receiving Part H services under an IFSP. She also was receiving aquatic and equestrian therapies. As part of the required transition planning the school district offered to continue the child's IFSP. While the parents believed the latter services were included in her IFSP, the school district refused to provide them, arguing that those services had been funded by a separate grant and were not part of the IFSP. A hearing officer ruled in favor of the parents, holding that the services were integral parts of the IFSP that had to be continued until an IEP was developed.

The review officer reversed on appeal. Even assuming the services were part of the IFSP, the school district had no obligation to continue to provide them. "No statutory link between [the lead agency] is responsibility to develop and implement the IFSP, and similar mandates to [the Department of Education] regarding the IEP makes the latter responsible for the actions of the former." 2 ECLPR ¶ 47 at 192.

That review officer was one of three on the review panel deciding *Chester County Intermediate Unit,* 23 IDELR 723 (SEA Pa. 1995), the next year. Using almost the exact same language as in the *Boyertown* decision, that panel ruled there was no such thing as a "stay-put" concept when a child is transitioning from Part H to Part B. The IU was not obligated to continue the services in the Part H IFSP pending the parent's due process challenge to the proposed IEP.

11.   If a child with a disability receiving Part H services turns three during the summer, may the school district wait until the beginning of the next school year to initiate the child's Part B programming?

No, not if the child needs extended year services. In such a case, to prevent an interruption in services, the school district must begin to provide needed services upon the child's third birthday.

---

[3] *See* Question 8 in this chapter, *supra.*

That was the opinion of OSEP in *Letter to Ash,* 18 IDELR 786 (OSEP 1992). For children eligible for special education and related services, an IEP (or an IFSP) must be developed and implemented by the child's third birthday, specifying the programming needed upon that birthday. If extended school year services are required for that child to receive FAPE, then they must be addressed in that first programming document, called the "transition IEP," and provided by the school district or other responsible pubic agency under Part B. *Accord Letter to Anonymous,* 22 IDELR 980 (OSEP 1993).

Other Agencies and Service Providers

12. Does the IDEA make the school district the public agency responsible for developing the IEP and providing FAPE to a student with a disability?

No, the IDEA does not create the local school district's legal responsibility for either developing IEPs or providing FAPE; state law, state regulations and interagency agreements do. The IDEA fixes responsibility on the states. 34 C.F.R. § 300.600. The states, in turn, through statutes and regulations determine the responsibilities of LEAs and other state units which have assigned roles in carrying out the IDEA mandates. These departments and units may have established interagency agreements or compacts which further complicate the real world practicalities of delivery of IDEA-supported special education and related services.

13. Which public agency is responsible for developing the IEPs for students with disabilities served by agencies other than the school district?

As the Notice of Interpretation on IEP Requirements makes clear, the IDEA does not require that the same agency responsible under state law for providing FAPE for a student with a disability also develop his or her IEP. The identification of the appropriate agency depends on the particular state law, policy or practices. As long as internecine disputes among agencies do not result in denial of FAPE to a student with a disability, then the state has flexibility to structure its own arrangements. Appendix C to 34 C.F.R. Part 300, Question 1. *See, e.g., Tennessee Dep't of Mental Health & Mental Retardation v. Doe,* 20 IDELR 347 (Tenn. Ct. App. 1993) (state's failure to identify agency responsible for providing FAPE resulted in SEA being ordered to assume financial responsibility for student with a serious emotional disturbance placed by state mental health agency in group home located outside his school district of residence).

The Notice provides:

The SEA, through its written policies or agreements, must ensure that IEPs are properly written and implemented for all children with disabilities in the State. This applies to each interagency situation that exists in the State, including any of the following:

(1)   When an LEA [school district] initiates the placement of a child in a school or program operated by another state agency . . . ;

(2)   when a State or local agency other than the SEA or LEA places a child in a residential facility or other program;

(3)   when parents initiate placements in public institutions; and

(4)   when the court makes placements in correctional facilities. . . .

Frequently, more than one agency is involved in developing or implementing the IEP of a child with a disability (e.g. when the LEA remains responsible for the child, even though another public agency provides the special education and related services, or when there are shared cost arrangements). It is important that SEA policies or agreements define the role of each agency involved in the situations described above, in order to resolve any jurisdictional problems that could delay the provision of FAPE to a child with a disability. . . .

Appendix C to 34 C.F.R. Part 300, Question 1.

The sad truth is that the type of complex situations discussed in Question 1 of the Notice of Interpretation frequently concern children with disabilities who have the greatest needs for educational services. The 20-year-old woman with a moderate to severe social and emotional maladjustment whose programming was at issue in *In re Child with Disabilities,* 20 IDELR 222 (SEA Conn. 1993), was one such student.

In that case an administrative hearing was held to determine if the young woman should continue to reside at an adult psychiatric facility (Connecticut Valley Hospital or CVH) operated by the state's department of mental health (DMH), which state agency was financially responsible for her placement and whether the local school district failed to provide her FAPE. After a review of the evidence, the hearing officer found that the young woman had been denied FAPE and ordered both the local school district and DMH to provide compensatory education and assume the educational and financial responsibility for same.

The hearing officer specifically found that interagency feuding and conflicts between the local school district and DMH made the development and implementation of a coordinated program of special education and related services impossible.

Under the [state interagency] agreement the Board [school district] is responsible for holding [IEP] meetings, developing IEPs and implementing them. However, those related services which are or should be provided by CVH staff are not included in the student's IEP. Nor are CVH staff members required under the agreement to participate in [IEP] meetings. Testimony at the hearing revealed that the Board's personnel and CVH staff not only fail to cooperate but are overtly hostile, thus greatly complicating integration and coordination of the respective aspects of a patient's program.

20 IDELR at 225.

14. Must the school district itself directly provide the services set out in the IEP it develops?

No, while a school district, or other public agency responsible for developing the child's IEP, must ensure that the child receives FAPE, it does not have to provide the services. Thus, for example, IDEA regulations at 34 C.F.R. § 300.401 makes the SEA responsible for assuring that students who are publicly placed in a private school or facility receive FAPE.[4] The Notice of Interpretation on IEP Requirements makes this point clear, stating that "the public agency responsible for the education of a child with a disability could provide IEP services to the child (1) directly, through the agency's own staff resources, or (2) indirectly, by contracting with another public or private agency, or through other arrangements." Appendix C to 34 C.F.R. Part 300, Question 46.

15. If the school district places a student with a disability in a State school, who is responsible for reviewing and revising IEPs?

Consistent with 34 C.F.R. § 300.600, while the school district is responsible for developing the IEP initially placing the student in the State school, the SEA has discretion to decide whether the State school or the local school district will thereafter be responsible for the provision of FAPE, including conducting reviews and revisions of IEPs.

In the Notice of Interpretation, though, the Department of Education states that "both agencies should be involved in any decisions made about the child's IEP (either by attending the IEP meetings, or through correspondence or telephone calls)." Appendix C to 34 C.F.R. Part 300, Question 1. Failure to assure cooperative review of the IEPs of two students placed in the state school for the deaf resulted in the decision in *Brimmer v. Traverse City Area Schools*, 22 IDELR 5 (W.D. Mich. 1994), that the local school district's conduct of a meeting to review the student's IEPs violated the IDEA.[5]

16. Must the school district assume financial responsibility for the services set out in the IEP?

Not always. While the school district remains responsible for providing all special education and related services identified in the IEP of a student with a disability, it

---

[4] *See* chapter 9, *supra,* in connection with public placement in private schools or facilities.

[5] *See* Question 6 in chapter 5, *supra.*

may use whatever state, local, federal or other private sources of support (such as parents' health insurance) are available for these purposes, assuming there is no cost to the parents. Appendix C to 34 C.F.R. Part 300, Question 46.

Provisions of the IDEA, other than those concerned with development and implementation of IEPs), make it clear that the school district is the payor of last resort. 34 C.F.R. § 300.600(c) states that "[The IDEA] may not be construed to limit the responsibility of agencies other than educational agencies for providing or paying some or all of the costs of FAPE to children with disabilities in the State." Similarly, 34 C.F.R. § 300.301(a) states that "each State may use whatever State, local, Federal, or private sources of support are available in the State to meet the requirement of [the IDEA]."

17. Should the IEP include services that other agencies are responsible for providing to students with disabilities?

No, if the services are not part of a student's educational program they should not be included in the IEP. In fact, the IEP does not even have to describe the total education of the student. Appendix C to 34 C.F.R. Part 300, Question 47.

Nevertheless, according to the Notice of Interpretation, when another federal agency is responsible for providing the service under a written individualized plan, then "it may be possible to develop a single, consolidated document" if two conditions are met: (1) the consolidated document contains all the information required in an IEP; and (2) all the required IEP team members have participated in the development of the document. Appendix C to 34 C.F.R. Part 300, Question 57.

The Notice of Interpretation gives four examples of individualized service plans that might be consolidated with an IEP: (1) an Individualized Care Plan under Title XIX of the Social Security Act (Medicaid); (2) the Individualized Program Plan under Title XX of the Social Security Act (Social Services); (3) the Individualized Service Plan (Title XVI of the Social Security Act (Supplemental Security Income); and (4) the Individualized Written Rehabilitation Plan (the Rehabilitation Act of 1973).

One notable example of a student with a disability receiving services under another program is the profoundly disabled student who was the subject of the influential decision in *Timothy v. Rochester School District,* 1987-88 EHLR 559:480 (D.N.H. 1988). Prior to being ruled eligible for educational services under the IDEA, Timothy received services, including medical care, physical therapy, tactile stimulation, feeding therapy and respite care (for his mother) under an Individualized Service Plan.

18. What is a school district's responsibility for providing services to a student who is receiving special education services according to an approved IEP, after the student becomes hospitalized?

A student's educational program should follow wherever he or she may go, whether to a hospital or even to jail.[6] Special education is defined under the IDEA as "specially

---

[6] *See* chapter 8, *infra,* for a discussion of incarcerated students and IEPs.

designed instruction . . . to meet the unique needs of a child with a disability, including instruction conducted in the classroom, in the home, in hospitals and institutions, and in other settings." 20 U.S.C. § 1401(16).

An IEP is designed to identify the child's unique needs and the specially designed instruction appropriate to meeting those needs. The IEP presents the student's educational objectives and describes the program elements appropriate to accomplishing those objectives. The actual physical location of the program becomes important only incidentally because it may enhance, or limit, the availability of appropriate program elements. Schools may group students with a common but unusual need in one central location, for example, to make more efficient use of a highly skilled specialist.

The principle which requires the program to follow the student must be tempered, however, by real world practicalities. There may be educational activities incorporated into a student's IEP which simply could not be accomplished, at least in the same way, in a more restricted setting such as a hospital. It is also possible that the priorities assigned to educational objectives may change because of the medical or psychological needs which prompted the hospitalization. It seems likely that the problem which led to hospitalization or the restrictions imposed by this change in location could demand some appreciable alteration to the student's IEP. Schools are more likely, for example, to send only one, more generally qualified home or visiting teacher to institutionalized students than several specific-field teachers. For these reasons, it is more accurate to say that it is the school's responsibility to make FAPE available to follow the student; the specifics of the IEP may need to vary as the location changes.

As discussed in Question 13, the IDEA fixes responsibility on the states. The states, in turn, through statutes and regulations determine the responsibilities of LEAs and other state units that have assigned roles in carrying out the IDEA mandates. These departments and units may have established interagency agreements or compacts. In short, the IDEA does not create the local school district's legal responsibility for hospital based instructions; state law, state regulations and interagency agreements do.

To fix the school district's responsibility, at least four basic questions must be worked through the regulatory maze.

- For what reason was the student hospitalized?

- Who made the hospitalization decision?

- Is the hospital a private institution or an arm of some state agency?

- What kinds of educational services are available at the hospital?

The greater the role that education played in the rationale for hospitalization and the greater the role played by the school district in that decision, the greater the school district's financial responsibility is likely to be. On the other hand, the clearer it is that the child was hospitalized for purely medical or psychological reasons, the less financial responsibility the school is apt to assume. If the student's IEP recommended hospitalization as essential to the student's educational growth, the school may be responsible for all costs except those that are strictly medical in nature. Conversely, if a student's physician orders hospitalization for an acute health reason, the school will be responsible for little more than seeing that a program designed to provide educational benefits under the changed conditions continues to be provided.

The public-private distinction may affect the responsibility assigned the district in several ways, but public hospitals typically fall under the administrative jurisdiction of a different arm of the state than school systems. The existence, or absence, and the specific terms of prior interagency agreements by which such shared responsibilities are to be handled will be influential in determining the school's duty.

Finally, some hospitals have well-developed education programs, others do not. In some cases, then, the school's responsibility might be simply a financial or administrative one. Other questions then become important. Can the student's educational needs be served only in the hospital or might the student be transported, for example? In other cases, the school would have to transport and provide to the child all of the people and equipment necessary to accomplish the student's educational program.

All of these dimensions of the student's hospitalization—reason, decision-maker, public-private character and resource availability—interact to create a great number of factors which would influence or determine the school system's responsibility.

Chapter 12

IEP Disputes and Remedies

When a parent and a school district disagree about an IEP (or, generally identification, evaluation, educational placement or the provision of FAPE) for a child with a disability, either party may initiate a due process hearing, an administrative hearing conducted by either the state educational agency or the school district (or other public agency) directly responsible for the child's education.

Swift resolution of disputes brought to due process is vital from an educational perspective and imperative as a matter of law. (A hearing officer generally must reach a final decision within 45 days after receipt of the request for a hearing.) So is resolution that allows the parties to rebuild a cooperative relationship, no matter who "wins."

Such rebuilding is not an easy task. Once a party files for due process, day-to-day communication between the parents and school district staff is likely to become tense, if it is not already so. And the hearing itself, while not a judicial proceeding, is adversarial by design. The IDEA grants each party to the hearing the right to be represented by counsel, to present evidence, to confront and cross-examine witnesses, and to compel the attendance of witnesses. Presentation of one's own expert witnesses frequently is necessary for an effective presentation of the party's position, as is rigorous cross-examination of the other party's expert and fact witnesses, including sometimes the parents themselves. Sometimes the acrimonious atmosphere associated with high-stakes civil litigation pervades the hearing room. And, those due process disputes in which the relationship between the parties has become the most poisonous arguably have the greatest potential for continuing in judicial appeals, should the parents not prevail.

When the dispute is finally resolved, the parties face the challenge of taking off their battle garb, putting the acrimony behind them, and trying again to work in unison for the benefit of the student. Not an easy task, certainly. More frequently in recent years, decision-makers include in their opinions a plea for the parties to put aside their feelings of mistrust and anger to work together cooperatively, always keeping the student's best interests in mind. For a one such extended plea—after what seems to have been a particularly vigorous dispute—see the concluding remarks of the hearing officer's opinion in *Mount Horeb Area School District,* 25 IDELR 286 (SEA Wis. 1997).

Thus, from every perspective, it is far better to avoid special education litigation—concerning IEPs or any other IDEA issue—to the extent possible. As a start, consider this Top Ten List of Sure-Fire Ways to Invite Due Process,[1] accompanied by the related positive actions school districts can take to minimize risk.

1. **DON'T:** Segregate students with special needs into self-contained classrooms based on labels.

   DO: Make sure the IEP is completed first so that the student's needs are identified. Later, further discussion can take place to determine the best placement for the student.

2. **DON'T:** Give parents the impression that you don't offer services that aren't currently provided by the school district.

   DO: Provide the service if the student needs it.

3. **DON'T:** Assume discipline policies and procedures supersede special education law.

   DO: Have staff trained in positive approaches to behavior support.

4. **DON'T:** Assume that an accommodation is expensive.

   DO: Use teamwork to devise creative, viable and economic solutions that meet students' needs.

5. **DON'T:** Assume only your school district's attorney needs to know about special education law.

   DO: Know the law. Pull together a team of stakeholders, consisting of parents, teachers, administrators and others, to regularly review case law and legislation and to monitor the school district's compliance.

6. **DON'T:** Ignore your board policies and administrative procedures.

   DO: Review your policies regularly so you know your responsibilities. For example, it is not unusual for school administrators not to know their district's policy on discipline and how it fits in with special education.

7. **DON'T:** Support teachers who insist that a particular child doesn't fit in their classrooms.

   DO: Stress diversity and offer in-service sessions on inclusion.

---

[1] As featured in *Want To Avoid Special Education Litigation?,* THE SPECIAL EDUCATOR,® Vol. 12, iss. 14, at 5.

8. **DON'T:** Support teachers who claim they don't have time to make accommodations.

   DO: Communicate the message that it's the teachers' job to make the time. Provide teachers with opportunities to learn how to make better use of available time and resources and to meet with others who have successfully dealt with this challenge.

9. **DON'T:** Support classroom teachers who say that all children—regardless of ability or needs—must be treated equally.

   DO: Ensure that all teachers are aware of your school district's policies and know their roles and responsibilities in supporting special education students. Make sure that general education teachers participate in IEP conferences and retain a copy of students' IEP goals.

10. **DON'T:** Give a student's parents the impression that you have all the answers about what's best for their child.

    DO: Conduct IEP meetings and other meetings with parents in a true team spirit. Recognize that each team member has important viewpoints that must be considered in order to make the best decision for the student.

When it comes to disputes about IEPs, in particular, a certain level of due process and judicial proceedings is unavoidable. Parents understandably want the best for their children with disabilities. While some states may mandate provision of "the best," other states follow the federal FAPE standard; school districts in those states do not have to provide "the best." Some parents may appreciate this distinction on an intellectual level, but not emotionally.

Even when there is an agreement in principle that the school district does not have to maximize their child's educational opportunities, parents may yet dispute the contours of the appropriate education to which their child is entitled. FAPE is an amorphous concept—purposely so. Twenty years of litigation show that on this issue both educators and jurists can reach different supportable conclusions.

Parents do not bring a due process action only to contest procedural violations. Clearly they believe the program proposed for their child would have been substantively superior had the school district complied with the IDEA's procedural safeguards. There is no comprehensive data base of all IEPs available for meaningful analysis, but the author thinks it reasonable to conclude that school districts, by and large, propose and provide FAPE as a substantive matter, even in those instances in which the IEP process is less than 100 percent compliant.

Nonetheless, school districts should no longer be surprised that parents seeking a substantively different educational program put the IEP process under which the program was developed under the microscope. The U.S. Supreme Court decision in *Board of Education of Hendrick Hudson Central School District v. Rowley*, 1981-82 EHLR

553:656 (1982), makes a successful attack on procedural compliance virtually a necessity.

Thus, school attorneys talk about the need for districts to "bulletproof" their IEPs. In essence, school districts must not allow procedural missteps to put them on the defensive when their officials have acted in good faith and in the best interests of the child in developing appropriate programming.

When considering how to bulletproof the IEP, districts should pay particular attention to the following points. Failure to follow the IDEA's procedural requirements and to document compliance has been a source of much litigation.

- Provide appropriate notice to parents.

- Convene the IEP meeting to permit timely development of the IEP.

- Include all appropriate staff and other personnel in the IEP meeting.

- Base the IEP on a proper evaluation.

- Discuss all elements of the IEP at the IEP meeting.

- Include in the IEP all programming and services required to provide FAPE, as determined by the IEP team, even if not currently available at the school or within the district.

- Fully enumerate all the required elements of the IEP in the IEP document.

- Always consider at the IEP meeting if the student needs extended school year (ESY) services.

- Select the student's placement only after development of the IEP.

- Provide all programming and services included in the IEP in accordance with implementation timelines.

- Communicate the agreed IEP to everyone involved in its implementation.

1.   If both divorced parents participate in the IEP meeting, what should the school district do if only one parent agrees to the IEP?

Federal law offers no specific answer. There are many references to parental rights in connection with disputes with the school district, but nowhere does the law address what we might term "interparental disputes."

There are no statutory requirements that both parents must agree with the recommendations of the rest of the IEP team. Stated differently, a school district may take the position that if *a* parent has agreed, the IEP may be implemented. While this problem may become more common, the author is aware of only two reported administrative decisions about school districts confronting this issue. In the absence of state or district law or policy dictating otherwise, the approach taken by the administrative decision-maker in *Lower Moreland Township School District,* 18 IDELR 1160 (SEA Pa. 1992), seems consistent with the IDEA.

In that case, the review officer recognized the right of a father with shared legal custody to bring a due process challenge to the IEP approved by the child's mother. While the father lived some distance from his daughter, he was an active participant in the educational decision-making process. His right to participate apparently was acknowledged by both the mother and the school district prior to the time he objected to the then-proposed program and placement. At that point, both the school district and the mother joined in asserting he was not a "parent" for purposes of the IDEA. The review officer found otherwise, holding the father's right both to attend IEP meetings and to file for due process was established by the terms of the order granting him shared legal custody.

The potential problems that would be created by applying this ruling to other situations where a parent without physical custody wants to challenge an educational decision approved by the custodial parent was acknowledged eloquently by the officer.

> By this decision, we are not suggesting that every noncustodial parent can exercise a veto over the educational decisions for his or her child. Such a blanket rule fairly invites abuse while burdening the school district with the near impossible task of securing the approvals from absent and possibly uninterested parents.

18 IDELR at 1161.

As a matter of law and common sense, if a properly composed team of educators develops an IEP with which the custodial parent agrees, the team should implement the IEP, while advising the parent who disagrees that he or she may have the right to challenge that decision. The school staff should, however, remain sensitive to the domestic situation of the student and make an effort to work with both parents to the extent authorized under any binding court order or court-approved settlement.

2. May a parent who refuses to attend an IEP meeting bring a due process claim challenging the substantive adequacy of the resulting IEP?

The question, in effect, becomes: Is the IDEA's requirement that parents be equal participants in the IEP process an obligation, as well as an entitlement? The better view is that the IDEA establishes a parent's right, but not an obligation, to participate in the IEP process.

Arguing in favor of the parent's absolute right to contest the provision of FAPE is the long-standing pronouncement of the U.S. Supreme Court in *Burlington School Committee v. Massachusetts Department of Education,* 1984-85 EHLR 556:386 (1985). The Court ruled that the stay-put requirement is not a mutual obligation and that school districts have a duty to develop and offer appropriate educational programs to students with disabilities each year, whether they are currently enrolled in the district or not. 34 C.F.R. §§ 300.342(a), 300.343(d).

In *Susquentia School District v. Raelee S.*, 25 IDELR 120 (M.D. Pa. 1996), the District Court for the Middle District of Pennsylvania held unequivocally that "the absence of parental participation in the IEP process does not excuse a district from developing and offering an appropriate IEP in accordance with the IDEA and its regulations." 25 IDELR at 127. *But see Philadelphia Sch. Dist.*, 21 IDELR 1193 (SEA Pa. 1994) (even when a child is in a private placement, the parent is obliged to participate in IEP development; the parent could not decline to participate in the IEP meeting ordered by the hearing officer and file an appeal of the decision instead).

The court in *Vipperman v. Hanover County School Board*, 22 IDELR 796 (E.D. Va. 1995), almost had this issue before it. In that case the parents of a learning disabled student brought an action seeking tuition reimbursement for the district's failure to identify their daughter as eligible for services and, once her eligibility was recognized, proposing an IEP that failed to include objective criteria and evaluation procedures. 34 C.F.R. § 300.346(a)(5).

The parents had not attended the IEP meeting at which the school district developed the allegedly inadequate IEP. On that basis, the administrative decision-makers refused to consider their objection. In fact, it rejected the parents' claims on all grounds, resulting in their filing a civil action. In its response the school district relied on the substantive appropriateness of the IEP. Because the district did not assert the procedural defense of nonparticipation by the parents, the court found it unnecessary to decide this troubling issue.

The 1997 Amendments do not make parental participation in IEP meetings a condition precedent for bringing a due process action. Further, there is no suggestion that districts can decline to offer to provide FAPE to children with disabilities as a result of the conduct of their parents.

Section 612(a)(10)(C)(iii) does authorize decision-makers to reduce or deny tuition reimbursement awards to parents who do not work cooperatively with the school district, even if the child was denied FAPE. That section sets out three circumstances under which parents, by their own actions, can lose some or all of the tuition reimbursement award to which they would otherwise be entitled. (Subsection 612(a)(10)(C)(iv) sets out four exceptions.) The first two circumstances seem straightforward, but the third is amorphous. In all events, no further guidance is offered in the statute about when an award should be reduced, rather than denied, and, if reduction is appropriate, by how much.

> (iii) Limitation on reimbursement—The cost of [tuition] reimbursement . . . may be reduced or denied—
>
> (I) if—

(aa) at the most recent IEP meeting that the parents attended prior to removal of the child from the public school, the parents did not inform the IEP team that they were rejecting the placement proposed by the public agency to provide a free appropriate public education to their child, including stating their concerns and their intent to enroll their child in a private school at public expense; or

(bb) 10 business days (including any holidays that occur on a business day) prior to the removal of the child from the public school, the parents did not give written notice to the public agency of the information described in division (aa);

(II) if, prior to the parents' removal of the child from the public school, the public agency informed the parents, through the notice requirements described in section 615(b)(7), of its intent to evaluate the child . . . but the parents did not make the child available for such evaluation; or

(III) upon a judicial finding of unreasonableness with respect to actions taken by the parents.

3. May a school district involved in a dispute with parents communicate with the parents through district counsel rather than convene an IEP meeting?

No. According to a California hearing officer, communication through attorneys is not an adequate substitute for the IEP process. *Soquel Union Elementary Sch. Dist.,* 22 IDELR 646 (SEA Cal. 1995). In that case, the school district made an offer of programming or services at an IEP meeting in December 1993. The parents rejected the offer and the district did not convene another IEP meeting until February 13, 1995, the first day of the due process hearing. In the interim, the district, through its attorneys, offered several written revised IEPs. When the parents claimed that the failure to convene an IEP meeting within one year of the last IEP meeting was a denial of FAPE, the school district claimed otherwise, arguing that it had met the requirement of *Union School District v. Smith,* 20 IDELR 987 (9th Cir. 1994), because it had made formal written offers to the parents.

Yes, the school district did make formal written offers, the hearing officer agreed, and thus it complied in that sense with the IEP document requirement of the IDEA statute and *Union School District.* But that was not enough. "[I]t is the responsibility of the IEP team and not an attorney to develop, review, and revise the IEPs of special education students." 22 IDELR at 662. In choosing to communicate through its attorney, the school district denied the parents their right under the IDEA to present information to an IEP team and participate in its decision-making.

4. If a parent does not challenge the proposed IEP at the IEP meeting, does he or she waive the right to due process?

Some courts have so held, although the author believes the better view is otherwise.

Some courts have overruled parents' objections to deficiencies in an IEP on the ground that the parents did not raise the objections at the meeting when the IEP was formulated. For example, the court in *Gorski v. Lynchburg School Board,* 1988-89 EHLR 441:415 (4th Cir. 1989), rejected the parents' objections to the lack of short-term objectives in the IEP because the parents failed to object to the omission at the IEP meeting, signing the IEP while recognizing the objectives were not included. *Abney v. District of Columbia,* 1987-88 EHLR 559:308 (D.C. Cir. 1988), held to the same effect. *See also Garland Indep. Sch. Dist. v. Wilks,* 1986-87 EHLR 558:308 (N.D. Tex. 1987) (refusing tuition reimbursement for period before parents objected to IEP); *see generally Hall v. Freeman,* 1986-87 EHLR 558:248 (N.D. Ga. 1987) (parent's signature on IEP is her agreement that the goals stated therein were appropriate).

Courts that take this position arguably place an undue burden on parents, many of whom are unrepresented at IEP meetings or who fail for other reasons to appreciate the significance of the omissions or the possibility that they will waive an objection by not raising it during the meetings. Administrative decision-makers have taken the position in some published opinions that requiring parents to raise objections at IEP meetings as a condition precedent to bringing a due process claim is overly burdensome to parents. For example, in *School Administrative Unit # 66,* 20 IDELR 471 (SEA N.H. 1993), the hearing officer found for the parents, stating that:

> Testimony of School District witnesses that the Parent failed to raise issues in the [IEP] meeting, when given the opportunity is not persuasive. [State law concerning special education] puts the duty on the school district to give the opportunity to participate to the Parent. The School District will not shift the burden to the Parent by saying the Parent did not mention it.

20 IDELR at 475.

In *W.G. v. Board of Trustees of Target Range School District No. 23,* 18 IDELR 1019 (9th Cir. 1991), the Ninth Circuit Court rejected the school district's argument that the parents could not challenge the appropriateness of the proposed IEP because they voluntarily left the meeting prior to its completion without raising the objections they brought in their due process action. While the court found that argument to be "without merit," its holding may be limited to the unusual circumstances of that case. The school district's conduct of the IEP meeting blatantly violated the procedural requirements of the IDEA and the parents had previously fully informed the school district about their concerns.

When considering how the 1997 Amendments modify the answer to this question, the same considerations discussed in Question 3 above apply.

5. Must the school district send the parents written notice of their rights following every IEP meeting?

Technically no. The school district must send a written notice meeting the content requirements of IDEA regulations at 34 C.F.R. § 300.505 every time it changes the student's IEP programming or placement or refuses to accede to any parental request for change. But best practice is to establish a routine of sending the notice to parents following every single IEP meeting, whether or not the parents attended the meeting or agreed to an unchanged IEP. This preserves a written record of the school district's actions and diffuses any later parental complaint alleging a notice defect.

IDEA regulations at 34 C.F.R. § 300.504 require that school districts provide a written notice to parents within a reasonable amount of time before initiating, or refusing, a change in placement, evaluation, identification or provision of FAPE. The regulation does not leave the content of that notice to the discretion of the states or local agencies. Specific pieces of information must be contained in every written notice, and they must be communicated in an understandable manner.

Required information is as follows:

1. A full explanation of:

- the school district's obligation to obtain the parents' written consent prior to initial evaluation and placement;

- the parents' right to examine their child's educational records;

- the parents' right to obtain an independent educational evaluation at public expense;

- the parents' right to receive prior written notice of any proposal or refusal to evaluate, change placement or affect the provision of FAPE;

- the parents' right to request a due process hearing to resolve disagreements with the school district and to appeal the hearing decision to court;

- the stay-put provision;

- the school district's obligation to appoint a trained surrogate parent, if necessary; and

- the parents' right to seek recovery of attorneys' fees if they prevail in a due process hearing or appeal.

2. A description of the action proposed or refused by the school district.

3. An explanation of why the school district proposes or refuses to take the action.

4. A description of any options the school district considered and the reasons those options were rejected.

5. A description of any data used by the school district to reach its decision.

6. A description of any other factors relevant to the school district's decision.

See Question 27 in chapter 5 concerning the impact of the 1997 Amendments.

6. Must the written notice of parental rights be provided in the parents' native language?

Yes, 34 C.F.R. § 300.504 carries over the native language requirement found in the requirement for the written invitation to the IEP meeting and the IEP meeting itself. And, as the decision in *Easton Area School District,* 24 IDELR 1077 (SEA Pa. 1996), shows, what matters for this purpose is whether the parent's native language for *written* communication is or is not English. In *Easton* the parent understood spoken English, making the conduct of the IEP meeting in that language compliant. Because he did not have mastery of written English though, translation of the notice was necessary.

7. Can the IEP document itself serve as the written notice to parents?

As a matter of federal law, the IEP may contain information over and above the content requirements of 34 C.F.R. § 300.346; thus the IEP could contain all the information required by 34 C.F.R. § 300.505 and properly serve as the written notice. Accordingly, the parent in *Tennessee Department of Mental Health and Mental Retardation,* 18 IDELR 694 (M.D. Tenn. 1992), could not prevail on his claim that he did not receive the required notice of intent to change placement because the IEP itself contained all the required elements of notice.

Chances are, though, that a school district does not include in the IEP each and every piece of information the parents must receive. Much of the notice information is superfluous to the provision and monitoring of the program itself. Including it in the IEP would make the document needlessly unwieldy.

8. Can public placement in a private school be ordered as a remedy for procedural violations of the IEP process?

No. According to a well-reasoned opinion by the state review officer in *Philadelphia School District,* 21 IDELR 1193 (SEA Pa. 1994), such relief is not authorized under the IDEA as a remedy for procedural violations of the IEP process. The school district must be given the opportunity to remediate past violations and to provide FAPE in the future.

The school district in this case clearly failed to adhere to the procedural timelines of conducting the preplacement evaluation and implementing the resulting IEP for a

12-year-old student with a learning disability and ADD. As a result, the student lost opportunity to make meaningful educational progress. A remedy was in order, and the school district offered compensatory education. The hearing officer, however, ordered two remedies: The district would reimburse the parents for their past private tutoring expenses as compensatory education and it also would place the student in a private school. On review, the obligation to place the student in a private school was reversed.

> Although . . . we can understand the Hearing Officer's sympathy for the parents in this case, we can find no legal basis for the remedy provided by his decision. Indeed, we must agree with District counsel that the order places the District in double jeopardy. The Hearing Officer is constrained, as are we, in terms of the remedies he can offer. The District has acknowledged its procedural defects with regard to [the student's] previous programming and has offered compensation. No remedy can be offered, by the Hearing Officer or by this panel, for the perception that the District may in the future commit some infractions. When unable to independently resolve their concerns with a District, parents, as provided by law, may invoke their right to due process by requesting a hearing. However, the District is also entitled to due process. It cannot be deprived of the right to correct its deficiency, nor can its offer of compensatory education for past omissions be used to indict it for presumed future transgressions.

21 IDELR at 1194.

9. Can an IEP be both inadequate and appropriate?

Yes, in the sense that some defective draftsmanship of some IEP elements, such as current levels of educational performance, annual goals or short-term objectives, will not prevent an administrative or judicial reviewer from concluding that the special education programming, related services and regular classroom modifications contained in the document provide the requisite level of individually designed educational opportunity. This principle is, in effect, analogous to a finding that flaws in the IEP process are merely technical.[2] As explained by the state review officer in *Philadelphia School District*, 21 IDELR 1193 (SEA Pa. 1996): "Some lack of specificity or detail in aspects of the IEP may produce an 'inadequate' IEP, but does not automatically render the IEP 'inappropriate.' " 21 IDELR at 1195.

But when the substantive adequacy of the program of services is involved, an opinion from the District Court for the Eastern District of Pennsylvania (the district that contains the City of Philadelphia) held that an IEP cannot be both inadequate and appropriate. In *Rose v. Chester County Intermediate Unit*, 24 IDELR 61 (E.D. Pa. 1996), the hearing officer, affirmed by the review panel, found that the IEP proposed for a preschooler with pervasive developmental disorder was "inadequate but appropriate"

---

[2] *See* Question 10 in this chapter, *infra*.

because it did not provide sufficient speech and language services to meet the child's needs, as reflected in his evaluation. As a remedy, the school district was ordered to reconvene the IEP team to modify the IEP consistently with its order.

The parents, still seeking tuition reimbursement, appealed. This time the court agreed with them. Under Pennsylvania law, incorporated into the IDEA by 20 U.S.C. § 14101(a)(18), an IEP must provide services to meet the child's needs, as evaluated. Thus, the IEP for the student at issue was inappropriate as a matter of law. Both the hearing officer and the review panel incorrectly characterized that deficiency as "inadequacy" in a purely procedural sense. While a court or administrative decision-maker may direct modification of an IEP that is procedurally flawed, such relief is insufficient when the IEP is inappropriate.

10. Do procedural inadequacies in the IEP process automatically necessitate a finding of a denial of FAPE?

Not always. If a court or due process decision-maker determines that the failure to follow the proper procedures was significant, the school district will be found to have violated the law. But if the violation is determined to be merely technical, then no intervention is warranted.

In *Board of Education of Hendrick Hudson Central School District v. Rowley,* 1981-82 EHLR 553:656 (1982), the U.S. Supreme Court established the importance of the procedural requirements of the IDEA, including those concerning the development of IEPs, stating that the elaborate provisions of the Act "demonstrate the legislative conviction that adequate compliance with the procedures prescribed would in most cases assure much if not all of what Congress wished in the way of substantive content of an IEP." 1981-82 EHLR at 553:670.

Thus, the *Rowley* court set out a two-part analysis to decide appropriateness:

First, has the State complied with the procedures set forth in the [IDEA]? And second, is the individualized educational program developed through the [IDEA's] procedures reasonably calculated to enable the child to receive educational benefits? If this two-part analysis is met, the State has complied with the obligation imposed by Congress and the courts can require no more.

1981-82 EHLR at 553:670.

Authoritative court decisions have established the principle that some procedural violations may be so significant that the court (or the hearing officer) does not even have to analyze whether the resulting program provides the requisite quantum of educational benefit. The procedural violations, standing alone, deny FAPE. In a sense, these are the easier cases for the courts, for they do not have to step in the quagmire of educational methodology and conflicting expert opinions. By the same token, these can be the most frustrating cases for school districts, for they may believe the proposed program provides educational benefit.

Courts generally have agreed on the standard for when a violation is significant enough to automatically result in a finding of a denial of FAPE, although application of the standard to particular situations still generates decisions on the administrative level and, less frequently, in the courts.

That standard is perhaps most frequently articulated by reference to the decision of the Ninth Circuit Court of Appeals in *W.G. v. Board of Trustees of Target Range School District No. 23,* 18 IDELR 1019 (9th Cir. 1992).[3] In that case, the court stated that, where procedural inadequacies result in the loss of educational opportunity or seriously infringe upon the parents' opportunity to meaningfully participate in the IEP process, the result is a denial of FAPE. Other federal circuit court cases adopting essentially the same standard include: *Schuldt v. Mankato School District No. 77,* 18 IDELR 16 (8th Cir. 1991); *Burke County Board of Education v. Denton,* 16 EHLR 432 (4th Cir. 1990); *Roland M. v. Concord School Committee,* 16 EHLR 1129 (1st Cir. 1990); *Hall v. Vance County Board of Education,* 1985-86 EHLR 557:155 (4th Cir. 1990).

In a most amazing recent case, the school district's blatant violations of the IEP procedural rules were excused as "merely technical." *Board of Education of City School District of City of New York,* 23 IDELR 165 (SEA N.Y. 1995), involved a 13-year-old student with learning disabilities who was being educated in the regular classroom with resource room support. His mother expressed concern about her son's low grades and posed questions about the IEP at a parent-teacher conference. The resource room teacher responded by saying it was "time-consuming" to go over an IEP and asked the parent to sign the blank page of a new IEP, telling the parent not to worry because she (the teacher) would take care of it. The next thing the parent knew, she received a completed IEP that indicated that the IEP meeting had been held on the date of the parent-teacher conference. In addition to the signature of the parent, the IEP now had the signatures of the resource room teacher, the special education administrator and the health coordinator, although the latter two individuals did not attend the meeting with the parent. The programming was slightly different than that contained in the student's previous IEP, formulated in April 1994.

The parent wondered how this could be legal. It wasn't. Both the hearing officer and state review officer held that the so-called IEP meeting was a nullity and the resulting IEP consequently void. The school's customary procedure, as described by the resource room teacher at the due process hearing, involved the teacher reviewing a draft IEP with the parent and then submitting it to the special education office for "printing." This procedure violated the IDEA because the IEP meeting was not properly

---

[3] *See* Question 11 in chapter 9, *supra,* for discussion of the particular violations at issue.

constituted, there was no prior notice and the mother was not advised of her procedural rights.

But the student was not entitled to compensatory education on the basis of these violations, despite their being "a serious breach in the cooperative relationship between the child's parents and the school district" because there was no denial of FAPE. The district did not have to convene an IEP meeting in November 1994 in the first place. The student's April 1994 IEP still was valid and not yet due for annual review. Further, the IEP proposed in November was very similar to the April IEP and provided FAPE. In essence—no harm, no foul.

11. When are violations of IDEA procedural requirements concerning the IEP considered "merely technical"?

Following the standards discussed in Question 10, several authoritative court decisions have found a district's violation to be merely technical when the parents have not been impeded from meaningful participation in the IEP process and the student with a disability has not been deprived of educational opportunity. *See, e.g., Doe v. Alabama Dep't of Educ.,* 17 EHLR 41 (11th Cir. 1990) (technical violation by school district regarding notice of rights to be provided to parents did not warrant relief where parents had actual notice and participated fully and effectively in IEP process); *Doe v. Defendant I,* 16 EHLR 930 (6th Cir. 1990) (failure of IEP to include statement of child's present level of educational performance and appropriate criteria for determining achievement of educational objectives did not invalidate IEP where parents were aware of the relevant information).

Most recently the Eighth Circuit's opinion in *Independent School District No. 283 v. S.D.,* 24 IDELR 375 (8th Cir. 1996), coined a new test to determine whether procedural violations are merely technical: Has the school district met the IDEA's "core procedural requirements"? If it has, then any deficits are either harmless or remediable without setting aside the IEP.

The student at issue in *Independent School District* was an elementary school student with severe dyslexia and attention deficit disorder. The parents challenged the adequacy of the programming offered by the district and unilaterally enrolled the student in a private school limited to students with learning disabilities. The local level hearing officer rejected the parents' claim for tuition reimbursement, finding that placement there did not comport with the IDEA's LRE requirements. The review officer reversed, however, on the grounds that the district's IEPs were substantively and procedurally invalid. The district court put the parents back to "square one," upholding the local level due process hearing officer.

The next appeal—to the Eighth Circuit—again held for the school district on both substantive and procedural grounds. While written opinions in the administrative or lower court proceedings are unavailable, the circuit court opinion accepts a district court finding that there was an "astounding number of procedural inadequacies" in the IEPs. Nevertheless, the circuit court, like the district court, did not find the procedural violations compelled judgment in the parents' favor.

> Congress intended that IDEA's procedural safeguards be enforced so that parents of a handicapped child will have adequate input in the development of the child's IEP. The district court concluded that the School District substantially complied with those statutory safeguards. S.D.'s IEPs set out educational goals and the special services to be provided. The School District maintained open communications with S.D.'s parents and allowed them to play an "aggressively participative role" in the developments of the IEPs.

24 IDELR 375 at 377 (citation omitted).

12. How should the school district proceed if it is unable to reach agreement with the parents at the IEP meeting?

The IDEA does not address this specific issue. If the parents opt to file for due process, as is their right, then the stay-put provision of 34 C.F.R. § 300.513 requires that the last agreed-upon IEP continue in effect, assuming the parties cannot agree to an interim program pending resolution of the dispute. Assuming the parents have not yet filed for due process, neither the IDEA statute nor its regulations provide a clear directive. Instead, the Department of Education's Notice of Interpretation on IEP Requirements suggests how a school district might proceed.

> As a general rule, the agency and the parents would agree to an interim course of action for serving the child (i.e., in terms of placement and/or services) to be followed until the area of disagreement over the IEP is resolved. The manner in which this interim measure is developed and agreed to by both parties is left to the discretion of the individual State or local agency. However, if the parents and agency cannot agree on an interim measure, the child's last agreed upon IEP would remain in effect in the areas of disagreement until the disagreement is resolved.

Appendix C to 34 C.F.R. Part 300, Question 35.

The Notice of Interpretation recognizes that the areas of disagreement may be either central to the program as a whole, or arguably marginal, such as a specific related service. In the former case, the DOE suggests the school district do three things: (1) remind the parents that they may file for due process; (2) work with the parents to develop an interim course of action; and (3) recommend mediation or other informal dispute resolution. In the latter case, the school district might do three other things: (1) implement the agreed aspects of the IEP; (2) document the IEP to indicate the points of disagreement; and (3) initiate procedures to resolve the dispute.

13.   Must a school district initiate due process if the parents do not agree to a proposed IEP?

As discussed in chapter 3, programming and services must be provided under an IEP that is considered to be "in effect"—meaning approved by parents. On the other hand, under IDEA regulations at 34 C.F.R. § 300.504(b) parental consent is required in only two circumstances: prior to conducting a preplacement evaluation and prior to the initial placement of a child with a disability in a program providing special education and related services.

Thus, in theory, under the IDEA a school district is not required to initiate due process to override lack of consent when the parents do not consent to a revised IEP, although it may. 34 C.F.R. § 300.506(b). Instead, a school district may take the actions discussed in Question 35 of the Notice of Interpretation,[4] including urging the parents to initiate due process or pursue alternative means of dispute resolution.

In practice, if provision of all the services described in the proposed IEP is necessary to provide FAPE, then the school district must take action to resolve the matter if the parents do not. As OSEP stated in *Letter to Williams,* 18 IDELR 534 (OSEP 1991), when a parent refuses to consent or revokes consent to services the school district believes are needed for FAPE, then it may use informal means, such as conferencing, minor adjustments or mediation, initially, but may have to invoke due process. *See also* Note 3 to 34 C.F.R. § 300.504.

IDEA regulations at 34 C.F.R. § 300.504 make it clear, though, that states may impose more demands on school districts facing parental objections to proposed IEPs. For example, New Hampshire state law[5] (in 1994) required a school district to initiate due process when parents either disagree or fail to agree to the IEP proposed by the remainder of the IEP team, assuming it believes implementation of that IEP is in the child's best interest. The goal of that provision, as explained by the court in *Murphy v. Timberlane Regional School District,* 20 IDELR 1391 (1st Cir. 1994), is to prevent an impasse—neither parents nor school districts seeking resolution of their disagreement—that may injure the child.

14.   How should the parents proceed if they are unable to reach agreement with the district at the IEP meeting?

Basically, parents have five choices:

1. They can, in effect, vote with their feet by withdrawing their child from public school and unilaterally enrolling him or her in a private school or facility

---

[4] *See* Question 12 in this chapter, *supra.*

[5] N.H. Code Admin. R. Ann. 1125(b)(3)-b.

while filing a due process claim for both prospective relief—an IEP that provides FAPE—and tuition reimbursement. In *Burlington School Committee v. Massachusetts Department of Education,* 1984-85 EHLR 556:389 (1985), the U.S. Supreme Court made it clear that the stay-put requirement of 34 C.F.R. § 300.513 applies only to school districts, not to parents. A number of issues can arise in claims involving tuition reimbursement, over and above the appropriateness of the school district's IEP. The equitable considerations involved are, to some extent, discussed in Question 6 in chapter 6, but overall the topic of the law concerning tuition reimbursement—and other remedies for the denial of FAPE—are beyond the scope of this publication. Once the 1997 Amendments take effect, parents need to be mindful of the limitations on tuition reimbursement awards discussed in Question 2 of this chapter.

2. Not all parents can afford to take what the Eastern District of Pennsylvania called the "Burlington gamble." *Rose v. Chester County Intermediate Unit,* 24 IDELR 61 (E.D. Pa. 1996). In these instances, the parents can file a due process claim while the child remains enrolled in public school, demanding prospective relief that may include different or additional services or compensatory education. As discussed in Question 12 above, the stay-put provision of 34 C.F.R. § 300.513 generally results in the student remaining in his or her last approved placement and being served under his or her last approved IEP, unless the parties can agree on interim measures.

3. Either in lieu of or in addition to due process, the parents can file a complaint under the state complaint procedures required by 34 C.F.R. § 300.660. According to OSEP, under Part B parents of children with disabilities may file a complaint under the complaint management system (34 C.F.R. § § 300.660-300.662) concerning the identification, evaluation, educational placement or provision of FAPE (including design and content of an IEP) to their child. *OSEP Memorandum 94-16,* 21 IDELR 85 (OSEP 1994). It is not altogether clear what relief is available to a parent pursuing a complaint on behalf of his or her individual child—the complaint procedure has been used mainly for systemic issues or others that do not involve the provision of FAPE to a particular child. Nonetheless, in *Letter to Murray,* 19 IDELR 496 (OSEP 1992), OSEP opined that an SEA is authorized to award compensatory education for a student with a disability upon a determination that the student has been denied FAPE.

4. Under the IDEA, mediation—an intervening step that may be used prior to conducting a formal due process hearing—is an option that may be available to parents, should they so choose, at the discretion of the state. The Comment to IDEA regulations at 34 C.F.R. § 300.506 endorses mediation, stating that "[i]n many cases, mediation leads to resolution of differences between parents

and agencies without the development of an adversarial relationship and with minimal emotional stress." The 1997 Amendments make a much stronger statement in favor of mediation, requiring that all states offer parents the opportunity (but not the obligation) to resolve disputes about, *inter alia,* IEP programming through mediation, assuming the district is also agreeable. Section 615(e). As stated in the Committee Report to accompany the Senate's Reauthorization bill, "[i]t is the committee's strong preference that mediation become the norm for resolving disputes under IDEA." S. Rep. No. 105-17, at 26 (1997).

5. While it may be a questionable choice, the parents could opt to indicate their disagreement but otherwise take no action.[6]

Undoubtedly, all this can be confusing to parents. Thus, the Department of Education's Notice of Interpretation states that, if the parents have not already received notice of their right to challenge the IEP at due process (34 C.F.R. § 300.504-300.505), the school district must remind parents with whom they are unable to reach agreement at the IEP meeting. The district "should remind the parents that they may seek to resolve their differences through the due process procedures under [the IDEA]." Appendix C to 34 C.F.R. Part 300, Question 32.

---

[6] *See* Question 13 in this chapter, *supra.*

Table of Cases

B

C

F

G

H

I

Index

C

D

E